Jane Corbin is an award-winning senior reporter for the BBC's flagship current-affairs programme *Panorama*, and has c[...] major news stories around the world. In recent years she[...] made a speciality of studying the growth of terror movemen[...], particularly in the Middle East. Following the September 11 atrocities Jane's series of special *Panorama* programmes revealed in meticulous detail how the hijackers plotted their attacks on the World Trade Center and the Pentagon, and how the West prosecuted the subsequent 'war on terror'.

Jane has won the Royal Television Society award four times, and has been nominated several times for Emmy awards in the US for her films about war crimes in the former Yugoslavia and for her trilogy of investigative programmes which revealed the existence of Saddam Hussein's 'Super Gun' and his nuclear and chemical weapons programmes.

Jane is married with two children.

THE BASE

Al-Qaeda and the
Changing Face of
Global Terror

Jane Corbin

POCKET
BOOKS

LONDON • SYDNEY • NEW YORK • TOKYO • SINGAPORE • TORONTO

First published in Great Britain by Simon & Schuster UK Ltd in 2002
This updated edition published by Pocket Books in 2003
A Viacom company

PICTURE CREDITS
1, 2, 7, 9, 21: Getty Images (UK) Ltd
3, 4, 5, 6, 16, 17, 18, 19, 20: PA Photos
Every effort has been made to trace copyright-holders.
If copyright has been inadvertently infringed please
contact the publishers at the address below.

3 5 7 9 10 8 6 4 2

Simon & Schuster UK Ltd
Africa House
64–78 Kingsway
London WC2B 6AH

Simon & Schuster Australia
Sydney

www.simonsays.co.uk

A CIP catalogue for this book is available
from the British Library.

ISBN: 0-7434-4942-8

Maps by Neil Hyslop

Typeset in Palatino by M Rules
Printed and bound in Great Britain
by Cox & Wyman Ltd, Reading, Berks

In memory of the 3,700 known victims of al-Qaeda and the many tens of thousands injured and bereaved by its acts of terror.

Contents

Part III: WAR ON TERROR

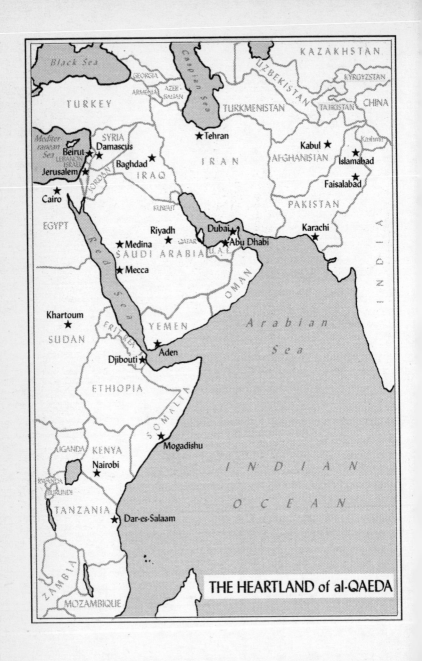

THE HEARTLAND of al-QAEDA

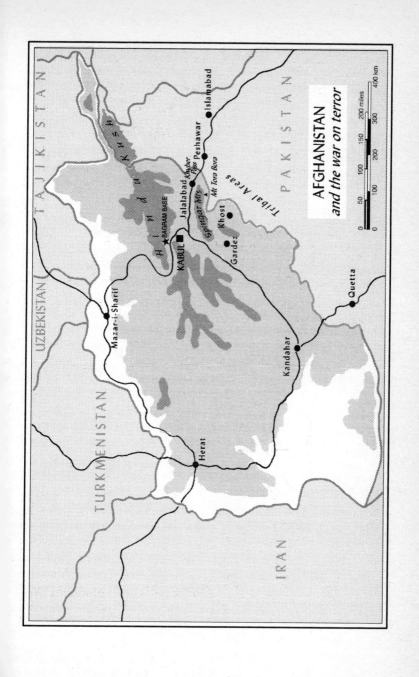

AFGHANISTAN
and the war on terror

Dramatis Personae

Senior personnel

Osama bin Laden	'The Director'
Ayman al-Zawahiri	head of Islamic Jihad and Bin Laden's deputy
Mohamed Atef	head of the military committee
Mustafa Ahmed al-Hawsawi	finance chief
Khalid Sheikh Mohamed	mastermind behind September 11 plot
Wadih al-Hage	Bin Laden's secretary
Tawfiq bin Atash ('Khallad')	Bin Laden's bodyguard
Abu Talal	trainer in Afghan camps
Abu Zubaydah	chief recruiter and head of Khaldan camp
Hamzallah al-Liby	documents expert
Khaled al-Fawwaz	propaganda unit, London
Omar Abdel Rahman	the 'blind Sheikh'

World Trade Center attack, New York (1993)

Ramsi Yousef

Embassy bombings, East Africa (1998)

Abu Ubaidah al-Banshiri
Ali Mohamed
Fazul Abdullah Mohamed
Mohamed al-Owhali
Mohamed Odeh

USS *Cole* attack, Yemen (2000)

Mohamed Omar al-Harazi

September 11, New York and Washington DC (2001)

The Hamburg cell
Mamoun Darkanzali
Mohamed Haidar Zammer
Mounir al-Moutassadeq
Ramsi bin al-Shibh
Saïd Bahaji
Zacharias Essebar

The Madrid cell
Abu Dhadah

The hijackers

Mohamed Atta (pilot)	American Airlines Flight 11
Abdulaziz al-Omari	(crashed into North Tower of
Satam al-Suqami	World Trade Center)
Wail al-Shehri	
Waleed al-Shehri	

Marwan al-Shehhi (pilot)	United Airlines Flight 175
Ahmed al-Ghamdi	(South Tower of World Trade
Fayez Benihamed	Center)
Hamza al-Ghamdi	
Mohand al-Shehri	
Hani Hanjour (pilot)	American Airlines Flight 77
Khalid al-Midhar	(The Pentagon, Washington
Majed Moqed	DC)
Nawaf al-Hazmi	
Salem al-Hazmi	
Ziad Jarrah (pilot)	United Airlines Flight 93
Ahmed al-Haznawi	(crash-landed in a field near
Ahmed al-Nami	Pittsburgh, PA)
Saïd al-Ghamdi	

South-east Asia

'Amrozoi'	Bali nightclub bomber
Abdul Hakim Murad	Operation Bojinka plotter (with Ramsi Yousef)
Abu Bakr Bashir	'spiritual head' of Jemaah Islamiyah
Imam Samudra	Bali plotter
Omar al-Faruk	al-Qaeda agent in south-east Asia
Riduan Isamuddin ('Hambali')	Bali plotter; link man between JI and al-Qaeda
Ustaz Muklaz	Bali plotter

Others

Djame Beghal	Paris embassy plotter
Jamal al-Fadl	Sudanese defector
Zacharias Moussaoui	the 'twentieth hijacker'

Richard Reid	the 'shoe bomber'
Abu Qatada	London-based cleric
Omar Saïd Sheikh	British militant, Kashmir

Preface

For three years he was my screen-saver. Every time I switched on my computer at the BBC's west London offices an austere figure in long robes appeared, smiling enigmatically as he stared directly at the camera. Osama bin Laden already looked the part of a fanatic, sitting in a room lined with religious texts, his Kalashnikov by his side. But his mission to destroy America was, as yet, ominously unfulfilled. So I kept him on my computer screen even when I finished making my first film about al-Qaeda following the US Embassy bombings in East Africa in 1998. I knew the world, and America in particular, had not heard the last of him. Osama, or 'Usama' as his name is also spelled, had first been mentioned to me in 1996. During discreet lunches in anonymous hotels Whitehall contacts would increasingly murmur 'UBL', warning me that the intelligence services had put his initials at the top of the list of terrorists emerging in the post-Cold War world of rogue states and resurgent Islamic fundamentalism. Reports were filtering back from Afghanistan that Bin Laden was building a formidable organisation there. It was called al-Qaeda, Arabic for 'The Base'.

Some gremlin in the BBC computer system had destroyed my screen-saver during August 2001, while I was away on holiday. On my return to the *Panorama* office at the beginning of September, I considered possible replacements as I wondered what unexpected news events would claim my attention that autumn. I did not have long to wait. At lunchtime on 11 September the television monitor in the office announced a newsflash: a plane had crashed into the North Tower of the World Trade Center in New York, but first indications were that it was an accident. I walked into the office of the programme's editor. 'It could be Bin Laden,' I warned him, remembering that our research in 1998 had turned up documents revealing that a member of al-Qaeda had dreamed of flying his plane into the CIA headquarters in Virginia. As I spoke I turned back to the television screen to see the second plane fly into the South Tower, a fireball blooming as people around me gasped in shock. 'It has to be al-Qaeda' was my reaction now – the terror group had already proved itself capable of carrying out sophisticated and near-simultaneous attacks, as the East African truck bombs, minutes apart, had demonstrated. Telephones began ringing all around as we started gearing up for a special programme to be broadcast that night. The third flight had yet to reach the Pentagon and the hijackers had not even revealed their presence on the fourth plane.

During the next year I was to make four more films for *Panorama*, investigating further al-Qaeda and its history, discovering how the network planned the September 11 attacks and covering the 'war on terror' which America and the West prosecuted in their aftermath. This book is the product of my research, my interviews and my travels and draws on the experience of the 1998 film and the watching brief I have on both the Middle East and terror organisations, as a specialist in this area. I have travelled widely and spoken to hundreds of people from

the Middle East to the Far East, from America to Africa, from
Europe to Afghanistan, Pakistan and the Central Asian states.

This book reveals who and what al-Qaeda is: its philosophy,
its tradecraft, and its malevolent aims. I have tried to find the
human beings behind the names on wanted lists. I have sought
to reveal the childhood secrets of the young men who penned
the 'martyrs' slogans, and I have explored the causes of the
hate-filled diatribes on grainy videos. It is no easy task for a
Westerner, or a woman, but then there are no easy answers to
the problem of international terrorism.

My book is also about the West's response to the threat of al-
Qaeda over the last fifteen years. It is a tale of weakness and
exploitation and a failure of imagination. Al-Qaeda, fundamentally a product of the Arab world, could only flourish in a
free and forgiving climate, unlike that of many Middle Eastern
countries, where harsh regimes stick to the only form of rule
recognised and respected by militant Islamic organisations. Bin
Laden's group turned instead to the softer underbelly of the
West; to democracies with respect for human rights, more open
immigration policies and laws that restricted intelligence and
law-enforcement agencies. Bureaucratic turf wars, complacency, military timidity and political weakness, not to mention
political correctness, contributed to our inability to deal with
these extremists, until it was too late to save the lives of thousands. Al-Qaeda, as the apogee of international terror, came to
represent, in my view, the greatest threat to democracy since
the Cold War. Combating that threat with new laws and a new
determination, post-September 11, has in turn undermined
some of the pillars supporting our democratic and open societies. There is also the very real fear that even if the West
eventually wins the battle against al-Qaeda, it is in danger of
losing the war. Just as Osama bin Laden himself intended,
many have come to see this as an epic struggle between East
and West, between the Muslim and the non-Muslim world.

This is not a biography of Osama bin Laden himself,
although he, of course, plays a large part in it. Neither have I

dwelled on the human tragedy of the events of September 11, the thousands dead and injured in the attacks on New York and Washington. This is in no way to diminish the loss and suffering of the victims and their families but there are other books which relate their terrible story. There are other books too which deal with al-Qaeda in its earlier years, accounts which were published before or just as the September 11 attacks occurred. A great deal has happened since then; the revelations of the details of the plot itself and discoveries made in Afghanistan have shed new light on the organisation and its previous attacks on American interests around the world. The reaction of the US and the coalition to the apocalyptic events of September 11 has fundamentally altered not just the network but also its future prospects.

'Our enemies made the mistake that America's enemies always make,' President George W. Bush said in December 2001. 'They saw liberty and thought they saw weakness. And now they see defeat.' It took the loss of three thousand lives on September 11 for the United States and Europe to face the danger of al-Qaeda head-on. Hundreds more victims – mainly from countries other than the United States – had died in earlier attacks, with barely a response. Hundreds more have died since September 11 as governments around the world scramble to uncover new plots while al-Qaeda strikes – again and again. Is Bush's certainty that al-Qaeda now 'sees defeat' justified? I hope the following pages will allow readers to decide for themselves.

'The wise learn many things from their enemies.'
—Aristophanes, *The Birds*, c. 414 BC

THE BASE

Part I

THE GATHERING STORM

1

The Seventeenth Son

'Every grown-up Muslim hates Americans, Jews and Christians. It is part of our belief and our religion. Since I was a boy I have been at war with and harbouring hatred of Americans.'

—Osama bin Laden, 1998

Saudi Arabia, 1959–79

'God Almighty was gracious enough for me to be born to Muslim parents in the Arabian peninsula in al-Malazz neighbourhood, in al-Riyadh, in 1377 *hegira*.' In this one sentence Osama bin Laden, the leader of and inspiration behind the al-Qaeda terror network, summed up the three factors which shaped his destiny. First, the religion he was born into – Islam; second, the place of his birth – the Arabian peninsula, or the land of the Holy Mosques; and third, the time of his arrival in the world – 1377 *hegira*, by the Muslim calendar, or on the cusp between 1957 and 1958, in Western terms. It meant he would pass into manhood during a period of great change in the Middle East.

Osama bin Laden was born the seventeenth son of an illiterate labourer from the Wadi Hadromawt valley, a remote tribal area in the north of the Yemen, which borders Saudi Arabia. The modern Saudi state was revived in 1902 by Abdul-Aziz Ibn

Saud, the great desert fighter, and became a kingdom in 1926. With his Wahhabi warriors, and the support of the British, Ibn Saud had unified much of the peninsula around the strict and austere principles of Wahhabism, which sought to regenerate Islam through a return to the original purity of the religion founded in the sixth century by the Prophet Mohamed and his companions.

Mohamed Awad bin Laden, according to family tradition, walked a thousand miles north in 1925 to find work in Saudi Arabia. Working as a bricklayer on the new palace, Mohamed came to Ibn Saud's attention by devising ways of getting the now-elderly monarch around the palatial complex in his wheelchair. Bin Laden senior seized his chance to ingratiate himself still further; soon he was building a road from Mecca to Taif, in the Asir mountains, where the royal family had their hitherto inaccessible country retreats. And so the BinLaden construction company was born on the back of a deepening relationship with the royal family. Substantial building contracts flowed from that relationship, including projects to extend the Holy Mosques on which the Saud family based their religious and political legitimacy. The BinLaden construction company's success brought Mohamed bin Laden vast wealth and also considerable prestige in the Islamic world.

'It is no secret that my father was responsible for the infrastructure of Saudi Arabia,' his son, Osama, once said proudly. 'God blessed him and bestowed on him an honour that no other contractor has known. He built the Holy Mecca Mosque where the Holy Kaba'ah is located and . . . he built the Holy Mosque in Medina for our Prophet.'

Mohamed bin Laden cemented further strategic alliances within the Kingdom, much as Ibn Saud himself had done, by marrying three Saudi wives. One of them, an al-Khalifa, was from the family of the Prophet Mohamed himself. But the fourth wife, the last allowed by Muslim tradition, was a more moveable fixture, frequently finding herself divorced to make way for a new favourite. In this way Mohamed accumulated twenty-one wives in his long and fruitful parallel career as patriarch of a family of fifty-four children, twenty-four of them sons.

The position of the final wife was always somewhat precarious, and this was the situation in which a young Syrian woman, Alia, found herself when she caught the eye of Mohamed bin Laden in Jordan. He was there to tender, successfully, for the refurbishment contract for the al-Aqsa mosque in East Jerusalem. Al-Aqsa is Islam's third holiest shrine, one over which the Hashemite Jordanian king always has guardianship. Alia became Mohamed bin Laden's fourth wife and bore him one child only, a son, his seventeenth, named Osama.

Osama bin Laden was to spend his life in the strictly conservative part of Saudi Arabia known as the Hejaz, moving between Mecca, Medina and the bustling, and more cosmopolitan, Red Sea port of Jeddah, where the BinLaden Group was based. His time in the sun was short. His mother was soon replaced as the fourth consort, although she and her son continued as satellites in Mohamed bin Laden's orbit, remaining in the extended family compound where wives and their offspring each had their own houses.

The family would like to erase the name Osama from the public record as effectively as it has been erased from the family history. Not only do they feel betrayed by his crimes, they believe Osama has violated a special relationship, the closeness between the Houses of Saud and Bin Laden, by his calls for the overthrow of the Saudi regime. The reluctance of family members to speak openly, however, has spawned a rash of speculative stories which have gone uncorrected in the media or even become received wisdom: the rejected, embittered son of a slave mother; the drinker and womaniser amid the brothels of Beirut; holiday snaps of a schoolboy 'Osama', clad in bell-bottoms, leaning against a purple Cadillac on a family holiday in Sweden. None of these colourful accounts is true, and the latter photograph is that of another brother.

The reality – both the opportunities and the frustrations of being within the Bin Laden clan, as relayed to me by those close to the family – is more complex. It centres on the commanding figure of Mohamed bin Laden. A photograph taken in the 1960s shows him relaxing on carpets in a Bedouin tent, his hands clasped behind his head; his eyes are screwed up against the harsh desert sunlight and a large signet ring flashes on his left hand. He is laughing: a real sensuous belly-laugh of enjoyment. He exudes power and charisma. His sons remember him as a strict but somewhat distant figure, although he would sometimes take the boys with him on trips to the desert. Inevitably, in the strict pecking-order of large Saudi families, a seventeenth son would have received less attention than the oldest boys, sons of more favoured wives. Some in the family believe that the frustrations Osama experienced as a boy rankled for ever, the outsider whose position was fixed, not at the centre but on the fringes of the clan.

Osama remembers his father as a devout Muslim whose material success enabled him to capitalise on his religious devotion. 'Sometimes,' Osama marvelled, 'using his helicopter, he prayed in all three of the Holy Mosques in a single day.'

As a boy, Osama bin Laden was quiet and intense, diligent at school. A teacher from Britain, Brian Fyfield-Shaylor, who taught him English for a year, remembered him both for his manners and his commanding presence, even at an early age. 'He was singularly gracious and polite, with a great deal of inner confidence,' said the tutor. 'Physically he was outstanding because he was taller, more handsome and fairer than the other boys.' His friends remember Osama as an avid reader of religious and historical texts. He was raised as a strict Sunni Muslim, in accordance with family and Wahhabi practice, based on Qur'anic teaching and the Shari'a law.

Mohamed bin Laden was on his way to building a $5 billion business with more than 30,000 employees. The unique relationship he enjoyed with the royal family was one of mutual advantage, the BinLaden Group acting as unofficial bankers, paying the wages of thousands of civil servants in the late 1950s when the royal family's finances were hit by a drop in the price of oil. But the family suffered a severe shock in 1966, when Osama was nearly ten: his father was killed in a plane crash while surveying his latest project on the border between Saudi Arabia and the Yemen. Osama would inherit a fortune, estimated at around $80 million, $50 million of it tied up in the company, $30 million in cash – although it would be more than a decade before the whole family came to an agreement on the division of the inheritance.

The royal family effectively adopted the Bin Laden children as their own, paying school and college fees and keeping an eye on their progress, as well as supervising the company. 'Your family will be my family,' King Faisal, Ibn Saud's successor, had promised Mohamed before he died. The new head of the Bin Laden household, and the business, was Salim, the eldest son – like his father, he was a charismatic and forceful personality. Salim was very Westernised, having been educated at the exclusive English boarding school, Millfield. He would later marry an English girl. A friend recalled a night spent in the Mirabelle nightclub in London's Mayfair. 'Salim handed round harmonicas and insisted everyone played "God Save the Queen",' he told me. 'He was a great guitar-player, too. Osama was very different, you didn't hear much about him.' Even his brothers did not see much of the seventeenth son, who remained ensconced in Saudi Arabia, rarely travelling abroad and then only within the Middle East.

Osama bin Laden has never been averse to subtly re-writing his own history, or less subtly re-writing religious texts, for the benefit of his Muslim audience. He told a Syrian interviewer in 1998, 'Every grown-up Muslim hates Americans, Christians and Jews. It is part of our belief and our religion. Ever since I was a boy I have been harbouring feelings of hatred towards America.' There is, however, no evidence of his harbouring any

political feelings at all as a boy or in his early teenage years;
these do not seem to have appeared until he emerged from the
protective cocoon of the Bin Laden clan to spread his wings in
the outside world. Osama bin Laden took his first wife when he
was seventeen, a cousin from the same Syrian clan as his
mother. Her name was Najwa Ghanem and she would bear his
first son, Abdullah.

At the age of nineteen, Osama bin Laden enrolled at the King
Abdul Aziz University in Jeddah to study management and
economics. It was 1977, a time of unparalleled change within
Saudi Arabia and upheaval across the Middle East. At the same
moment another young Saudi, the same age as Bin Laden, had
begun his medical studies at university in the capital, Riyadh.
Dr Sa'ad al-Fagih would himself become a Saudi dissident in
exile and his path would cross many times, through the years
and the continents, with that of his more infamous compatriot.
Al-Fagih, a scholarly man with a neat beard, invariably carries
a copy of the Qur'an. He does not support Bin Laden's violent
creed but offers insight into the events which shaped the terrorist leader. Al-Fagih described to me the atmosphere of the late
1970s in Saudi Arabia, a time when a new ruler, King Khaled,
was seen as a more liberal force, opening up the country and
lifting the ban on travel. The oil price was high and the economy
boomed. Some young Saudis chose to fling their money around,
indulging themselves in the nightclubs of London and Paris –
but others found a different kind of freedom.

'There was an atmosphere of increasing openness, but at the
same time a resurgence of Muslim thinking, inspired by people
from countries like Egypt and Syria as well as in Saudi,' Dr al-
Fagih explained. 'There was a desire to use existing educated
communities, in high schools and universities and mosques, to
influence the population socially and culturally, to bring them
back to Islamic thought.'

Ever since forming an alliance with the religious reformer
Mohamed Ibn Abdul Wahhab, the founder of Wahhabism, in

1744, the Saudi royal family has relied on inspiring religious fervour to consolidate their power. It has been a delicate balancing-act and whenever the scales threatened to tip in favour of religious extremists challenging their authority, the royal family has quickly called for foreign aid to destroy the upstarts. In 1929, when ultra-conservative elements in his army who were opposed to modern innovations like aircraft and telephones rose in revolt, Ibn Saud quickly crushed them with the help of the British. The authority of the king, as imam, or leader of the Muslim community, was paramount.

The resurgence of Muslim thinking in the late 1970s was, however, allowed a freer rein, especially in the Islamic universities of the kingdom where opponents of secular Arab nationalism, as practised in Gamal Abdel Nasser's Egypt, were allowed to spread their message. With the new prosperity, pamphlets and audio cassettes espousing their views were freely distributed. These were heady days of debate and deception, too; for the first time, groups dared to gather clandestinely to discuss the most seditious ideas. This was the environment that the young Osama bin Laden found himself in when he began taking his degree course in business and economics and, at his insistence, Islamic studies as well.

Bin Laden started attending meetings at Jeddah University addressed by key thinkers in the Muslim Brotherhood movement – the Islamic party which had been a thorn in the side of Nasser's regime in Egypt. Since the 1930s the Brotherhood had been agitating to establish an Islamic state based on Shari'a law. One of the Muslim Brotherhood speakers was Abdullah Azzam, the man who would become Bin Laden's mentor and the ideological figurehead behind the establishment of al-Qaeda.

Azzam, a Palestinian born in Jordan, offered his listeners an intoxicating blend of violent rhetoric and zealotry. His version of Islamic history was aggressive and militant. He railed against the forces which had brought about the disintegration of the Ottoman Empire after the First World War, and the creation of the state of Israel after the Second. He held up the life of Saladin, the twelfth-century military hero who checked the progress of the Crusaders and re-took Jerusalem, as an inspiration to a new generation.

The second significant figure who passed through Jeddah University at the same time as Bin Laden was Mohamed Qutb, another radical Islamist, from Egypt. A Saudi student who attended his lectures but preferred not to be identified told me: 'The auditorium was packed, there was standing room only. He was very popular and you gained prestige if you could attend one of his lectures.' Mohamed preached the views of his brother, Sayyid Qutb, who has been called the father of the *jihadi* movement. It is Qutb's views, polemical, anti-American and revolutionary, which, together with Azzam's fiery historical rhetoric, shaped Osama bin Laden's philosophy.

Sayyid Qutb was a small-town teacher, a school inspector and a publisher of literary criticism. But all that changed in 1948 during a fateful visit to America. He decided on the trip that his salvation lay in devotion to Islam; a vow that was immediately tested when a drunken American matron tried to seduce him on the ship that carried him westward. Qutb was not won over by her charms – or the charms of the American way of life. Their churches were 'entertainment centres and sexual playgrounds'; their women scandalously free. 'Western civilisation is unable to present any healthy values for the guidance of mankind,' Qutb concluded. He joined the Muslim Brotherhood and became the most influential advocate in modern times of *jihad*, or Islamic holy war. The strict meaning of *jihad* within Islam is 'a struggle', and the word can apply to both a physical and a psychological striving. For Qutb and later for Bin Laden, *jihad* was always associated with conquest, a war sanctioned by Islamic tradition.

Qutb harked back to the era of Ibn Taymiyya, a thirteenth-century Islamic purist whose opposition to everything he considered not to be sanctioned by the Qur'an had led him into conflict with the Mamluke Sultans of Egypt. However, he ruled in their favour against the Mongols, fellow Muslims who were threatening war. He declared the Mongols *jahili*, pagans, like the Arabs before the coming of the Prophet, because they did not follow all the guidelines laid down in the Qur'an. *Jihad*, he declared, could therefore be waged against them.

The judgement of Ibn Taymiyya echoed down the ages but found real resonance in the twentieth century. It became the justification for Islamic fundamentalists to declare even Muslim rulers corrupt, Westernised, unfit to govern and therefore ripe for overthrowing. Ibn Taymiyya's doctrine was taken up by Sayyid Qutb to justify his struggle against the secular regime of Gamal Abdel Nasser.

Qutb's views landed him in trouble with the Egyptian President. He was tortured and detained in a concentration camp and eventually executed in 1966. But his best-known work, *Milestones*, written in prison in 1962, became a seminal work for the *jihadi* movement. 'If we look at the sources and foundations of modern ways of living it becomes clear that the whole world is steeped in *Jahiliyyah* [ignorance of divine guidance], and all the marvellous material comforts and high-level inventions do not diminish this ignorance,' Qutb wrote. 'This *Jahiliyyah* is based on rebellion against God's sovereignty on earth.'

While the Qur'an instructs Muslims to treat the People of the Book, Jews and Christians with respect and courtesy, Qutb concluded from his reading of the Prophet's words – and, no doubt, his experiences in America – that all Christians are destined for damnation. Jews too were declared the enemy. For Qutb, everyone was a target; both the West, as the civilisation of the infidel, and the rulers of modern Arab states, who had proved themselves effectively infidel as well – *jahili*, like the ignorant Arabs in the dark ages before the coming of the Prophet.

This was a heady brew which the Saudi royal family, who claimed to run a truly Islamic state, allowed to ferment in their universities. At the same time the liberalisation of the country resulted in pictures of more scantily-clad women in magazines, more daring films on television. It was causing mutterings in a population acknowledged to be more conservative than its ruling family. The un-Islamic high jinks abroad of some of the royal princes could not be entirely hidden.

Then, in 1979, Bin Laden's final year in university, a bomb-shell dropped in the Middle East. In neighbouring Iran an Islamic Revolution led by Ayatollah Khomeini, supported by students and the poor, ousted the Shah. The shock-waves were felt throughout the region as Khomeini's Muslim theocracy replaced the monarchy, declared with such pomp by the Shah's Pahlavi dynasty. The House of Saud shivered next door. In universities throughout the kingdom, student gatherings were electrified by what popular power, harnessed to Islam, could achieve.

The Saudi royal family's fears were realised in December 1979, hard on the heels of the Iranian Islamic Revolution. A group of religious militants, students and tribesmen seized control of the Grand Mosque in Mecca. King Khaled, alarmed at the genie he had released from the bottle, resorted to the time-honoured tradition of calling for foreign help. An elite group of French paratroopers eventually wrested back control and the bloody uprising was brutally quelled.

The families of many fervent young students were alarmed at the spread of this religious fever, and wondered how it would next manifest itself. An outlet arose that very same month, December 1979, when the Soviet Union invaded Afghanistan to prop up the Communist regime there. Now there was a new and exhilarating war to be fought, a true *jihad* between the forces of Islam and the secular armies of Communism.

Osama bin Laden was a witness to these tumultuous times, as junior observer in the radical new Islamic circles which were developing. He graduated from university shortly afterwards with an assured and prosperous future in the family firm before him. But he chose differently.

'When the invasion of Afghanistan started, I was enraged and went there at once,' he later said. 'I arrived within days, before the end of 1979.' Osama bin Laden had taken the fateful step which would launch him on his career as the mastermind of a worldwide terrorist organisation.

2

The Dark Defile

'We are young, we don't know anything; let's go, it's an adventure!'

—L'Houssaine Kerchtou, Moroccan member of
al-Qaeda and US federal witness, 2001

Afghanistan, 1979–89

It was Rudyard Kipling who immortalised the experience of 16,500 British troops and their Eton-educated officers, at the mercy of Gilzai tribesmen and their jezails, or long muzzle-loaded rifles:

> A scrimmage in a border station,
> A canter down some dark defile,
> Two thousand pounds of education
> Drops to a ten-rupee jezail.

In 1840 Afghanistan, in the mountain cockpit of Asia, found itself a pawn between the imperial ambitions of two great powers, the Russians and the British. Blood flowed when the British tried to install a puppet royalist regime to halt Russian expansion southwards to threaten the riches of India. Thousands of British troops and untold numbers of Afghans died. Two more wars were to follow, leaving a nineteenth-century British Secretary of State to sourly sum up: 'All that has been accomplished has been the disintegration of the state which it was desired to see strong, friendly and independent. There is a condition of anarchy throughout much of the remainder of the country.' It is a remark which still stands as a description of Afghanistan two centuries later.

In 1979 Afghanistan found itself again in the cockpit, this time caught between rival twentieth-century superpowers. When the Russians invaded to prop up a puppet regime of their own, America did not stand idly by. The Russians would meet the descendants of those invisible tribal marksmen whom Kipling had described as 'Being blessed with perfect sight, / Picks off our messmates left and right.' In the 1980s, with new allies, and fighting under the banner of Islam, the tribes would pick off Russian helicopter gunships, using Stinger missiles supplied by the US Central Intelligence Agency. For ten long years Afghanistan became the Soviets' 'bleeding wound', in the words of Mikhail Gorbachev.

Seven fractious Afghan warlords and their followers, from different ethnic groups, formed an alliance of *mujahideen*, 'warriors of God', to resist the Soviet invaders. A triumvirate of outside nations – Pakistan, Saudi Arabia and the United States – provided the bulk of their weaponry, finance and training. Britain, Egypt and China also participated in the coalition. The CIA, operating a policy of 'plausible deniability', organised a massive airlift of arms – several hundreds of thousands of tons in the first five years of the war. An estimated $2 billion flowed from Saudi coffers, both government funds and private charities. The Pakistanis, in the shape of the ISI, the all-powerful Inter Services Intelligence agency, were the front men, handing out the arms, arranging the training and attempting to adjudicate between the quarrelsome Afghans and the Muslim volunteers who had come to join them.

The town of Peshawar, thirteen miles from the Afghan border in the tribal area of Pakistan, guards the entrance to the

Khyber Pass, the route through the Hindu Kush into Afghanistan. Always an arms market for the tribal areas, where the love affair with the gun is deeply rooted in history, Peshawar in 1979 became a veritable arms bazaar, with Kalashnikov rifles spilling out of doorways and more exotic and lethal weaponry tucked away inside.

Osama bin Laden came to this dusty, Wild West town in the early 1980s. He was one of an estimated 10,000 young Saudis who went to Afghanistan to volunteer for battle against the Soviets, according to the Saudi Interior Ministry. A hefty discount was offered on Saudi Airlines flights from Riyadh to Peshawar. Some volunteers stayed for years, some professionals for a few weeks at a time, to lend their expertise as engineers and doctors. Some even went for their holidays, just to say they had been there.

Together with his mentor from Jeddah, Abdullah Azzam, the father of the new *jihad* teaching, Bin Laden formed the *Maktab al-Khidmat*, known as the MaK or the Afghan Services Bureau. It provided accommodation and logistical services to transport the flood of volunteers to the front and provide for their needs. Twenty-two-year-old Osama became the organisation's chief fund-raiser.

The volunteers from abroad, as many as 25,000, who joined the local *mujahideen* became known as the 'Afghan Arabs'. Milt Beardon, the CIA's local station chief, watched them pass through the staging post of Peshawar and on to the battle front. 'Some were genuine, on missions of humanitarian value,' he decided, 'while others were adventure-seekers looking for paths to glory, and still others were psychopaths.' Osama bin Laden, running his aid agency for *jihad*, at this time fitted into the first category. In the next decade Afghanistan would turn him into a man looking for paths to glory. Ultimately he would find his niche in the final category, that of the psychopath.

From the Islamic perspective these were heady days, days never experienced before. A coming-together of young men from all over the Muslim world, they were characterised by fervour, excitement, a sense of duty – and a sense of history. Essam Deraz, an Egyptian film director and former army officer, was one of the many volunteers who came to Afghanistan, via Bin Laden and Azzam's MaK. 'It was something new when he started to gather Arabs together,' Deraz told me. 'It was my duty as a Muslim and as a film-maker to go and experience it.' Now a middle-aged man, balding and rotund, Essam Deraz had a wistful look in his eyes as he showed me the grainy footage he had shot of Osama bin Laden and his men in the Tora Bora cave complex in the south of Afghanistan.

The soldiers look amateurish: men wandering around in *shalwar kameez*, the loose pyjama-style shirts and trousers, with turbans on their heads and bandoleers slung round their shoulders. They casually cradle RPGs, rocket-propelled grenade-launchers, in their arms, as they bounce along the rocky scree in rusty jalopies. But time, the weather and the terrain were on their side. Deraz's pictures show a scene of indescribable beauty: green plains, the tinkling of bells from herds of animals moving below, the Hindu Kush blue and smoky along the horizon. The *mujahideen* are literally wedged in cracks in the rocks high up in the mountains, laughing at the attempts of the clumsy Soviet bombers to find them. 'We are young, we don't know anything; let's go, it's an adventure!' L'Houssaine Kerchtou told a US court ten years later. He was explaining how, as a young Moroccan, he got sucked into the world of *jihad* in Afghanistan, a thousand miles away from home, and became a follower of Bin Laden.

During the first years of the war, Osama bin Laden spent more time roaming the Arab world fund-raising than he did in Afghanistan. At the height of the foreign Arab influx into Peshawar, between 1984 and 1986, Bin Laden and the MaK channelled several billion dollars' worth of Western financial and material resources into the war. They worked closely with the ISI, the Pakistani intelligence service, and with the Saudi government. Bin Laden proved to be an able organiser and used his contacts in the construction business to bring in machinery.

'We transported heavy equipment from the country of the two Holy Places, hundreds of tons including bulldozers, loaders, dump trucks and equipment for digging trenches,' Bin Laden said later. 'When we saw the brutality of the Russians bombing *mujahideen* positions, we dug a good number of huge tunnels and storage places. We also built a hospital.'

Abdullah Azzam was Bin Laden's mentor, but Osama had a second confidant, a royal friend from Saudi, the powerful chief of security. Prince Turki bin Faisal bin Abdul-Aziz was in charge of 'the Afghan file' – the Saudi campaign to help the drive against the Soviets, channelling up to $2 billion through twenty Islamic charities and two Saudi-owned banks, set up by the royal family for the purpose. 'Osama was a model, we wanted more of him,' said Prince Turki recently. 'He was very upright, a very friendly and amenable fellow in the 1980s.'

By 1986 Bin Laden was playing a more active role, becoming involved in military action himself, and setting up his first military training camp, at Jaji. 'The longer he spent here, the more Osama was determined to stay and to fight himself,' Essam Deraz recounted. Deraz would spend a week at a time with Bin Laden and his fighters in the mountains. His film footage shows a tall rangy figure in khaki *shalwar kameez*, towering over the others in the group; Deraz points out his Saudi head-dress. Bin Laden speaks on a field radio, clearly the commander: 'Send water and food to the other post,' he orders. Stooping, he enters what looks like a horizontal crevice in the rock. Inside the cave, dark but for a beam of light filtering through a crack in the roof, he squats with the others in a circle as they eat from a plate of mutton and rice. There are sleeping bags on the floor. Bin Laden is smiling, shy, waving his hand at the intrusive camera. 'Enough, Essam,' he protests. 'I will shut off your electricity supply.'

The scene is in its own way romantic, presenting an ideal of male camaraderie and noble purpose, a small band battling the

enemy in a harsh landscape. It appealed to Essam Deraz and
thousands of other Arabs, steeped in a tradition of rigid hierar-
chies and remote and repressive rulers. Here was a rich man,
almost a prince, from a far-away country come to suffer the same
hardship as the poor man beside him. Deraz is nostalgic for those
days: 'It was unheard of, to bring together Arabs from many different countries in the middle of battle, to eat and sleep and fight
together in the same place,' he told me. 'I had little but my life to
give but he came with a great deal of money, from a life of
luxury, which he left behind him to fight in the mountains.'

Osama bin Laden's actual military experience was limited,
although this has not stopped his propaganda machine from
extolling his exploits. The most significant battle he was
involved in occurred in 1987 at Jaji when, in the face of over-
whelming odds and despite the loss of twenty-four of their
number, a small group of Afghan Arabs stopped a Soviet
advance.

'It was at the military camp called al-Ansar, the Lions' Den,'
Bin Laden later recounted. 'The Arab fighters led by Abdullah
Azzam and myself, a group not exceeding more than thirty-five
people, held their ground during two weeks of fighting.' The
legend of Bin Laden and his Arab fighters was born. It was the
beginning of al-Qaeda, Arabic for 'The Base', a group of
Muslim warriors fighting a *jihad* that would eventually expand
to challenge the Western world. The men who came together in
these early days, from all over the Muslim world, formed the
hard core, the loyalists around Bin Laden. Their names would
come to dominate the 'wanted' lists in years to come. Their
leader trusted them to take his message to the four corners of
the world – and to act on it.

By the late 1980s, however, Bin Laden's relationship with
Abdullah Azzam was becoming strained. Bin Laden preferred
Gulbuddin Hekmatyar, leader of the Hizb-i-Islami, the Islamic
Party which was both anti-Communist and anti-Western.
Azzam supported Ahmed Shah Masoud, the more pragmatic

warlord backed by the British intelligence service, MI6. Masoud was a brilliant strategist and canny alliance-builder but his more moderate brand of Islam did not suit Bin Laden. Despite their differences the two directors of the MaK continued to work together. But Bin Laden was beginning to shift his attentions from the more logistical concerns of the Services Bureau towards training active fighting units, which would go on to form the fledgling al-Qaeda.

Bin Laden was also coming under the influence of a man who would ultimately replace Azzam as his religious and political mentor. Ayman al-Zawahiri, an Egyptian doctor, had met Bin Laden in Peshawar when he treated him for high blood pressure. Al-Zawahiri, the leader of the Egyptian militant group Islamic Jihad, which was responsible for the assassination of President Sadat, recognised Afghanistan as fertile ground for developing the new ideology of *jihad* resistance. Al-Zawahiri had settled in Peshawar using his medical skills to treat Afghan refugees in the hospital and his political skills to expand his creed of violence against the Egyptian state. Of all the many extremist Muslim groups which ended up comparing notes in Peshawar, the Egyptian Islamic Jihad and al-Zawahiri would have the most far-reaching impact on Osama bin Laden. Ultimately they would merge with al-Qaeda to inspire, plan and perpetrate atrocities which would kill thousands.

'Al-Zawahiri is the brains, Bin Laden the body,' Montasser al-Zayyat, a Cairo lawyer who has defended many Egyptian militants, told *Panorama*. 'He has had the biggest influence on Bin Laden's world-view.'

By 1988 Bin Laden had split from Abdullah Azzam and the Services Bureau completely and established a separate guesthouse in Peshawar. He established a proper database to track the thousands of Afghan Arabs in the country, classing them as fully-fledged fighters, volunteers in Peshawar, or visitors, which no one had yet done. It meant the families of those missing in Afghanistan could receive proper documentation on their sons; the database would also become invaluable to Bin

Laden, establishing the identity and whereabouts of thousands of willing recruits to the cause of *jihad*. The vast financial resources and technical expertise amassed throughout the ten-year war against the Soviets also benefited the new group he was forming.

The most detailed evidence about the al-Qaeda of those early days in Afghanistan comes from a defector who gave evidence in a New York court, in 2001, against four of Bin Laden's terrorists. Jamal al-Fadl, a Sudanese, was in his twenties when he fought on the Afghan front lines. He was trained in the use of explosives and taught how to shoot down helicopters. He was approached to become the third member of al-Qaeda in 1989.

'I had to take the *bayat*, the oath of allegiance to the group's philosophy of *jihad*, and I signed papers swearing my allegiance to the *emir*, Bin Laden,' he said. At the trial al-Fadl detailed the early operational structure of al-Qaeda, describing it as being split into four committees: military, religious, financial and media. They all came under a consultative council headed by Bin Laden. Formal military training, in special camps, was established as a hallmark of al-Qaeda.

On 15 February 1989, in a carefully choreographed ceremony which could not disguise their ignominious defeat, the last Russian to leave Afghanistan crossed the Friendship bridge over the Amun Darya river into Uzbekistan. General Boris Gromov was greeted by his fourteen-year-old son, Maksim, bearing a sheaf of red carnations. Fifteen thousand of their countrymen had been killed in action, thousands more by disease and hundreds of thousands had been wounded. The once-mighty Red Army had been vanquished; Bin Laden both revelled in that victory and drew from it inspiration for the future.

'The lesson here is that *jihad* is a duty for the nation,' he said. 'We believe that those who waged *jihad* in Afghanistan performed a great duty. They managed with their limited resources of RPGs, anti-tank mines and Kalashnikovs to defeat the biggest legend known to mankind, to destroy the biggest war machine and to remove from our minds the so-called big powers.'

In Bin Laden's mind a religious force which could defeat the Russians could also overcome the other superpower, America, which exerted such power and influence – politically, militarily and culturally – on the Islamic nations.

The pride, and the notion of invincibility, aroused in the hearts of many Muslims by the defeat of the Soviets, cannot be underestimated. Dr Sa'ad al-Fagih, the Saudi contemporary of Bin Laden's, came to Afghanistan as a volunteer in the last stages of the war. He worked, like Ayman al-Zawahiri, in a hospital in Peshawar and stayed with other Egyptian medics in an Afghan Arab guesthouse. Al-Fagih was taken over the border to witness one of the final battles in Afghanistan, and watched the victorious firing of a rocket launcher which the *mujahideen* had captured. In the Beit-al-Ansar guesthouse, in Peshawar, he heard of the legendary exploits of Osama bin Laden, wounded in battle at least three times but unbeaten.

'He believed, from those days forward, that he is living in what football fans call "extra time",' al-Fagih told me. 'He reckons that he should have died in Afghanistan in the Eighties and that whatever happens to him after that is somehow a bonus.'

Within months Abdullah Azzam was dead, killed in a mysterious bomb blast in a market in Peshawar. Suspicion centred on Bin Laden, although some believed the Pakistani intelligence services had carried out the killing. A rival for Bin Laden's position as the head of a new international *jihad* had been conveniently removed from the scene at just the right moment.

What Bin Laden drew from his experience with Abdullah Azzam and the MaK drawing together Muslims from all over the world was a realisation that real power lay in forming a pan-Islamic, rather than just a pan-Arab, organisation. The men who had flocked to the Afghan *jihad* were mostly Arabs, from Saudi Arabia, the Gulf States, Egypt, the Yemen and the Sudan. But Bin Laden understood the potential of embracing Muslims from outside the Middle East, from North Africa and the extensive Islamic communities in Asia and the Far East. By building a broad base al-Qaeda could attract extensive support and construct a wide-ranging operational infrastructure.

Jamal al-Fadl, the Sudanese defector, testified that Osama bin Laden set al-Qaeda an ambitious goal: 'To create an empire of all the world's one billion Muslims, ruled by a single leader.' In Bin Laden's own words his purpose was to 'unite all Muslims and establish a government which follows the rule of the Caliphs', the Islamic empire so ignominiously allowed to disintegrate eighty years earlier. The instrument to accomplish this would be al-Qaeda. The method they would use would be *jihad*, Holy War, drawing inspiration from the works of Sayyid Qutb, the Egyptian polemicist who had used the judgements of a thirteenth-century Islamic purist to justify his call for war against the 'infidel'. Al-Qaeda's enemy would be twofold: first, the Muslim governments they accused of being un-Islamic; second, the power which supported them, the United States of America.

'The acme of this religion is *jihad*. The nation has had a strong conviction that there is no way to obtain faithful strength but by returning to *jihad*,' Osama bin Laden told CNN some years later when asked about the influence of the Afghan war on his thinking. 'The influence of the Afghan *jihad* on the Islamic world was so great and it [demonstrated] that people should rise above many of their differences and unite their efforts against the enemy.'

'Blowback' is the graphic term the CIA use to describe what happened to both the United States and, to a lesser extent, the Saudi regime as a result of their exploits in Afghanistan. The most extreme example of 'blowback' is seen in the murderous career of Bin Laden, which would come to haunt both his own countrymen and the United States, which had once applauded his actions. Prince Turki, then the Saudi security chief, has claimed, 'Bin Laden went to Afghanistan of his own accord . . . we supported the *mujahideen*, we did not support Bin Laden.' Western intelligence officers, who worked on the ground in Afghanistan, laugh hollowly at that statement.

Both the CIA and Bin Laden himself have rejected suggestions of any relationship between them. 'Contrary to what has been said and written, the CIA never recruited, trained or otherwise used the Arab volunteers who arrived in Pakistan,' says Milton Beardon firmly. 'That includes Osama bin Laden.' Beardon agrees, however, that, like the Saudis, American officers involved in the secret war in Afghanistan regarded Bin Laden as an asset at the time, because of his success as a fundraiser.

Bin Laden himself cannot afford, as a self-styled champion of Islam, to be seen as owing anything to America and scoffs at media charges of CIA support. 'What they are saying did not occur at all. Regarding their support for the *jihad*, that support actually came from the Arab states, especially the Gulf States,' he fumed in an interview in 1998. 'Americans are lying, in fact they were a burden on the *mujahideen* and us in Afghanistan. We were just performing a duty to support Islam, although this duty crossed with US interests – without our consent.'

So much money was flowing directly from Saudi Arabia and other Muslim countries through Bin Laden's Services Bureau that in all probability there was no need for CIA funding. But one aspect of the 'blowback' scenario that the CIA are less keen to talk about is the whereabouts of several hundred deadly Stinger missiles supplied to the *mujahideen* by the Americans. On the ground the British SAS showed local fighters how to use the missiles. Some of the Stingers subsequently ended up in the hands of al-Qaeda. A witness in a terror trial in 1995 recounted seeing a Stinger in one of al-Qaeda's camps in eastern Afghanistan five years earlier. Bin Laden would try unsuccessfully to ship some Stingers to the Sudan in 1993, and he told a group of journalists in 1998 that some of his followers had been arrested in Saudi Arabia in possession of one of the American missiles.

Stinger missiles would be found near a British troop base in Kabul in the spring of 2002, and a senior British military source confirmed to me that al-Qaeda had tried to use Stingers against the coalition forces in Afghanistan after September 11. The ultimate nightmare – that American-supplied missiles could be used successfully against Western forces on the ground in Afghanistan – has now become a reality. Following the September 11 attacks, with President Bush's declaration of a 'war on terror', a superpower and its allies have once again entered that dangerous cockpit in the Hindu Kush.

The film footage which Essam Deraz shot of Osama bin Laden marked the start of the Saudi dissident's Afghan adventure; a shy young man, neatly dressed, looks awkwardly at the camera as he drives his bulldozer slowly along a dirt track, a plateau dotted with khaki army tents behind him. This was the image of the fund-raiser, using his contacts to build a military infrastructure.

There is another piece of film that captures the man that Bin Laden had become eight years later. A black horse gallops headlong towards the camera, enveloped in a cloud of dust. Then it slows and its rider, dressed in flowing robes, raises his hand in greeting. '*Sala'am aleikum,*' he says courteously as he passes. Osama bin Laden inclines his head graciously, almost regally; he is relaxed and totally at home in the wild landscape. The symbolism is already there; it is Saladin, the Islamic warrior prince on horseback in the desert.

3

Terror Incorporated

'We want our land to be free of enemies. We want our land to be freed of the Americans.'

—Osama bin Laden, 1998

Saudi Arabia, 1990–91

The modern state of Saudi Arabia under the House of Saud has been blessed with two rare gifts of incalculable worth. The first is its custodianship of the Holy Places of the Islamic faith: Mecca, where the Prophet Mohamed was born in the seventh century; and Medina, where he is buried. The second is the largest reserves of crude oil in the world – 260 billion barrels and an even larger reservoir of undiscovered black gold. These two treasures have combined to give the Saudi nation a unique status, both in the eyes of the Muslim world, which despatches more than 2 million people annually to Mecca for the *Haj* pilgrimage, and in the eyes of the West, which considers the stability of Saudi Arabia vital to its commercial and political interests. But in 1990 the presence of these natural gifts brought an external threat to the nation and also sparked internal conflict which would have far-reaching consequences.

On 2 August 1990, Saddam Hussein, the President of Iraq,

invaded Kuwait, threatening the oil supply in neighbouring Saudi Arabia. The royal family were in a quandary as they saw the stunned al-Sabagh royal family of Kuwait, forced to flee their palaces, pitch up in Saudi. The al-Saud family were fearful for their own lives as well as their own oil-fields. They wanted, in the time-honoured tradition of the House of Saud, to call for outside protection. However, the strict Wahhabi interpretation of Islam, on which their power and support was founded, forbade non-Muslims from setting foot in the places of the Holy Mosques of Mecca and Medina. 'Let there be no two religions in Arabia,' said the Prophet Mohamed, and many Saudis considered that non-believers should not live anywhere on the Arabian peninsula. These were desperate times and the pliant *ulema*, or Islamic clergy, in the shape of the Grand Mufti of the Saudi state, Abdul-Aziz bin Baz, was prevailed upon to issue a religious decree making an exception for American forces invited into the kingdom to protect it from the threat posed by another Muslim ruler.

Osama bin Laden had returned from Afghanistan that year and settled back in Jeddah, working for his family firm. He immediately offered the royal family the services of his Afghan veterans, the new al-Qaeda, in the fight against Iraq. In the royal palace in Riyadh, the young Saudi contractor was received by Prince Abdullah, the effective regent of the country. The prince's words were conciliatory: 'The family of Mohamed bin Laden have always been faithful subjects of our kingdom and helped us greatly in our time of need,' he murmured. 'We are sure that nothing will be allowed to mar our good relations in the future.' Bin Laden was 'seething', according to one of his veterans present at the meeting. The meaning was clear: the services of the Afghan Arabs were not required. Instead, the royal family invited 300,000 American troops to defend the kingdom.

For weeks military hardware poured off the giant US C-130 transporters into the airbase at Dhahran, the Saudi city that became the gateway to occupied Kuwait. Lines of troops marched endlessly down the ramps and on to the holy soil of Arabia. These were strange days in the kingdom: hotel rooftops, commandeered by the Western press, sprouted satellite dishes; and women soldiers in military uniform, wearing trousers and rolled-up sleeves, directed the stream of khaki-coloured vehicles roaring north on specially built roads to the border.

'We're here to protect freedom, we're here to protect our future and we're here to protect innocent lives,' declared President George Bush. The Saudis were both relieved and appalled.

I was one of that female, infidel, influx eleven years ago, reporting on the impending Gulf War. In Jeddah, despite my long skirts and long sleeves, I was pursued into a shop by the *mutawa*, the feared religious police, and whacked around the ankles with a stick for displaying too much hair under my headscarf. I learned of the audiotapes circulating in the mosques which preached sedition, arguing against the American presence in the country and accusing the royal family of desecrating the birthplace of Islam. Safar al-Hawali, one of the most influential radical preachers, broadcast this message from Mecca: 'We have asked [for] the help of our real enemies in defending us. The point is that we need an internal change. The first war should be against the infidels inside, and then we will be strong enough to face our external enemies,' al-Hawali said. 'Brothers, you have a duty to perform. The war will be long, the confrontation is coming.'

Dr Sa'ad al-Fagih was by now also back in Saudi Arabia after his Afghan experience. 'During the 1990 Gulf crisis the US crossed the psychological barrier by bringing in their forces,' he told me. 'They failed to remember the sensitivities. Worse, the Saudi government was never brave enough to remind them.'

Osama bin Laden, capitalising on the celebrity status his Afghan exploits had earned him and his extensive contacts, began to lecture openly against the royal family. Tapes of his speeches were widely circulated. He canvassed religious scholars for their views and he started lobbying Muslim activists. Defiantly, he began recruiting volunteers and sending them to his camps in Afghanistan for military training in preparation for joining al-Qaeda. His anger was directed not only against the United States for 'occupying' the Holy Places, as he saw it; his rhetoric had developed overtones of resentment against America's wider cultural dominance, and a sense of grievance that Islam was somehow being emasculated by depending on non-Islamic warriors to defend Arabia.

'We believe that we are men, Muslim men who must defend the greatest place in existence, the Holy Kaba'ah,' Bin Laden later explained. 'We want to have the honour of defending it. We do not want American women soldiers, including American, Jewish and Christian women soldiers, defending the grandchildren of great Muslim leaders.'

The ground war against Saddam's forces was over in days but the US troops stayed on after the Iraqi withdrawal from Kuwait. The Bin Laden clan were embarrassed at the strident tones and provocative actions of their black sheep. 'You must remember that the family was so close to the ruling clan, by virtue of Mohamed's relations with Ibn Saud,' a family insider explained. 'It was seen as the ultimate act of disloyalty for Osama to preach against a king and a prince who had effectively been his guardians when his father died.'

The CIA, who until then had only a vague knowledge of Bin Laden as a fellow-traveller in the Afghan war against the Soviets, now noted his anti-American statements with interest. On the fifth floor of the CIA headquarters in Langley, Virginia, the Counter-Terrorism Center, or CTC, was beginning to find his name regularly cropping up in reports from Saudi Arabia about internal dissent.

At that time the CIA's focus was still firmly fixed on state-sponsored terrorism from more secular, often left-wing groups, which still looked to Moscow and Russia's satellites in the Middle East for sustenance. The CTC had been created in response to a rash of hijackings and bombings of American targets in Europe in the mid-1980s, and it brought together agents from the CIA, FBI, Defense Department and other US government agencies in a unique attempt at turf-sharing. Above the rows of desks hung tongue-in-cheek 'street signs' like Tamil Tigers Terrace and Abu Nidal Boulevard. There was as yet no sign reading al-Qaeda Alley.

Stanley Bedlington, a dapper Englishman who was an expert in Muslim groups in the Far East, went to work for the CIA and became the chief analyst in the CTC. 'It was a turning-point for Bin Laden when our troops entered Saudi Arabia,' Bedlington now acknowledges. 'We knew what his views were then, but he didn't attract much attention. We did not know he was building up his own force, al-Qaeda, at that point.'

In Saudi Arabia the royal family, with its all-pervasive security apparatus, had more information on their renegade subject. Their alarm increased when they discovered that Bin Laden was using his veterans to help create the first *jihadi* group in neighbouring Yemen, under the warlord Tariq al-Fadli, who was openly defying the Communist government. The pressure mounted on Bin Laden. Essam Deraz, the Egyptian film-maker, remembers visiting the Saudi dissident, now thirty-three, at the home he shared in Jeddah with his four wives and growing family. 'It was a small house, just two storeys, with his wives in four small flats on the top floor and his offices beneath. I slept on the floor there for the night,' Deraz recalled. 'Osama was depressed about the situation in Saudi – he knew they wanted to get rid of him. He wouldn't say much. He felt they were following his every move.'

At the beginning of 1991 an escape route materialised. In the Sudan, the National Islamic Front had seized the reins of government in a coup in 1989. The real power behind the throne was an Islamic scholar, Dr Hassan al-Turabi. He dreamed of establishing a pure Islamic government across the Muslim world and saw Bin Laden as an influential, and wealthy, figure whom he could use in his campaign.

Dr al-Turabi offered the dissident a refuge and, with the Saudi government pushing relentlessly for his removal, Bin Laden cracked. His assets were frozen by the state but he was allowed a passport to travel – with only a one-way visa, out of Saudi Arabia. He left Jeddah and travelled back to Afghanistan to collect his fighters. All over the Middle East, in Saudi, the Yemen and Egypt, restless Afghan Arabs had tried to settle back at home. But fired up with proselytising zeal for the *jihad*, they were considered dangerous and were unwelcome. They became social misfits, as out of place as many Vietnam veterans had been on their return to America. The Afghan veterans formed a new pool of recruits for al-Qaeda. By the end of 1990 Osama bin Laden had brought many of them to the Sudan, where he set about shaping an international terror organisation along corporate lines, one which would have a truly global reach.

Sudan, 1991–94

The figures wheeled in circles, their black mantles swirling in the dusty golden light. The drummers and flute-players paraded in front of them, urging them to dance on into oblivion. It was the end of my first day in the Sudan and I was standing in front of the Great Mosque at Omdurman on the banks of the Nile, lost in the amazing spectacle of the whirling dervishes, the Sufi celebration of the *dhikr*, in which the participants enter a trance in order to lose their personal identities and attain union with God. This mystical devotional ritual of Sufi Islam, based on Persian poetry, is very different from the ascetic, puritanical practices of Wahhabism, with its prohibition on music and dancing, to which Osama bin Laden ascribed.

Khartoum lies at the crossroads in East Africa, the confluence of the White and the Blue Niles, between the Islamic nations of North Africa and the Christian and animist South. It is an overwhelmingly Islamic city and Osama bin Laden found it a convenient springboard for his opposition to the forces of the West. From here he would attack America's interests and its citizens in Africa and signal his intentions to wreak death and destruction inside the United States itself.

I had come to Khartoum in 1998, in the aftermath of the bloody bombings of US embassies in Africa – suspected to be al-Qaeda's handiwork but as yet unproved. I knew the terror organisation still had a significant presence in the city, although Bin Laden himself had returned to Afghanistan. I wanted, above all else, to speak to the man who invited Bin Laden to Khartoum, and who became his Sudanese mentor and, in many ways, his *alter ego*.

Taking tea with the ideological ruler of Sudan, no one would guess that Dr Hassan al-Turabi was the man accused both of inspiring Sudan's state sponsorship of terror in the 1990s and also of drawing up the blueprint for what al-Qaeda would become, an umbrella organisation of Islamic terror groups. The Sorbonne- and London university-educated scholar of Islam was keen to show off his razor-sharp intellect in witty repartee. Al-Turabi clearly had a soft spot for the BBC and even the Foreign Office – 'Our former colonial masters,' he called them. 'Bad history at least is some history between our countries,' he said, dismissing Americans as 'Wild West cowboys, stupid, naïve people, prone to shoot from the hip'.

Small and energetic in a spotless white turban, he was genial, smiling cheerily as he dispensed the tea and biscuits. With his trimmed grey beard and heavy black-rimmed glasses he looked like an earnest university don.

'Well, I wouldn't say that he focused on advancing Islamic thoughts or new programmes and policies for a new society, actually,' he mused, somewhat condescendingly, when I asked him what kind of man his friend Osama bin Laden was. 'But when he hears about Muslims suffering anywhere, being oppressed or attacked, he will go there and try to put as much money as he can behind any Muslims fighting for a cause . . .' Al-Turabi's giggle was incongruous. He seemed to be enjoying some kind of private joke at the expense of his Saudi friend. I suspected it was on account of Bin Laden's legendary gullibility when it came to underwriting the cash-strapped Sudanese regime's ambitious projects.

Dr al-Turabi had persuaded his wealthy Saudi guest to fund road-building programmes and to undertake construction work on the airport. 'His company was working for this and that, agriculture and building roads. It was a good relationship,' the doctor confirmed. Did Bin Laden get his money back, I wondered? 'Well,' he admitted, giggling again, 'our government couldn't follow up, actually, I mean on the payment instalments . . . Most of our debtors find that, but Osama didn't seem to mind. I suppose he thought he could generate more income in the long run in our country.'

The Sudanese defector, Jamal al-Fadl, painted the most detailed picture of al-Qaeda's development and day-to-day affairs during the Sudan years at the trial of the US Embassy bombers in New York in 2001. He described how Bin Laden used his management training and his business acumen to build a conglomerate whose tentacles stretched across the Middle East. It was a kind of 'Terror Incorporated', established and run on a framework similar to that of multinationals in the West, with a business and financial arm, a public relations or media department and even a strategic group, in the shape of its *fatwa* or religious department. The fourth arm was the all-powerful military committee. Bin Laden, whose alias had been 'The Contractor' in the days of bulldozers and tunnel-building in Afghanistan, now became known as 'The Director' – the man at the apex of the pyramid.

Bin Laden first established a company called Wadi al-Aqiq, 'the mother of other companies', according to al-Fadl, which effectively became the holding company for the terror corporation. There followed a trading company called Laden International and a vehicle for currency trading, Taba Investments, which had no compunction in trading weak Sudanese pounds for the mighty dollar. Bin Laden turned his hand to agriculture, growing sunflowers and peanuts and securing the lucrative sesame seed concession, in lieu of the government's defaulting on the road project repayments. The al-Hijra subsidiary imported explosives, al-Qadurat was a trucking venture, and al-Themar al-Mubaraka ran fruit and vegetable farms that doubled as training camps. Other ventures were less successful; a plan to import bicycles from Azerbaijan flopped.

On the second day of my stay in Khartoum I set off for the district of Riyadh, a quiet and affluent enclave in the city. The three-storey cream-coloured stucco villa that Bin Laden had lived in and run his business from was deserted, its windows barred. Television aerials and a communications antenna still sprouted from the white dome on the roof. I peered through the iron fence ringing the compound to see a few dusty oleander bushes struggling to survive in the baked earth.

The house was in a street next to the mosque where Bin Laden's wives taught local children their Qur'anic studies. Three neighbours, worshippers with Bin Laden at the mosque and, like him, prosperous merchants, invited me to take tea with them on a terrace filled with flowers. The grandson of one helped out with the translation. 'He was a very good man, a good Muslim, not a terrorist at all,' said one man. 'The house was simple, no furniture, just carpets on the floor,' his friend added. They could not decide if this was a result of Saudi tradition, as practised in Bedouin tents, or whether it was a sign of the Bin Laden family's frugal lifestyle. 'He had lots of security, bodyguards provided by the government,' said one former neighbour. 'He was of course a famous Saudi Arabian and a rich businessman.' A portrait was emerging of a quiet family who kept themselves apart but who were still respected in the middle-class Sudanese community around them.

A few blocks away I found a modern, glass-fronted office where, it was whispered, Bin Laden's holding company had been headquartered. A few young men lounged outside, leaning against two shiny black four-wheel-drives. Al-Fadl, the defector, admitted in court three years after my visit that he had been in charge of the al-Qaeda payroll here; he was in effect the personnel officer, and as such was witness to the office politics, the petty jealousies and strains and stresses inside the organisation which would be familiar to any Western office manager.

'A visitor would hand over his business card and the secretary would check the appointments list,' he said, describing an ordinary day inside Terror Inc. 'There was a front hall with all the secretaries, and they would ask you to wait if the person you came to see was busy.' Some of the employees thought they were working for a regular trading company but others, like al-Fadl, were involved in the darker side of al-Qaeda's business.

There were the inevitable grumbles about money. Al-Fadl earned $200 a month, like all the regular al-Qaeda members, but got a bonus of $300 monthly for his payroll work. He found himself the conduit for complaints to the Director. Bin Laden was obviously feeling the pressures of corporate poaching and skills shortages and explained, with a sigh, that in order 'to keep people happy' he had to offer some of the *jihadis* a pay rise to keep them from returning to their own countries, where they could earn better money.

There were company perks arranged by Bin Laden, who also looked after his employees' welfare with a medical scheme. 'Sometimes al-Qaeda workers would be given sugar and tea and oil and other stuff to help them, because it was hard to get these things in the Sudan,' said al-Fadl. He described a network of ten guesthouses in a square mile area of the Riyadh suburb, where the young, mostly single, al-Qaeda recruits lived.

Al-Qaeda even had its own in-house magazine, the *Newscast*, published daily and also in a special weekly edition, which carried news of Islam in the world and *jihad* studies. Some sense of humour seems to have permeated al-Qaeda in those early days; the editor of the paper was dubbed Abu Musa

Reuter, after the famous American news agency. The newspaper was staffed by members of another of al-Qaeda's four arms, the media committee. In the years to come this would become a powerful tool of the terror group, making recruitment and propaganda videos to spread the message.

The day I visited, two years after al-Fadl left, the office was quieter but clearly still functioning. The reflective glass glowed in the sun, blank and unwelcoming, like the bodyguards outside. As I left with my camera crew, our car was followed by one of the black jeeps. It swept past us on the highway, forcing us off into the sand, a warning that al-Qaeda still had a presence in Khartoum even though the Director had gone.

Bin Laden looked up to his host, Dr al-Turabi, who had expansive plans for a new *jihad* which would establish a true Islamic government across Muslim countries in Africa and further afield. According to Western intelligence agencies, and the testimony of Jamal al-Fadl, there were moves to bring representatives from the Shi'a Muslim group Hizbollah and its state sponsor, Iran, to meet Sunni Muslim groups like Bin Laden's in the Sudan. There was vigorous debate, terror 'seminars' to thrash out doctrinal differences and discuss whether these disputes between Sunni and Shi'a should be set aside in the interests of attacking the common enemy, the secular Muslim government in Egypt, and ultimately the Great Satan, the United States of America.

There was talk of involving other state sponsors of terror, particularly Iraq, which had struck an unholy alliance with Sudan following the Gulf War and moved some of its chemical weapons research programme there in an effort to shield it from the prying eyes of UN arms inspectors. Khartoum became a kind of radical university campus for disseminating al-Turabi's ambitious plans for terror alliances.

'Do you categorically deny that Sudan supports terror in any way?' I asked al-Turabi. He was clearly enjoying the debate, and gave a senior-common-room-style rejoinder. 'Well, it depends what you mean by terror. Do you mean any resistance fighter is a terrorist? Of course the Europeans, if they don't like someone, will call him a terrorist. He's a revolutionary if he seizes power but if they don't like him, he's just a terrorist. What about America and Vietnam? What about Christianity and those wars of Christian terrorism?' Al-Turabi was warming to his theme – Americans were stupid, aggressive, alienating everyone in the Muslim world, turning young men into 'terrorists'. It was exhausting, but strangely hypnotic, listening to his tirade. I was not surprised to learn from al-Fadl's testimony that Bin Laden and the hierarchy of al-Qaeda were fascinated by al-Turabi's arguments too, influenced by his passion and his revered position as an Islamic scholar of forty years' standing.

From the start Osama bin Laden was conscious of his own credibility gap, despite his exploits in Afghanistan. He was not a respected Islamic scholar, and needed religious authority to give cover to his developing philosophy of terror. Jamal al-Fadl recounted how, during 1992 and 1993, al-Qaeda developed a hierarchy under Bin Laden in which members with more religious training formed the 'fatwa and religious committee' to codify, and justify, with fatwas or religious rulings, the jihad against America and more secular Muslim governments. As it became clear that US troops were not in a hurry to leave Saudi Arabia, al-Fadl recalled that 'the religious committee said we had to do something, in a fatwa. We could not let the US Army stay in the Gulf area and take all our money and oil. We had to do something, we had to fight them. They also said that the Prophet Mohamed did not allow two religions in our land.' One of the fatwa 'authorities' for al-Qaeda, according to al-Fadl, was a Palestinian cleric known as Abu Qatada; an unknown figure at that time, he would later surface in Britain from where he issued decrees endorsing the murder of 'infidels', including women and children.

Once Bin Laden and the hierarchy of al-Qaeda had concocted a self-serving fatwa to give cover to their violent aims, they began establishing military training camps on the Afghan model in the Sudan. Initially they were to offer the Afghan veterans 'refresher' courses, as al-Fadl put it, but increasingly they began to train new recruits drawn to the Sudan by the extremist policies of al-Turabi.

Jamal al-Fadl was the intermediary in the purchase of land at Soba, north of Khartoum on the banks of the Blue Nile. He paid $250,000 for the plot, where a farm was established. The source of the money was Bin Laden's old friend from Afghanistan, the Egyptian doctor, Ayman al-Zawahiri, whose Islamic Jihad now effectively merged with al-Qaeda. Two Egyptian stalwarts of Islamic Jihad – an ex-policeman called Mohamed Atef and Abu Ubaidah al-Banshiri, who had been 'on loan' to Bin Laden since the days of the Afghan war – became key members of the inner circle, with a brief to run the military committee. Al-Zawahiri assumed the position of Bin Laden's second-in-command. The Egyptians were feeling the heat from President Hosni Mubarak's crackdown on their organisation, and the Sudan, on Egypt's southern border, was close enough to maintain links and to offer protection under al-Turabi's wing. There were the usual merger arguments and jockeying for position. 'Some wanted to change the name to the "Islamic Army",' according to al-Fadl, 'but in the end we went with "al-Qaeda".' There was unhappiness in some quarters about the number of Egyptians inside al-Qaeda and more grumbles about the unfairness of the pay scale.

I headed out of Khartoum with my BBC colleagues to find the farm, a burly Sudanese at the wheel of our van. He could not possibly have been anything other than a secret policeman, although he claimed to be just a driver. He was not keen to go to Soba, but I was determined to discover the al-Qaeda camps which Western intelligence had pinpointed through their satellite trawls. At a peaceful, uninhabited spot by the Nile where bullocks ploughed the rich, silty soil, the air was heavy, pulsing with heat and flies as I woke a guard dozing by a forbidding but rusty iron gate. He was unarmed and open to the promise of some *baksheesh*, a tip. I reckoned we had a good half an hour to film before someone raised the alarm.

Inside the deserted compound of several acres there were half a dozen whitewashed barracks, each two storeys high. A parade ground in the middle had obviously been used as a practice area. The walls around it were riddled with bullet holes and larger pock-marks made by something more power-ful. Inside, cobwebs festooned the wash basins in what looked like dormitories. It would be three years before al-Fadl gave his detailed testimony to the New York court to confirm it, but I had no doubt I was standing in one of al-Qaeda's training camps.

Al-Fadl described how Bin Laden would visit his trainees at Soba. 'Every Thursday, after the sunset prayer, any al-Qaeda members in Khartoum had to come to the farm meeting. Osama bin Laden would give a lecture, and others too, about *jihad* and our agenda.' The practical course consisted of weapons training and lessons in how to fire Stinger missiles and Milan rockets from the Afghan arsenal which the Sudanese government had so obligingly transported back on Air Sudan.

There was a farcical flavour to some of the incidents at the camp. The neighbours complained to the local police station at the noise of explosions, as neighbours tend to do, even in Dr al-Turabi's Sudan. The police were fobbed off by the Sudanese intelligence services. 'We had a good relationship with intelli-gence,' al-Fadl said, 'and they told the police, "Don't worry, we'll handle it." The intelligence men were angry and told us, "You shouldn't do that – we told you just to do a refresher course, not to let off real explosives!"' But al-Qaeda was diffi-cult to control, the ambitions of its Director hard to contain. He sent representatives to the Lebanon, to the training camps of Hizbollah, the Iranian-backed terrorist organisation. Hizbollah specialises in massive truck bombs: one destroyed the American Marine Corps barracks in Beirut in 1983, killing 241 people and precipitating the US withdrawal from the Lebanon. Videos were brought back to teach the Soba camp residents

Hizbollah's technical secrets. Truck bombs would soon become a deadly hallmark of al-Qaeda too.

There was more subtle training as well, in the art of deception. Forgery was becoming an al-Qaeda speciality; trainers in the camps in the Sudan showed recruits how to create false passports and alter documents. The organisation quickly realised that its strict Islamic observances would easily mark out its members. Abu Talal, one of the trainers, told the recruits to shave off their beards and wear Western clothes while travelling. They should make a point of carrying packs of cigarettes, despite al-Qaeda's injunction that smoking was *haram*, forbidden, and they should wear cologne when passing through airports. 'He said it makes you look more like you are interested in women,' said al-Fadl. 'Also if you are smoking cigarettes, the customs man would be less likely to think you are [a member of] an Islamic group.' Ten years later, the leader of nineteen al-Qaeda hijackers on September 11 would instruct his men to apply cologne before the terror group launched its most ambitious terror attack to date.

As 1993 began al-Qaeda was beginning to shape itself into a formidable force; but it was still off the radar screen of the CIA and Western intelligence. That would change within weeks. Jamal al-Fadl was present at a meeting with Osama bin Laden when he gave an ominous speech to the weekly al-Qaeda gathering. 'He said that we have to cut off the head of the snake,' al-Fadl explained. 'The snake is America, their army has come to the Horn of Africa and we must stop them. We must cut off the head.'

4

War Against America

'Our duty is to rouse the Muslim nation for jihad *against the United States, Israel and their supporters, for the sake of God.'*

—Osama bin Laden, 1998

Somalia, 1992

In the early hours of 9 December 1992 American troops waded ashore on the beaches of Somalia. The press pack was there before them and they were greeted by the glare of television lights. It was an inauspicious beginning to an operation which would end in ugly scenes of humiliation as the bodies of American Rangers were dragged through the streets of Mogadishu in front of the world's cameras. It scarred the new President, Bill Clinton, on his first foray into global territory and branded his administration as weak in the eyes of Osama bin Laden and al-Qaeda.

The US intervention, so optimistically christened Operation Restore Hope, was launched with the best of intentions by a rich and civilised nation. It was supposed to shore up a United Nations peacekeeping effort that was struggling to keep food aid out of the hands of the Somali warlord, Mohamed Farah Aideed, and rival clan factions. But al-Qaeda saw it differently.

There was consternation within the ranks, according to Jamal al-Fadl, the Sudanese defector. 'The religious committee said the American army is in Somalia,' said al-Fadl. 'They already took the Gulf area and now they go to Somalia. If they succeed, it could be the south of Sudan next and then they could take all the Islamic countries.'

Mohamed Atef, Bin Laden's trusted Egyptian aide and second-in-command of the military committee, went secretly to Somalia to meet local militants in their training camps. 'Everything that happened there in Somalia was our responsibility,' Atef told al-Fadl on his return to Khartoum.

The first blow was struck in Aden, the southern port in the Yemen, a staging-point for US troops bound for Somalia. On 29 December a bomb killed an Austrian tourist and a hotel worker but failed to harm the American soldiers who had already left for Mogadishu.

The religious committee had already found a justification for the unfortunate 'collateral damage' that al-Qaeda was beginning to inflict on innocent civilians. The thirteenth-century Islamic sage, Ibn Taymiyya, who had so influenced the revolutionary thoughts of Sayyid Qutb, was again called upon to provide historical justification. 'Those around the invader who sell to and buy from him are fair game,' said a top aide of Bin Laden's. 'If there is anyone around them, a non-military person, and you kill him, you don't have to worry about that. If he is a good person he will go to Paradise and if he is a bad person he will go to Hell.'

Abu Talha, an instructor with special skills in using mortars, was sent to Somalia to help train local militants. He told al-Fadl when he returned that he had received a 'reward' with which he bought a house in the Sudan. Another Afghan veteran and al-Qaeda member, Mohamed Odeh, was sent to train the Somalis in using weapons and explosives. From there he moved along the coast of Africa to become a key figure in the Kenyan cell which Bin Laden was already forming to carry out later terrorist attacks.

On 3 and 4 October American troops in Mogadishu were caught in a vicious firefight with the Somali clans, their helicopters shot out of the sky in a bloody skirmish later described in *Black Hawk Down*, a book on the disaster which was also made into a Hollywood movie. Eighteen US servicemen died and seventy-five were injured. According to the US court indictment issued later against Osama bin Laden, the killings were the work of men 'trained by al-Qaeda and trainers trained by al-Qaeda'.

The al-Qaeda specialists sent to Somalia, Abu Talha and Mohamed Odeh, could have been the key to the downing of the US helicopters. Afghan fighters had learned, from US and British military advisers in the war against the Soviets during the 1980s, that a helicopter's weak spot is its tail rotor. They had also been shown how to alter the fuses on rocket-propelled grenades so that they exploded in mid-air. The first Black Hawk helicopter was brought down by a man hiding in a tree exploding a grenade in such a way. It appeared to be another catastrophic example of 'blowback' against the West, which had backed the *mujahideen* in the Afghan war and sent its military advisers to train them in the use of such weaponry.

There is some doubt, however, about just how deeply al-Qaeda was involved in the actual firefight with the Americans in Mogadishu. It may have proved too good a propaganda opportunity to pass up when the pictures of the bodies of US servicemen were shown around the world. Bin Laden made no claims at the time, but then he has rarely spelled out his responsibility for any terror outrages.

It was not until 1997, in his first interview with an American television network, that Bin Laden first gave a hint of the involvement of his Afghan veterans. 'With Allah's grace, Muslims over there co-operated with some Arab *mujahideen* who were in Afghanistan,' he told CNN. 'They participated with their brothers in Somalia against the American occupation and killed large numbers of them.'

Later he was more specific with a Pakistani journalist from

the *Dawn* newspaper. 'My associates killed the Americans in collaboration with Farah Aideed,' Bin Laden stated. What is perhaps more significant than the exact role played by Bin Laden and al-Qaeda is the lesson they took from the American humiliation in Somalia.

'We believe that the United States is a great deal weaker than Russia. We have learned that from our brothers who fought in Somalia,' crowed Bin Laden later. 'They saw wonders about the weakness, feebleness and cowardliness of the US soldier. Hardly eighteen of them were killed, when they fled in the dark of the night, despite the uproar that was created world-wide about the New World Order.'

Bin Laden was closer to the mark than Americans would like to admit, for there is no doubt that the Somalia incident dramatically changed foreign policy. George Bush senior, whose forces re-took Kuwait and pursued Saddam's army back into Iraq, had heralded the dawn of the 'New World Order' under the firm but benevolent leadership of America. After Somalia Bill Clinton and his generals shrank from involving US forces in the former Yugoslavia to halt ethnic cleansing lest more flag-draped coffins marred his administration.

Clinton, however, refused to withdraw his soldiers from the one place dearest to Bin Laden's heart, the Arabian peninsula. Three years after Operation Desert Storm 5,000 troops remained in Saudi Arabia, with 3,000 more in Kuwait. Eventually the situation would embolden al-Qaeda to openly declare war on America – not only on its soldiers but its civilians too. For the moment, though, Bin Laden appeared content to stay in the shadows, using his money and his military training facilities to encourage others to strike at America through acts of terror. His strategy was to make al-Qaeda part of a loose association of militant Islamic groups, all fuelled by hatred of the superpower which supported 'un-Islamic' governments and which was Israel's great protector. Al-Qaeda would never be a monolithic structure; its strength would lie in its fluidity, its ability to strike alliances with other groups which supported its philosophy and its goals. Myriad affiliates would make it harder to track and almost impossible to eliminate.

If Somalia gave Bin Laden a clear indication of America's 'weakness' on the battlefield far from home, another act of terror that year gave him even more confidence that he could successfully carry out audacious attacks inside the United States itself. For the freedom, the rule of law and the safeguards enjoyed by American citizens and the citizens of other Western allies would make them fatally vulnerable to the religious fanaticism of al-Qaeda. America was a sleeping giant and she would prove remarkably slow to wake.

New York, 1993

On 26 February 1993, a massive bomb was detonated in the underground garage of the 107-storey complex which, above all others, symbolised the economic might and the confidence of America, the Twin Towers of the World Trade Center on the tip of Manhattan. Six people died and 1,042 were injured, but the skyscraper complex was largely undamaged.

'We crawled under pipes when we arrived and everything was on fire,' said Edward Bergen, one of the first firefighters to enter the station beneath the towers which bore the brunt of the blast. It was closest to 'Ground Zero', the name explosives experts give to the epicentre of the blast. 'Suddenly a guy came walking out of the flames like one of those zombies in *Night of the Living Dead*. He was a middle-aged man and his flesh was hanging off,' Bergen recalled.

The mastermind behind the bombing – and a follow-up terror campaign intended to destroy other New York land-marks including the UN building in Manhattan and the Lincoln and Holland tunnels – was a Muslim man thought to have been born in Kuwait to a family from the wild Baluchistan province of Pakistan. Some have argued that he was a tool of Iraq or Libya or a creation of rogue elements inside Pakistani intelligence. He may well have been a fanatical loner nursing a deep personal hatred, but what is indisputable is that this terrorist had links to Osama bin Laden's network, stayed in al-Qaeda guesthouses and received training in their camps. It has now emerged that key figures close to Bin Laden, members of the inner circle that surrounded him from the beginning in Afghanistan, played a significant role in the first and inconclusive attack on the World Trade Center.

To this day Ramsi Yousef remains an enigma. Incarcerated in 'Supermax', the Colorado prison which is the highest security institution in America, he is serving a 240-year sentence while politicians, investigators and journalists still argue about which of the forty aliases he has used is his real identity. Thin-faced and broken-nosed, with hypnotic, hooded eyes, Ramsi Yousef was also a charmer, a brilliant technician with a persuasive manner; 'a riddle wrapped in a mystery', concluded one of the investigators who chased him round the world. Another dubbed him an 'evil genius'.

Yousef's acts of terrorism against America seem to have been motivated primarily by the Palestinian cause and a hatred of Israel. He was a Muslim, but not a particularly devout or observant one, and seems to have been inspired by political as much as religious zeal. His early life in Kuwait was played out against the background of his father's strict Wahhabi beliefs. The family were immigrants, despised guest workers from Baluchistan, a land sucked into the vortex of the *jihad* fought in Afghanistan against the Soviets. Ramsi Yousef wound up, somewhat unexpectedly, in Wales at the West Glamorgan Institute of Higher Education, known as 'Wiggy' to its students. There the science-mad young man, whose hobby was experimenting with chemicals, took a Higher National Diploma in computer-aided electrical engineering.

From Swansea, where he came into contact with the Muslim Brotherhood and was exposed to radical Islam, he took the *jihadi*'s pilgrimage to Afghanistan in 1988, around the time Bin Laden was laying the foundations of al-Qaeda. Yousef trained in Bin Laden's camps near Peshawar and also taught others to make nitroglycerin bombs, his speciality. He formed close friendships with several militants there who would later figure in his terror spree across the globe. One of them was the leader of the Abu Sayyaf, a Muslim terror group in the Philippines which was receiving funding from Bin Laden to create an independent Islamic state in the southern part of the islands.

In 1992 Yousef travelled to New York and enlisted the support of a number of Afghan Arab militants who were disciples of a blind Egyptian Sheikh, Omar Abdel Rahman, an influential scholar in the world of *jihad*. Most of them were none-too-bright young men, susceptible to what the judge later acknowledged was Yousef's clever and persuasive character. One of the plotters not only crashed his car on a dummy run, leaving Yousef injured on the sidewalk, he then tried to claim back the $400 deposit on the rental truck which had been the vehicle for the gigantic bomb used in the attack on the World Trade Center.

Within hours of the bombing Ramsi Yousef fled New York and for two years went on the run. He ended up in the Philippines – at Bin Laden's request, according to American investigators; there he trained Abu Sayyaf militants in remote Basilan in the use of explosives. The Far East, with its large Muslim population, hardline rulers and ethnic strife, was one of the first areas identified as potentially fertile territory by al-Qaeda. From the organisation's inception in Afghanistan in the late 1980s, Bin Laden had begun to forge links with local Islamic extremist groups particularly in the Philippines, a Christian country where Muslim secessionist movements were waging a bloody campaign in the southern islands.

From Basilan, Ramsi Yousef gravitated to the capital, Manila, where he met up with two men from al-Qaeda's inner circle. One was Yousef's uncle, a Kuwaiti called Khalid Sheikh Mohamed. Mohamed is thought to have already been involved in planning, with Yousef, the bombing of the World Trade Center two years earlier. When that first attack failed to destroy the skyscrapers Khalid Sheikh Mohamed refused to give up, nurturing his ambition for many years with disastrous consequences. The second man, Riduan Isamuddin, an Indonesian known as 'Hambali', had fought in Afghanistan against the Soviets and was spearheading al-Qaeda's drive to establish a foothold in the Far East.

Together the three men formulated an even more audacious plan than the earlier attack in New York – to kill both President Clinton and the Pope on their forthcoming visits to the Philippines. The choice of targets – the leader of America and the head of the Catholic Church – illustrated the way al-Qaeda was already combining its own anti-US agenda with that of local Islamic groups in the area, for whom the Christians were the foremost enemy. Ramsi Yousef, a mercurial character, abandoned the assassinations as too personally dangerous for a mastermind who valued his own skin, so he coolly hatched a second plan to detonate bombs aboard eleven US airliners flying trans-Pacific routes to America. Yousef was deadly serious and even carried out a trial run, killing a Japanese engineer who had the misfortune to sit in the seat in which Yousef had planted the small test bomb.

Khalid Sheikh Mohamed and Hambali vanished when Yousef's chemical experiments started a fire in his rented apartment. Once more Yousef escaped, outwitting local police and the FBI, who were hot on his heels. But he left behind his laptop computer with details of the killing spree he had planned.

Eventually, in 1995, Ramsi Yousef was caught in Pakistan and taken back to New York to face trial. He only gave one interview, to a woman reporter, Raghida Dergam from *al-Hayat*, a newspaper widely circulated in the Middle East. Yousef claimed to be a warrior avenging the wrongs visited on Arabs by Israel and America. 'America finances these crimes,' he argued, 'and these funds are taken from the taxes which Americans pay' – thus making them 'logically and legally . . . responsible for all the killing crimes and the settlements and the torture which the Palestinian people are exposed to'.

Among the tons of paper evidence presented at the trial of Ramsi Yousef were several manuals and notebooks on bomb-making. Andrew McCarthy, one of the prosecutors at the World Trade Center conspiracy trial, told me, 'Those bombing manuals were festooned with a variety of annotations, included among them phone numbers that went back to Afghanistan and Pakistan. They included numbers that were regularly being called by the blind Sheikh who was in charge of a global terror network even then. And those numbers link up with Bin Laden players overseas.'

The World Trade Center bombing was the event that at last focused American investigators on Osama bin Laden and al-Qaeda. 'In 1993 when the Twin Towers were bombed we were very much behind the ball as far as what we knew about organisations like al-Qaeda,' admitted Andrew McCarthy. It would be another two years before Ramsi Yousef was actually caught and the jigsaw began to fall finally into place. But even as the FBI investigators unearthed the clues, not all the key information was passed on to intelligence officers at the CIA, or their counterparts in friendly capitals abroad. The lack of co-ordination between America's domestic law-enforcement and its foreign intelligence agencies, evident in the aftermath of the first World Trade Center bombing, would have far-reaching and fatal consequences.

The CIA was only privy to what its own intelligence-gathering brought it from spying in foreign parts or eavesdropping via its satellites. Material gathered within the United States, in the course of preparing a trial, was out of bounds. Grand Jury secrecy as codified under Rule 6(e) of the Federal Rules of Criminal Procedure permits material obtained in a Grand Jury investigation to be shared with certain law-enforcement authorities to help solve other cases, but there is no exception to permit intelligence officers to see such material while the trial is in preparation – in Yousef's case, a process that took several years.

James Woolsey, the then Director of the CIA, told me he did

not even recall hearing Bin Laden's name being linked to the World Trade Center bombing until early 1995, when he was leaving office. 'He was still in the Sudan and there was no word about his activities in Somalia,' said Woolsey, who has criticised the 'Chinese walls' maintained between the Justice Department, FBI and CIA until the aftermath of the September 11 attacks. 'Some of the key material was bottled up in Grand Jury secrecy rules, material which would have been vital to intelligence officers. It had an extremely detrimental effect.'

Within the FBI too there were sensitivities about the conduct of investigations into terror networks. In 1988 the Bureau had come under fire, accused of using illegal tactics in its attempts to penetrate a Salvadoran group suspected of links with terror. The case had become a *cause célèbre* and the effect was to make the FBI recoil from aggressively pursuing cases with political links for many years. According to Oliver 'Buck' Revell, a tough Texan, then the Deputy Director of the FBI, 'We almost went down to ground zero ourselves in carrying out our counterterrorism responsibilities.' Under the Privacy Act agents were prohibited from collecting public information even from groups who directly espouse the use of violence to accomplish their objectives. 'The FBI is in the very unusual position of being perhaps the only people in our society who cannot take official cognisance of what people say, and pronounce and promulgate what they'll do – until they do it,' says Buck Revell.

It was not just the law, with its protection of the rights of defendants, which helped terror groups to flourish in the United States. America's well-established sense of political correctness also made it difficult to target a group of immigrants or a minority religious leader.

Sheikh Omar Abdel Rahman came to the United States in 1990, with a history of alleged but unproven involvement in terrorism. He had been detained in his home country, Egypt, after the assassination of President Anwar Sadat in 1981 and was kept under house arrest for a time. His militant followers, the Islamic Group, had close links to Islamic Jihad. But the

Sheikh was nevertheless allowed a visa to enter the USA, where he began collecting money from all over the States, working from his base at a mosque in New Jersey. He also took control of a Brooklyn mosque after the imam there was mysteriously murdered.

Omar Abdel Rahman had first met Bin Laden in the 1980s in Afghanistan, and their paths crossed again in the Sudan during the 1990s. Two of his sons later went to Afghanistan to work with Bin Laden and became part of al-Qaeda's wider terror grouping. In late 1992, five months *before* the World Trade Center bombing, the FBI opened a formal investigation of the Sheikh following the killing of the Brooklyn imam. There had been interminable wrangling inside the Justice Department over the ramifications of focusing on a religious leader and Rahman himself was never questioned; neither were his offices bugged or his phones tapped. If they had been, Yousef's murderous spree might well have been prevented.

The two-year investigation following the Trade Center bombing eventually resulted in the blind Sheikh's conviction for 'directing others to perform acts' in the follow-up operation to bomb bridges, tunnels and buildings in New York. He was shown to be a central and inspirational figure for Ramsi Yousef and the others who carried out the bombing. The Sheikh has since been identified by other al-Qaeda members as a prime mover behind the religious decrees that inspired the 1998 US Embassy bombings in Africa.

Political correctness, a lenient immigration policy, legal safeguards to protect the rights of citizens which built walls between the FBI and CIA: a pattern was beginning to emerge which would repeat itself over and over again, until reality dawned on September 11. When I spoke to Prosecutor Andrew McCarthy after the embassy bombings, this veteran of the trials of Ramsi Yousef, the blind Sheikh and their band of Islamic militants was already doubting the wisdom of applying 'due process' to terrorist suspects. 'Under American law when you arrest people and bring them into the system they become vested with all the rights, including discovery rights, of American citizens,' he said. 'You have to reveal to them things you would prefer they didn't know if their successors are to be stopped from perpetrating further acts of terror.'

'So what's the answer?' I countered. 'A military response with missiles? Assassination of key figures like Bin Laden?'

'It's an option,' McCarthy said bluntly. 'It may well be a very good remedy in this situation.'

There are three details which stuck in my mind among the many incredible facts which I unearthed when looking at the life and times of Ramsi Yousef for a television programme four years ago. The first is that the New York judge who tried Yousef believes that he incorporated a cylinder of sodium cyanide in the truck bomb he made in the hope it would be sucked into ventilation shafts, lift shafts and stairwells. Luckily the explosion incinerated rather than vaporised the deadly cyanide. Six years later a video would be found in which Osama bin Laden gloated at the fact that burning aircraft fuel found just such pathways in the Twin Towers, killing even more people than he had expected.

The second fact was one I gleaned from an intelligence report from the Philippines which fell into my hands in 1998. It concerned Operation Bojinka – Serbo-Croat for 'the explosion', the name Yousef himself gave to his plan to blow up US airliners. The intelligence report contains a record of the debriefing of Abdul Hakim Murad, a co-conspirator and childhood friend of Yousef who was captured in the Manila flat which caught fire. Murad was a commercial pilot and said that he and the others had discussed a suicide mission in which Murad would fly a plane into the CIA headquarters in Virginia. The attack was intended, said the report, 'to demonstrate to the whole world that a Muslim martyr is ready and determined to die for the glorification of Islam'.

It seemed at the time even more far-fetched than Yousef's plan to blow up eleven US airliners, but it had a fanatically ambitious ring to it – the deliberate crashing of a plane into a building full of Americans. In the words of the intelligence officer to whom Murad revealed his plan, 'It is simply a suicide mission which he is very much willing to execute . . . the subject was observed to be very angry with Americans and the United States government.' Little did I – or, presumably, assorted intelligence and law-enforcement agencies worldwide – believe that using four planes as missiles would become Bin Laden's ultimate *modus operandi*. Yet there was one small clue – the disappearance of a key member of the planning team in Manila – Khalid Sheikh Mohamed, Yousef's uncle. He had been there when Murad discussed his willingness to die using his plane as a weapon against an American government building. Mohamed took this idea back to Afghanistan, where he and others in al-Qaeda would mull over it for five long years.

The third detail that struck me during the investigation was the story told to me by FBI investigator Louis Schaliro, who had sat with the securely handcuffed and bound Ramsi Yousef on the helicopter that brought him back to New York City. 'As we approached the Metropolitan Correctional Center in lower Manhattan we took the blindfold off him,' Schaliro said. 'It was just as the chopper flew in front of the World Trade Center. One of the agents on board said to him, "You see, it's still standing!" And Yousef said in a very chilling way, "It wouldn't be, if I had had more money."'

Ramsi Yousef had constructed and placed his bomb with the aim of generating enough explosive force in one direction to shear through the twenty-one steel columns on one side of the first tower, the North Tower, and topple it into the second, bringing them both down. He only spent about $15,000 and the operation was hastily planned with an amateurish team in New York. It was unfinished business as far as Ramsi Yousef was concerned but Osama bin Laden, al-Qaeda's leader, would one day fulfil his ambition to destroy the proud symbol of American might.

5

The Exile

'As for being driven from one land to another, that is the nature of war. You win some and you lose some.'

—Osama bin Laden, 1998

Sudan, 1994–96

'We came to the conclusion that he was some kind of financial Godfather,' said CIA analyst Stanley Bedlington, describing the belated awakening of the Counter-Terrorism Center in Langley to exactly what Bin Laden was doing in the Sudan. The capture of Ramsi Yousef in 1995 and the discovery of his contacts with al-Qaeda was soon followed by two bomb blasts in Saudi Arabia; twenty-four American servicemen, the 'occupiers' of the Holy Places, were killed. 'Bin Laden was on our radar screen now all right,' said Bedlington grimly.

In January 1996 the 200-strong CTC decided to set up a special 'Bin Laden Issue Station'. Ever since, the staff of a dozen federal agencies have been engaged in the largest, most costly and far-ranging investigation ever into a single individual engaged in terrorism. They have received and shared information with a number of other intelligence agencies including Britain's MI6, Israel's Mossad, the German BND, the Italian

DIGOS and the French DST and DGSE, all of whom have investigated Bin Laden's network.

Dr al-Turabi's Islamic state had become the perfect place for Bin Laden's operation and 'Terror Incorporated' expanded between 1994 and 1996. 'Sudan was very hospitable: al-Turabi gave him passports and a semi-official status, a base from which he could travel to other parts of the world,' says Buck Revell, the former Deputy Director of the FBI.

The Libyan Fighting Group, the Moro Liberation Front and Abu Sayyaf in the Philippines, Jemaah Islamiyah in Malaysia, the Syrian Jihad Group, the Groupe Islamique Armé of Algeria: Jamal al-Fadl, the Sudanese defector, reeled off lists of names during his trial, an alphabet soup of exotic places and different ethnic groups united by the philosophy of *jihad*. All these and more were the recipients of Bin Laden's largesse and were invited to send their foot soldiers to al-Qaeda camps for training. They came from Tajikistan and Tunisia, from the far-flung Comoros islands off the east coast of Africa, from Eritrea and Chechnya and Indonesia. Just as the Afghan conflict had provided the first pool of recruits to found al-Qaeda, so the new *jihad* – in Chechnya and Bosnia and in parts of the Far East – would provide a second flow of hardened Muslim fighters to swell the terror organisation's ranks.

Bin Laden made precise calculations and al-Fadl kept the books – $1,500 to equip each Chechen fighter with a Kalashnikov and fund his air travel, for example. There were more costly ventures, including an aeroplane which was purchased in America to transport weapons but which crashed in the Sudan. Undaunted, al-Qaeda's military committee loaded crates with weapons and despatched them by sea to the Yemen. Camel trains laden with guns were sent north to Egypt for Islamic Jihad, the backbone of al-Qaeda.

The Saudis were furious as news of their wayward citizen's exploits began to leak out. They had thought they could keep the lid on the Bin Laden problem by exiling him to the Sudan. Their concern was not with the rumours of terror attached to his name; it was stirred by the vociferous campaign he was conducting against the Saudi regime itself. Things came to a head in early 1994 when Bin Laden set up an office in London. He was following the example of other Saudi dissidents, like his contemporary Dr Sa'ad al-Fagih, who had set up the Movement for Islamic Reform in Arabia, campaigning against the Saudi regime. The British capital, with its open and tolerant attitudes, was an important centre for the Arab press and therefore for disseminating criticism of the Saudi government.

Late one evening in August 1998, in the wake of the bombings in East Africa, I knocked on the door of a neat semi-detached house in Dollis Hill, in north-west London. I was muffled up in a long coat and headscarf, as was my colleague, Fiona Campbell. We were ushered in to a comfortable sitting-room with a fax machine and computer in the corner. An illuminated model of Mecca, which gave out the call to prayer in somewhat tinny tones, dominated the room. For two hours Fiona and I were lectured on the history of Wahhabism and the evils of the al-Saud regime, which we were assured would soon be exposed and overthrown. Our tutor was Khaled al-Fawwaz, a plump Saudi with a lugubrious manner, an old friend of Osama bin Laden's and the gateway to the leader of al-Qaeda for journalists who wanted to travel to Afghanistan to meet him. Since 1994 al-Fawwaz had run the 'Committee on Advice and Reform', the ARC, an important part of Bin Laden's operation which acted as a propaganda arm and media information centre for al-Qaeda.

'With the Saudi regime the veil is getting thinner every day, like a woman not wearing the *hejab*,' he said, glancing disapprovingly at the two females sitting on his sofa; we were so obviously ill at ease in our makeshift version of the covering worn by women in the Islamic world.

Khaled al-Fawwaz had been with Bin Laden in the Sudan and had set up a company in Nairobi which investigators believed was a front for funding terror operations. He had moved to London in 1994 and immediately claimed political asylum, as a Saudi dissident, one of many extremists and sympathisers of Bin Laden's to take advantage of Britain's tradition of sheltering political opponents of repressive regimes in the Middle East. The Saudi royal family had ignored al-Fawwaz's actions until he turned up in London and started disseminating al-Qaeda's diatribes against the Saudis and their American protectors from his fax machine in Dollis Hill. 'We believe in the *umma*, one great nation and religion only,' al-Fawwaz declared. 'Non-Muslims are not allowed to stay in the Arabian peninsula. Even civilians are not allowed to stay. If there is a military presence it is completely unacceptable,' he told me. It was these views and other criticisms of their 'un-Islamic' behaviour which so incensed the Saudi regime and led them to sever finally the links which bound Osama bin Laden to his birthplace.

According to a family insider, Osama received at least three secret visits from the Bin Laden clan during his sojourn in the Sudan. The final trip came in January 1994, under pressure from the Saudi royal family, when they again tried to reason with their renegade son. The octogenarian Abdullah, the last surviving brother of Mohamed, Bin Laden's father, led the group. He was accompanied by Bakr bin Laden, a half-brother of Osama's, now head of the family firm. The fun-loving eldest son, Salim, had died in a plane crash.

'They told Osama, "You've got to end all this. Come back and we'll give you a responsible job in the company, one of the top five positions,"' a source close to the family told me. 'They thought he had chosen his path because he was too far down in the pecking order to make a real career in the business. They beseeched him to stop his diatribes against Saudi and the Americans. But he basically said, "Sorry, I have a mission – goodbye."'

In April 1994 the Saudi royal family stripped Bin Laden of his passport and his citizenship. His extended family sorrowfully cut him off although he would remain close to his mother, who had remarried, and to his half-sister and brother, children of her later marriage. It appeared that the gloves were off now, on both sides.

When a truck bomb exploded outside the National Guard Communications Center in Riyadh on 13 November 1995, killing five American servicemen and two Indians, the Saudi authorities arrested four men. Confessions were extracted from them in which they said they were supporters of Osama bin Laden's views, but they were beheaded before they could be questioned by American investigators. Three of the men were *mujahideen* veterans who had fought in Afghanistan, the fourth had joined the Bosnian Muslim army in the former Yugoslavia. The Americans were furious at the Saudi reaction and some intelligence sources suspected that Bin Laden's powerful friends in the Saudi establishment had acted to protect him. The executions may well have been to prevent embarrassing revelations about the extent of support for Bin Laden within the kingdom.

Jamal al-Fadl, the defector, was now the trusted international representative of al-Qaeda and Bin Laden sent him to Zagreb and Budapest with money and letters for others in the European network that al-Qaeda was starting to build. It was the beginning of the extensive courier service the organisation would use to communicate between its members; safer and more secure than telephones and faxes. Bin Laden and his associates held dollar bank accounts in Hong Kong, Malaysia and Dubai, and one with Barclays Bank in London. Some of the money, however, flowed through the *hawala* system, common in the developing world: cash advanced on trust with no incriminating records kept. A member of al-Qaeda, whom I shall call Ibrahim, told me in London in 1998 that Bin Laden kept large reserves of gold and also dealt in different currencies, including US dollars, as a hedge in case of the collapse of one of those currencies. Ibrahim also described how Bin Laden boycotted any American-made product, even enquiring of his dentist if the fillings he used had been made in the United States.

The purpose of all al-Qaeda's international activity was to raise the Muslim world to arms in order to establish a true Islamic empire, an empire with the military might to vanquish all others. There is evidence that as early as the mid-1990s Bin Laden was contemplating using the most extreme form of terror weapon, a nuclear device. 'It is the duty of Muslims to possess these weapons,' Bin Laden has said on more than one occasion.

Jamal al-Fadl testified that in 1994 he was the emissary in an attempt to buy uranium from a former Sudanese government minister. He was taken to a warehouse in Khartoum and shown a cylinder about three feet high, engraved with numbers and symbols on the side. The paperwork identified it as containing material from South Africa, a country with a secret nuclear weapons programme. The price was $1.5 million, plus the usual generous commissions. The tale has elements of black farce, as Bin Laden's top aides debated with al-Fadl how to get hold of a machine to check the nuclear material was genuine.

'They said, "Don't tell anyone about this, even inside al-Qaeda. You did a great job; everything's fine,"' said al-Fadl, who claims he does not know if the purchase was ever completed. Someone, somewhere must have been pleased with the result, for al-Fadl was given a $10,000 bonus for his work. Al-Fadl also revealed that al-Qaeda was involved with officers in the Sudanese army in trying to develop chemical weapons in an area of Khartoum called Hilat Koko. The CIA would later reveal their spies discovered that Bin Laden had hired a physicist from a Middle Eastern country to work on chemical and nuclear projects in Sudan.

Buck Revell, the former FBI Deputy Director, told me the American intelligence community feared that Bin Laden had tried to obtain nuclear material from sources in the Asian republics of the former Soviet Union, a leaky sieve which is the repository for hundreds of suitcase-sized, battlefield nuclear weapons. No one knows how capable al-Qaeda is of mounting a terror attack with radioactive material, but a 'dirty bomb', which scattered radioactive waste material, could render a whole urban area uninhabitable for many years. The use of crude devices incorporating nuclear material, chemical or biological agents is the ultimate nightmare terror scenario, and one which no one in the intelligence community can say is beyond al-Qaeda's means.

In June 1996 a second bomb rocked a Saudi base for US troops, in the city of Dhahran. The front of the Khobar Towers, a housing complex, was demolished, killing nineteen US servicemen and injuring many more. Bin Laden was immediately suspected although the Clinton administration later identified a pro-Iranian group as the most likely culprits. Bin Laden, who through Dr al-Turabi had held talks with Shi'a terror groups, may have given them logistical support in a joint terror attack. He certainly praised this effort to attack America as he lauded the Saudis who had carried out the National Guard bombing the year before. 'I hold in great esteem and respect these great men,' Bin Laden said, 'because they removed the brand of shame from the forehead of the Islamic nation when they carried out the bombings in Riyadh and al-Khobar.'

Sudan now came under enormous pressure from America and the Saudis to get rid of Osama bin Laden. The Counter-Terrorism Center task force was already under way and a Grand Jury was secretly empowered in New York to gather evidence on the involvement of al-Qaeda in international terrorism. By now Dr al-Turabi had reluctantly concluded that his guest and friend was becoming too hot even for him to handle; Sudan itself was under suspicion. Al-Turabi's government was implicated in a plot to kill President Hosni Mubarak of Egypt. Investigators had established that the Sudanese diplomatic mission in New York had been involved in Sheikh Omar Abdel Rahman's plot to bomb the UN complex in New York. Sudan was put on a US blacklist, the US ambassador was withdrawn and sanctions threatened.

Dr Hassan al-Turabi was somewhat reluctant to discuss his unmasking as a sponsor of terror with me in Khartoum in 1998. 'Oh, the Americans are ignorant people. Don't talk to me about their courts and their legal system!' he exploded. 'Once they look into the face of a nigger and someone says he's a terrorist, he gets found guilty because he's black—'

I tried to interject, reminding him of the evidence against the diplomats.

'They didn't have any evidence at all,' he countered, refusing to discuss the delicate matter of the Sudanese UN mission's preparedness to supply diplomatic licence plates to enable a truck bomb to enter the UN garage.

'Osama did not want to embarrass the Sudan in its relationship with Saudi Arabia, and of course, privately, the Americans put pressure on us,' he finally conceded, explaining Bin Laden's decision to leave Khartoum in May 1996. Internally there were disagreements between al-Turabi and President Omar Hassan al-Bashir about the troublesome guest who had in effect hijacked the Sudanese state, despite al-Turabi's insistence that he remained the master manipulator pulling the strings.

The Saudi dissident departed the Sudan a wiser but poorer man, estimating in an interview that he had lost $150 million in his Sudanese ventures. He had, however, gained a new notoriety to take back to the land where he had first become a hero. 'Afghanistan is the only place that he knew,' al-Turabi told me sadly. 'The only place you can go to without a passport. He didn't even have a nationality now.' Al-Turabi himself would also come to feel an exile, condemned to years of house arrest in Khartoum after President al-Bashir decided to curb the influence of his radical Islamic adviser.

There was a palpable sense of relief in Khartoum when Bin Laden loaded up his planes and flew his family and his al-Qaeda fighters out. The Sudanese immediately made an overture to the Americans: they were prepared to show them their intelligence files, with lists of al-Qaeda's members and details of the network. There were disagreements inside the White House as to the true intentions of the Sudanese, however, and the result was a curt refusal to accept the offer. The Americans made a mistake in not accepting the information, however flawed it might have been, however unsavoury the regime offering the files. For some members of al-Qaeda active in the Sudan, their details presumably contained in the Sudanese intelligence files, would eventually make their way to many Western capitals and dig in there as part of the underground terror network.

This was the height of the Clinton-era 'sensitivity' drive from which the CIA did not escape unscathed. That fastidiousness extended to keeping suspect regimes like the Sudanese more at arm's length, not always the wisest policy for intelligence agencies. John Deutch, the new Director, had succeeded Jim Woolsey, whose departure was hastened by exasperation at his failure to engage President Clinton's interest in intelligence matters. 'We didn't have a negative relationship,' Woolsey told me, 'I just never saw him.' Deutch set up a Human Resource Oversight Council after complaints from female staff and he drew up elaborate new procedures which all but ruled out the recruitment of agents who might have criminal backgrounds or less than true commitment to the CIA's new 'human rights' agenda. 'It's like telling the FBI they can recruit informants inside the Mafia but they can't recruit any crooks,' was Woolsey's verdict.

The mid-1990s marked a low point for the CIA, a 'de-fanged and dispirited organisation' according to Robert Baer, a veteran of the CIA's Directorate of Operations. Baer told *Panorama* that there was not a single reporting agent in any of the eight posts he supervised in Central Asia and the Caucasus and that American CIA personnel fluent in the local languages were non-existent. 'Desk jockeys were promoted at the same rate as field operatives,' complained Baer. 'All over the Islamic world, cells were forming, ancient grudges were boiling to new surfaces, the infidel West was being targeted for destruction and we didn't have a real ear to the ground anywhere.'

Afghanistan, 1996–98

It has been said that Osama bin Laden was a leader in need of a state and Afghanistan was a state in search of a leader when fortune threw them together again in 1996. Bin Laden was philosophical about the American success in driving him from the Sudan. 'As for being driven from one land to another, that is the nature of war. You win some and you lose some,' he said, with a shrug.

It is now clear that ousting Bin Laden from a country with at least some desire to obey the diplomatic norms was the biggest mistake the Clinton administration could have made. He was now ensconced in an impenetrable stronghold from which he could launch new attacks with impunity. Milton Beardon, the CIA's former station chief in Peshawar, sensed another repeat of the 'blowback' effect. 'So off he goes to Afghanistan, which is probably the best move since the Germans put Lenin in a boxcar and sent him to St Petersburg in 1917,' he quipped. 'By forcing him to leave he was out of the place where we might have been able to control him, or at least monitor him more closely, to see what he was up to.'

Bin Laden had tried living in the Sudan, a country which claimed to be the first modern Islamic state, melding together Sunni and Shi'a and Sufi in a common cause. It had not worked out but he was back in a place where he felt much more comfortable. Afghanistan was now a theocracy, ruled over by the Taliban and modelled on a medieval Islamic caliphate.

The Commander of the Faithful and Supreme Leader of the Taliban was a man already in Bin Laden's debt. Mullah Mohamed Omar's house in Kandahar had been purchased by Bin Laden during the Afghan war against the Soviets, when Omar was an obscure warlord. His only claim to fame in those days was his courage and personal bravery. Injured in the face when his mosque was hit by a Soviet shell, he is said to have ripped his eye out before it could become infected. And so a second blind Sheikh would become a central figure in the story of Bin Laden and al-Qaeda.

Mullah Omar retired to his house and studied the Qur'an as his country descended into an orgy of violence and lawlessness after the Soviet withdrawal. The tale of Mullah Omar's awakening is the stuff of legend. In early 1994, outraged at the rape of two girls by *mujahideen* outlaws, he rallied former Afghan veterans and hanged the offenders from the barrel of a tank. It was the beginning of a cleansing sweep throughout the land which would turn Afghanistan back in time to become a medieval and vengeful state, secretive and cruel. It would be like no other ever seen in the twentieth century with the possible exception of Cambodia under Pol Pot's Khmer Rouge.

Mullah Omar's chivalrous action struck a chord among a fearful population repelled by the anarchy, corruption and sexual licence of the warlords. Two *mujahideen* commanders, rivals for the affections of a young boy, had just let loose their tanks in the Kandahar bazaar, killing scores of bystanders. As Mullah Omar's avenging sword scythed through the rabble of the former *mujahideen*, thousands of Islamic students flocked to join his cause. They called themselves *Taliban*, the 'students of Islam'. Many came from the *madrassas*, religious schools in the border areas of Pakistan, hotbeds of Deobandi radicalism. This form of Islam had its origins in India in the nineteenth century and emphasised the value of learning in bringing about Islamic reform. But under the Taliban it was interpreted as justifying the establishment of a purist state, rejecting all forms of modernism and debate and relegating women to the status of chattels forbidden to leave home.

There were strong parallels between the Deobandi and Wahhabi models and the *madrassas* were liberally funded by Saudi Arabia. Again the royal family was playing a double game which would result in catastrophic 'blowback', just as their backing of radical Wahhabi elements in the battle against the Soviets had given rise to Bin Laden's movement and its ilk. They saw the Taliban as a bulwark against Shi'a influence in the region and so the Saudis became the first and virtually only regime to recognise the Taliban when, in 1996, Mullah Omar effectively took control of Afghanistan.

Once again, the Pakistan ISI, or Inter Services Intelligence, played a murky, meddling role, seeing an opportunity to manipulate events on its northern border. Many Western observers believe the Taliban was largely a Pakistani creation, a result of the close links between the Taliban and various extreme Pakistani factions sponsored by elements within the intelligence services.

In the early days of Taliban rule the American administration was inclined to give the new regime the benefit of the doubt, supported as they were by allies like Saudi Arabia and Pakistan. They seemed like messianic reformers who would get tough on 'drugs and thugs'; intelligence short-hand for the heroin trade and terrorist problem posed by the Afghan Arabs. There was a lack of direction in Washington on US policy towards Afghanistan until Hillary Clinton and Secretary of State Madeleine Albright, under pressure from feminist groups, accused the mullahs of beating women in an attempt to break their spirit.

On 4 April 1996 Mullah Omar appeared on a rooftop in Kabul, which the Taliban had finally taken, and literally wrapped himself in the cloak of Islam in front of the assembled mullahs in the courtyard below. Secretly shot video exists of this extraordinary scene, the blurry quality and distant figure giving it a surreal quality. The one-eyed Omar, his head swathed in a black turban, slowly and reverently wraps and unwraps the cloak of the Prophet Mohamed about him, as the monotone all-male crowd, in their grey and black and beige garments, shout, 'Amir-ul Momineen', Commander of the Faithful, their oath of allegiance to Mullah Omar. It was a politically inspired gesture which made it clear what kind of regime the Taliban would be; a regime which believed it had the right to lead all Muslims, not just the Afghans. No wonder that Osama bin Laden, exiled only a month later from the Sudan, felt he was indeed returning to his spiritual home.

Defiantly, on 23 August, Osama bin Laden issued his first official *fatwa* or religious ruling, theatrically headlined 'from the mountains of the Hindu Kush'. His message was that a global battle against the Americans had now been joined. 'To his

Muslim Brothers in the Whole World and especially the Arabian Peninsula; Declaration of *Jihad* against the Americans occupying the Land of the Two Holy Mosques; Expel the Heretics from the Arabian Peninsula,' declared the *fatwa*.

Khaled al-Fawwaz, Bin Laden's diligent press officer in Dollis Hill, made sure the press received copies of the *fatwa*. According to US court documents he also set about procuring an expensive satellite phone from America to enable Osama bin Laden and his military commander, Mohamed Atef, to keep in touch with their network abroad. Court records would later reveal that in the next two years 260 calls were made on the phone to 27 different numbers in Britain alone – more than in any other country.

Most of the calls made on the phone, more than 200, were to Khaled al-Fawwaz, al-Qaeda's representative in London, who was busy arranging for selected journalists to visit Bin Laden in Afghanistan.

Abdel Bari Atwan is the editor of the *al-Quds al-Arabi* newspaper in London: an engaging and expansive Palestinian, Atwan is always impeccably dressed in a well-cut dark suit. Over lunch near his office in Hammersmith he recounted his experience in Bin Laden's cave headquarters near Jalalabad, where he went to interview him in November 1996. 'It was awful,' he recalled with a shudder, 'damp and freezing cold and when I put my hand under my camp bed, hoping to find another blanket, there were mortars and Kalashnikovs stacked under there.' Bin Laden had two laptop computers, a satellite phone and a book-lined inner room within the cave complex where he posed with his own faithful Kalashnikov by his side. Legend had it that he had taken it from a Soviet soldier he had killed.

It was not only Arab journalists who beat a path to Bin Laden's door as, emboldened by the Taliban's protection, his tone became increasingly strident. The following year the American television station perceived by many in the Middle East to have been the mouthpiece of the Great Satan during the

Gulf War, CNN, came to talk to Bin Laden. Peter Juvenal, the British cameraman and a veteran of the Afghan conflict, had his camera taken away and substituted with one of al-Qaeda's own machines. Bin Laden, whose training camps turned out experts in the art of explosives, was clearly sensitive about his security. The interview brought the image of Bin Laden's face – ascetic, calm and almost saint-like – into American living-rooms for the first time. His audience heard him boast of al-Qaeda's involvement in Somalia and they heard his threats against Americans in his own homeland. His obsession with cleansing the Holy Places of the infidel seemed a bizarre notion, but comfortingly far enough away not to affect their daily lives.

The American government was already realising its mistake in pushing Bin Laden into the arms of the Taliban. The scale of al-Qaeda's activities and the extent of their organisation was becoming ever clearer to the officials at the Counter-Terrorism Center. In the summer of 1996 Jamal al-Fadl had fallen out with the Director of al-Qaeda over the number of Egyptians in the organisation and their favoured status. Al-Fadl had embezzled $110,000 and had been caught. More in sorrow than in anger Bin Laden told him he would have to pay it all back. Al-Fadl managed to scrape together $30,000 before he fled. He turned up on the doorstep of an American embassy in Europe, offering a goldmine of information about al-Qaeda. For two years he would help investigators piece together the puzzle, earning a $20,000 loan and a new identity under the Witness Protection Program. Jamal al-Fadl, the defector, would later turn out to be the FBI's star witness in the New York trials of several al-Qaeda terrorists.

For two years after his return to Afghanistan, Bin Laden rebuilt and extended his training camps and recruited thousands more men into al-Qaeda. He was also busy on the diplomatic front, creating a coalition of some of the world's most feared terror groups. In February 1998 a merger was announced under the rubric of 'The International Islamic Front for Jihad Against the Jews and Crusaders'. There was a photo-opportunity which brought Osama bin Laden and Ayman al-Zawahiri together again, smiling, on the podium. Bin Laden, not only the Director of al-Qaeda but now publicly the Chairman of 'Terror Incorporated', told the mainly Pakistani press who assembled that 'this Front has been established as the first step to pool together the energies and concentrate efforts against the infidels as represented in the Jewish–Crusader alliance, thus replacing splinter and subsidiary fronts'. And so he gave notice of his grandiose plan to bring together terror groups across the world to defeat America, Israel and the West, in order to establish a wide-ranging Islamic empire or caliphate.

The new coalition officially brought at least five groups together under al-Qaeda's umbrella, including al-Zawahiri's Islamic Jihad; the imprisoned Sheikh Rahman's organisation; the Egyptian Islamic Group, which also represented a number of North African Islamic movements; the Pakistani Harkut al-Ansar; and a Bangladeshi militant group. Their manifesto was as follows: 'For more than seven years the US has been occupying the lands of Islam in the holiest of places, plundering its riches, dictating to its rulers, humiliating its people, terrorising its neighbours and turning its bases in the peninsula into a spearhead through which to fight the neighbouring Muslim peoples.'

The *fatwa* which followed declared: 'Obeying the order to kill the Americans and their allies, both civilian and military, is the duty of every Muslim, providing that he is capable of doing so, everywhere it is possible to do so, in order to free the al-Aqsa mosque and the Holy Mosques from their stranglehold, in order that their armies shall depart from the lands of Islam, crushed and unable to threaten any Muslim.' Once again the *fatwa* was disseminated through London by Khaled al-Fawwaz.

It was the first time Osama bin Laden had made it clear that American civilians would be a target anywhere in the world. The Clinton administration interpreted the *fatwa* as a declaration of war – which it was – and the CIA made sure that a memo noting this was made public at a Senate Hearing on terrorism.

Prince Turki bin Faisal, the Saudi intelligence chief, was prevailed upon to visit his old acquaintance: 'My instructions were to ask him to hand over Bin Laden,' Turki said. After flying by private jet to Kandahar and some heated words with Mullah Omar, a meeting was finally arranged with Bin Laden, who had refused to see the prince. Osama again made it clear, as he had done to his family in the Sudan, that he was not interested in showing the 'restraint' which Prince Turki urged him to adopt.

Mullah Omar was also visited by a deputation of his own Taliban chiefs, muttering that they would never achieve United Nations recognition while harbouring al-Qaeda and its leader. Osama bin Laden himself offered to leave if his presence was considered too disruptive but Mullah Omar sealed his own fate, and the fate of thousands of innocent Afghans, Americans and others, when he replied, 'You are our own and one of our own you will remain.'

'Mistaken policy or accident of history – take your pick,' the Saudi Foreign Minister, Prince Saud al-Faisal, later said when asked about the outcome of his country's policy towards the Taliban in the critical years 1995–98. 'The stability of Afghanistan seemed a bigger concern than the presence of Bin Laden,' Saud went on. 'When the Taliban received him they indicated he would be absolutely prevented from taking any actions. We had unequivocal promises.' A director of the CIA would later ruefully remark, 'We often talk of two trends in terrorism – state-supported and independent – but in Bin Laden's case with the Taliban we had something completely new: a *terrorist* sponsoring a *state*.'

The training camps the Taliban allowed al-Qaeda to establish in Afghanistan formed the foundation of a worldwide network by sponsoring and encouraging extremists from many parts of the Muslim world to forge longstanding ideological, logistical and personal ties. 'In summary,' according to the CIA, 'what Bin Laden created in Afghanistan after he relocated there in 1996 was a sophisticated adversary – as good as any the CIA has ever operated against.'

Meetings were convened in Washington that spring to plan an operation to extract Bin Laden from his mountain retreat and bring him to America to face trial. The Justice Department was confident that the Grand Jury hearings and the testimony of defectors like al-Fadl had given them enough ammunition to mount a successful prosecution. The Pentagon was tasked with mounting a Special Forces operation, a snatch squad, in concert with Pakistani troops. The plan was discussed at a meeting between the President, senior army generals and representatives from the CIA and the Justice Department.

Clinton noted that the last time the US Army had invaded a country to arrest a suspect was the case of General Noriega, the Panamanian strongman, who was eventually worn down by the effect of music blasted through loudspeakers in front of his house, day and night. The President concluded they were hardly in the same ballgame with al-Qaeda. The shadow of Somalia still hung over the White House. Afghan history was revisited to remind them all of the fate of hundreds of Soviet commandos who had lost their lives trying to take the area of Zhawar Kili, the same spot where al-Qaeda now had its training camps. Stephen Simon, the Senior Director of Counter-Terrorism at the State Department, was one of the officials involved in the discussions. 'At the end of the day the President wasn't going to authorise the slaughter of innocent Afghan people,' Simon told me.

Buck Revell, the former Deputy Director of the FBI, offered a more expanded view of the deliberations inside the White House when he told me about the decision to abort the mission. 'They thought there would be too much collateral damage, too many civilian casualties and a high rate of casualties among American soldiers,' he said. 'Pakistan would not have supported it and Afghanistan would have opposed it. It was not like Noriega, where the population was basically supportive. And so the decision was taken to leave him there for the time being, although we knew we would ultimately have to deal with him.' Those were prophetic words even in 1998; in the aftermath of September 11 they have a haunting quality.

Bin Laden reiterated his call for *jihad* against America in front of journalists in Afghanistan in May 1998. 'There will be good news in the coming weeks, you will see,' he promised them. A young Saudi member of al-Qaeda was watching from the back of the room. Mohamed al-Owhali was then twenty-two years old. Born in Liverpool, where his father had been a student, he had just graduated from a religious university in Riyadh. After the press conference al-Owhali had a private audience with Bin Laden. 'I approached my *emir* and asked him for a mission,' al-Owhali later told investigators. Osama bin Laden graciously granted his request – the young Saudi graduate would be designated to become a martyr in an anti-American operation in Africa. In less than three months the threat implicit in the *fatwa* would become a bloody reality.

6

The Innocents

'My children want to know why someone would do this. I
can't answer them. I don't understand this "holy war" – all
I have is the fear.'

—Joanne Huskey, wife of US diplomat, Nairobi,
September 1998

East Africa, 1998

The red earth glowed, a raw gash in the green of cassava and
banana tree. I was brought up in Kenya, and the smell and the
sight of the Rift Valley soil always exhilarates me and makes
me feel I have come home. But this day was different. Moses
Rundu had come to visit the newly-dug graves of his father,
Peter, and twenty-year-old sister, Ruth, buried on the plot of
land this poor family own on the outskirts of Nairobi. 'My
father loved this place. He told me when he died he wanted to
be buried here,' Moses said. 'It was such a totally unexpected
event for us. Burying two people is so hard.'

Peter Rundu had been paying the fees for his daughter at the
secretarial college she attended next door to the US Embassy
when a massive truck bomb was detonated by al-Qaeda on 7
August 1998. Moses searched the city's hospitals and morgues
for five days before he found Ruth and Peter's bodies.

A devout Christian, Moses could not begin to understand

why the bombers had struck in the heart of an African city, killing 201 local Africans in order to claim their real prize, the lives of 12 Americans, diplomats and support staff in the embassy. Osama bin Laden's *jihad* against the 'infidel' was incomprehensible to a genuinely religious man like Moses. 'It is only Arabs who could do something like this. Africans could never have something like that in their minds,' Moses said simply.

The next day I was driven round Nairobi in a powerful four-wheel-drive, its doors and windows securely locked, by Joanne Huskey, the wife of the US First Secretary. We passed a scene of utter devastation beside a busy roundabout in the city centre. The five-storey secretarial college had collapsed, pancaked into a few layers of concrete; beside it the block-like fortress of the embassy was shrouded in canvas. FBI investigators in yellow safety helmets were busy scraping up ash and debris inside the cordon thrown up around the site. Mrs Huskey, an attractive, lively blonde in her thirties, was torn between tears and defiance: 'My children want to know why someone would do this. I can't answer them. I don't understand this "holy war" – all I have is the fear,' she said.

Joanne had been in the embassy with her two young children when the blast happened; they narrowly escaped death. She had searched in desperation for her husband but, unlike Moses Rundu, her story had a happy ending – the Huskeys found each other outside the ruin of the building. But other friends and colleagues were dead; there were many women and children to comfort. As they tried to help amid the mayhem of wailing ambulance sirens and blood-soaked victims, frantically digging to find survivors, they heard that the US Embassy in Dar-es-Salaam, capital of neighbouring Tanzania, had been bombed almost simultaneously, killing eleven Africans.

The al-Qaeda bombings of the American embassies in East Africa had been a classic 'sleeper' operation, planned and prepared over five years by individuals living undetected in the local community. It began in 1992, when Osama bin Laden and his top lieutenants decided to expand from their new base in the Sudan into the horn of Africa, to Somalia, and then further afield in East Africa. Abu Ubaidah al-Banshiri, the Egyptian who headed al-Qaeda's military committee in the early 1990s, was despatched to Kenya. It was another failing state, another suitable location in which to base a terror network; the government was corrupt and crony-ridden, the population poor, and law enforcement weak. In addition Nairobi was an important CIA listening station for the African continent and there was a substantial American presence in the capital.

Bin Laden's plans met a temporary setback in the spring of 1996 when al-Banshiri was drowned in a ferry accident on Lake Victoria. 'That put a spanner in the works for a while,' an intelligence source told me with some satisfaction, but within a year al-Qaeda had found a replacement, Fazul Abdullah Mohamed, from the Comoros islands off the African coast. He had been through the usual Afghan military training camp, was good with computers and fluent in Arabic, Swahili, French and English.

Other al-Qaeda figures close to Bin Laden became part of the growing operations in East Africa. Wadih al-Hage had taken over from Jamal al-Fadl as the paymaster in Khartoum and had then become Bin Laden's personal secretary. Al-Hage was Lebanese but became a naturalised American citizen when he moved to Louisiana to study urban planning. He worked part-time in a doughnut shop and married an American woman, April Ray, a convert to Islam. She dutifully followed her husband first to Afghanistan and then to the Sudan where, with her growing brood of children, she enjoyed picnics on the banks of the Nile with the other al-Qaeda families. She found the segregation of the women hard to take but described Bin Laden as 'a great boss'.

Wadih al-Hage was not a typical al-Qaeda fanatic: his

photograph shows a man with pleading eyes, a soft face and a somewhat defeated air. He was responsible for a number of al-Qaeda's failed business ventures, including the Azerbaijan bicycle import scheme. His American mother-in-law called him a 'sad sack' and there were fights between al-Hage and April Ray over her refusal to buckle down to the proper submissive role of a good Islamic wife. When al-Hage informed her he was going to take a second wife, as Muslim tradition allowed, 'I made his life pure hell,' Ray told the American magazine *Newsweek*, 'until he had to give up the idea.'

Wadih al-Hage moved his wife and seven children to Nairobi in 1994. His role was to supervise the logistics for the Kenyan cell and he set up an Islamic charity, 'Help Africa People', in Nairobi to provide false identity documents. He also invested in a Tanzanian gemstone business, a front for al-Qaeda to move money around the region. Khaled al-Fawwaz, head of Bin Laden's propaganda unit in London, was the co-director, with al-Hage, of an import–export company called Asma which supposedly dealt in animal hides; it was, investigators believe, another front company.

An even more unlikely figure in the plot than al-Hage, with his American wife and nagging mother-in-law, was a US Army sergeant who had been assigned to a Special Forces unit at Fort Bragg, North Carolina. Ali Mohamed was a former Egyptian intelligence officer who became a naturalised American citizen and a star pupil in the army, even giving lectures on Islamic culture to his fellow recruits. After he left the forces he became involved in the *jihad* in Afghanistan and was introduced to Osama bin Laden by Ayman al-Zawahiri, the leader of Islamic Jihad. Ali Mohamed trained fighters in al-Qaeda's camps in surveillance techniques and, in his own words, taught them how to 'create cell structures that could be used for operations'. Mohamed became a trusted lieutenant of Bin Laden's, helping him to transport his fighters to the Sudan from Afghanistan in 1991 and training his personal security detail.

Ali Mohamed carried out detailed reconnaissance of possible

targets in Nairobi, including the US Embassy. He took the resulting plans and photographs of the building to Khartoum, where Bin Laden examined them. 'He pointed out where a truck could go [with] a suicide bomber,' Mohamed said. The former US sergeant seems to have had a yen to become a secret agent. He had offered to work for the CIA in Egypt, but had been deemed unreliable. If the CIA had held its nose and recruited more men like Ali Mohamed, the penetration of al-Qaeda might have been more successful and more precise knowledge of its targets might have been gleaned.

The small plane touched down in the humid darkness on an airstrip running beside the Indian Ocean. I could smell the sea. The trip to the hotel took us through squalid road-side shanties, cooking fires illuminating the ragged forms of children and goats. Mombasa was far more impoverished than when I had come here on family fishing holidays long ago; the atmosphere was ugly and intimidating. Rioters had recently invaded the secluded compounds on the tourist hotel strip brandishing machetes. There was not much trouble getting a room at a knock-down rate these days.

The next morning at breakfast we were almost alone in the dining-room, a pastiche of a traditional Spice Coast house with a soaring palm-thatched roof, set on elegant ebony posts. The only other people there were half a dozen elderly German matrons, each sharing her table, champagne and orange juice with a handsome but uncomfortable-looking young African man. Sex tourism was clearly the most profitable employment in Mombasa now.

We headed out along the coast to the small fishing village of Witu, looking for the home of the key 'sleeper' in the Kenyan cell. Mohamed Odeh, a Jordanian, had been sent by al-Qaeda to Kenya in 1994 – fresh from his experiences tutoring Somalian Islamic militants how to use explosives – to attack American Rangers in Mogadishu. Odeh set up a business, married a local girl and settled down to await further orders.

As I stood on the white sand at Witu, two Arab dhows silhouetted against the glittering sea plied their trade across the straits to Zanzibar. Some women passed me, the breeze billowing their black, all-enveloping *burkhas* around them. It seemed Odeh had chosen his burrow well – the heart of East Africa's Muslim community. And he had the perfect business front, a fishing company which required long, unexplained absences away and the movement of small boats up and down the coastal strip. The explosives and detonators for the truck bomb were acquired from Tanzania in this way.

Odeh's in-laws were still living in the area, and I wanted to find the uncle who had given the local newspaper an interview about his niece's 'ultra-religious' husband who hated smoking and disapproved of watching television. As we hunted around for the house an ancient black Peugeot pulled up in the back street where we were lurking but sped off as soon as we approached. The family had no doubt been rattled by the FBI's discovery in Odeh's house, just days before, of sketches resembling the embassy compound.

There were almost a dozen men involved in planning and executing the Nairobi bombing and the near-simultaneous explosion in Dar-es-Salaam. By 1997 both the Kenyan police and American law-enforcement and intelligence agencies could not have failed to be aware that East Africa had become an area of al-Qaeda operations. The British intelligence service MI6 had information too. Yet none of the cell was apprehended, despite the increasing volume and clarity of the signals coming into the CIA's listening station inside the Nairobi embassy itself.

On 21 August 1997, a year before the bombings, an FBI agent together with Kenyan policemen searched Wadih al-Hage's house in Nairobi. They missed him because he was in Afghanistan at the time, but his outspoken mother-in-law from Louisiana happened to be visiting her daughter in Nairobi. 'Being Wadih, he had all these papers all over his desk, his little address books, his ledgers. They scooped them up – every single one of them. And his computer too,' she later said. The FBI advised her to return to America for her own safety.

FBI agent Robert Crisali, a computer technician, made a 'mirror image' of al-Hage's Apple PowerBook's hard drive. On it he found a letter from one of al-Hage's associates describing the existence of al-Qaeda's Kenyan cell. 'There are many reasons that lead me to believe that the cell members in East Africa are in great danger,' the letter read. 'My recommendation to my brothers was not to be complacent regarding security matters and that they should know that they have now become America's primary target.'

Following the seizure of his computer, Wadih al-Hage was summoned in spring 1998 before the Grand Jury in New York investigating Bin Laden. Although al-Hage admitted he was 'acquainted' with figures involved in the 1993 World Trade Center bombing, he denied recent knowledge of Osama bin Laden or of Abu Ubaidah al-Banshiri, the al-Qaeda man in Nairobi who had drowned in Lake Victoria.

Nine months before the bombings, in November 1997, an Egyptian called Mustafa Ahmed actually walked into the Nairobi embassy and volunteered the information that there were plans to detonate a bomb-laden truck in the garage underneath the building. He said he had already taken surveillance photos of the compound. Two CIA reports were duly written but could not link Ahmed to any specific group. Security was stepped up for a few weeks and Prudence Bushnell, the US Ambassador in Nairobi, lobbied the State Department in Washington in a December 1997 cable to move the embassy to a safer location. She followed up with a letter, a direct plea to the Secretary of State, Madeleine Albright, in April 1998, four months before the bombing. Her plea fell on deaf ears.

Meanwhile the young Saudi member of al-Qaeda, Mohamed al-Owhali, was receiving the equivalent of a Ph.D. course in Afghanistan. He had already received basic training at Bin Laden's Khaldan camp and gained military experience fighting alongside the Taliban for control of Kabul. Now he took an intensive course in explosives, hijacking, kidnapping and assassination techniques in readiness for receiving details of his 'mission' from the Director. He also received a month's specialised instruction in the 'operation and management of the cell'. Al-Owhali knew his would be a 'martyr mission', as he called it, and in June he prepared a video celebrating his anticipated death and claiming credit for the bombing in the name of a previously unknown group, 'The Islamic Army for the Liberation of the Holy Places'.

It was the job of Bin Laden's master recruiter to bring together the right men for the most ambitious al-Qaeda terror attack planned at that time: the assembly, transportation and near-simultaneous detonation of two massive truck bombs in East Africa. That master recruiter was a Saudi-born Palestinian known as Abu Zubaydah. Later members of the East African cell would tell prosecutors that Abu Zubaydah made the travel arrangements to bring them to and from Afghanistan and assigned them to the various camps. He showed that he was capable of supervising several complex operations simultaneously in conditions of the utmost secrecy, keeping the operational teams separate. Abu Zubaydah had quickly become a key man in the organisation, the man who kept the files of all the members of the terror network and who matched individuals to specific tasks.

There were three different categories of terror operatives: first, locals who were low on the totem pole, without specific knowledge of all the details of the plan; second, 'sleepers' sent to live and work in East Africa for some time, usually al-Qaeda members of long standing; and finally, the al-Qaeda specialists and 'martyrs' flown in from Pakistan and other Middle Eastern countries. Among them was the bomb-maker, who would make only a fleeting visit to Nairobi and Dar-es-Salaam. The last to arrive would be the men who had undergone heavy indoctrination and who could be relied upon to drive the trucks and press the button that would guarantee their own death.

That summer a Nissan refrigerator truck was purchased in

Tanzania and a Toyota bought from a Kenyan poultry farmer. In Tanzania, a local man called Khalfan Khamis Mohamed rented a house where the bomb could be assembled. He ground up between four and five hundred packets of TNT and packed them into crates. The al-Qaeda bomb expert, an Egyptian known as 'Abdel Rahman', connected them to oxy-acetylene cylinders to magnify the blast. These were then wired to a hundred detonators, linked to two truck batteries.

In Kenya, the head of the local active unit, Fazul Abdullah Mohamed, rented Number 43 Runda Estates, a large villa in a walled compound where the Nairobi bomb was assembled by 'Abdel Rahman' and another expert flown in by al-Qaeda. Before he left, Fazul Abdullah Mohamed took care to have a cleaning company thoroughly scrub the villa from top to bottom; however, residues of explosives were later detected in the house.

In the final few days before the bombing, different members of the team who would transport and detonate the bomb assembled in Nairobi. The grandly titled 'Hilltop Hotel' is a seedy flophouse in a street teeming with prostitutes and street children. No one was interested in the three men who rented a room here together on 2 August 1998. Mohamed al-Owhali had arrived from Afghanistan with a man he knew only as 'Azzam', another Saudi he had met in the camps. Mohamed Odeh, the fisherman from Mombasa, was also here; he left behind a fingerprint on the door frame. Al-Owhali and Azzam, who would drive the bomb-laden Toyota truck, made a last-minute reconnaissance of the embassy two days before the bombing.

Just after 9:00 A.M. on Friday 7 August the truck set off for the US compound. It was timed to explode between 10:30 and 11:00, when al-Qaeda reckoned most of Nairobi's Muslim population would be safely in the mosque. Faxes had already been sent in the early hours of that morning to Bin Laden's propaganda office in London claiming responsibility for the bombings in the name of 'The Islamic Army for the Liberation of Holy Places'. The PR angle had been carefully considered;

according to al-Owhali, al-Qaeda had already concluded that because the US Ambassador was a woman, her death would guarantee them more publicity.

Al-Owhali and Azzam chanted religious texts to keep their spirits up during the drive towards their deaths. Al-Owhali was armed with stun grenades and a handgun, and he had the keys to padlocks on the vehicle. The diplomat's wife Joanne Huskey arrived at the security gate to the underground garage at the same time as the truck. She was bringing her children to a dental appointment at the embassy, where her husband was working on the fifth floor. She noticed the security guard seemed edgy; she also noticed a truck alongside her, but thought nothing of it as she shepherded the children from the basement garage up the ramp into the building.

Behind Huskey, al-Owhali had got into an argument with the guard, who would not let the vehicle pass. The Saudi threw a stun grenade at the African. Then, realising they could not drive the truck into the heart of the underground parking area but reckoning it was close enough to do its work, al-Owhali abandoned his companion and his plans for martyrdom and ran away.

The bomb, containing several hundred pounds of TNT and aluminium nitrate, was detonated by Azzam at 10:40 A.M. precisely at the intersection of two of Nairobi's busiest streets, near the railway station. The area was packed with office workers and people shopping for the weekend. A *matatu*, or local bus, full of schoolchildren was just one of the vehicles caught in the carnage.

In the twenty-five-storey office building behind the embassy, the woman whose name was top of al-Qaeda's death-list that day was holding a meeting with an African minister when she heard the stun grenade explode followed by the massive bomb blast. 'Suddenly I was sitting on the floor with my hands over my head,' Prudence Bushnell, the US Ambassador, said later. Picking herself up, she made her way down the stairwell towards the ground floor along with hundreds of African

workers. 'They were singing hymns, a huge procession, bleeding all over each other. There was blood all over the banister. I
could feel someone bleeding on my hair and back,' the
Ambassador recalled.

Next door, the smaller secretarial college where Ruth and
Peter Rundu were was completely destroyed by the blast,
crumpling into a heap of fallen masonry. Before the dust had
settled passers-by were clawing at the rubble, desperate to
reach possible survivors.

Inside the embassy Joanne Huskey and her children struggled to escape, entombed in the dark by fallen walls with
exposed electric cables sparking in the air around them.
'Finally we made our way up a ramp towards the light, and
we saw the city on fire all around us,' Joanne told me, in tears,
weeks after her trauma. Miraculously, all three were unhurt.
Squeezing through the twisted steel railings around the compound the children found their father, who had made his way
down from the fifth floor. Inside, on the first floor, which had
taken the brunt of the blast from the truck, twelve Americans
lay dead.

Nine minutes after the Nairobi attack, the Dar-es-Salaam
bombers struck. Elizabeth Slater, who worked in the information section, recalled the moment: 'It went pitch-black and then
coming down the stairwell there were all kinds of body parts.'
She saw a security guard who was beyond all help. 'He didn't
have any skin left. I just wished he would hurry up and die.'
No Americans died in the attack – the eleven victims were all
African, most of them Muslim.

By now the senior members of al-Qaeda involved in the plot
were safely out of the country, or so they thought. The bomb-
makers had long since gone and Mohamed Odeh, the cell's
long-term 'sleeper' from Mombasa, had taken a flight to
Karachi in Pakistan, arriving in the early hours of 7 August,
before the blast. Odeh had taken the precaution of shaving off
his beard in an attempt to avoid attention. But his passport
photograph still showed a bearded man and he aroused the

suspicion of an immigration officer. Having heard BBC radio reports about the Kenyan bombing the officer bluntly asked Odeh if he was a terrorist. Much to his amazement, Odeh said nothing instead of denying it. He then began trying to persuade his Pakistani fellow Muslim that it was the right thing to do for Islam. Intelligence officers were called and Odeh made a full confession. It was an early and a lucky break for the investigation.

Nairobi's hospitals were full of hundreds of injured people. Moses Rundu heard the call that went out on the radio for all doctors to report to work at once and set off, with his uncle and his mother, to search the hospitals for Ruth and Peter. One of the many injured people queuing at the MP Shah Hospital that day was Mohamed al-Owhali. Dr John de Sousa told me that he was suspicious of the foreigner who spoke no African or Asian language and had injuries on his back, rather than his front, which suggested he had already been moving rapidly away from the area when the bomb went off. Later a hospital janitor would discover bullets and keys stuffed into a cupboard where al-Owhali had hidden them. Al-Owhali was trapped in Nairobi and in desperation made a phone call to an al-Qaeda contact. The same man also received a call from Osama bin Laden's satellite phone. The Kenyan police had been alerted by the doctor and five days after the blast they picked up al-Owhali when a local taxi driver remembered where he had taken the injured man.

The same day that al-Owhali was arrested Moses Rundu's nightmare journey through the hospitals and morgues ended when he found the bodies of his father and his sister. 'It was God's plan and God's plan is not man's plan,' were the only words he could say to comfort his mother.

After a week of interrogation al-Owhali cracked, confessing his part in the bombing. He was swiftly handed over to American authorities; by now the FBI were running the investigation. Odeh too was quickly relinquished by the Pakistanis and the two al-Qaeda suspects were taken to New York. At

Mohamed al-Owhali's trial the jury would reject the death sentence called for by the prosecutor, refusing to make the Saudi
the martyr to Bin Laden's cause that he had wished to be. The
arrests, confessions and subsequent trial of significant players
in al-Qaeda would give the Americans valuable insight into
the organisation and its methods. Next time Bin Laden would
ensure that none of the operatives on the ground would survive to give away valuable information to the enemy.

The net was closing and the two al-Qaeda plotters in the
United States were soon picked up. Wadih al-Hage was working at a tyre shop in Texas when the FBI came calling. Ali
Mohamed, the former Fort Bragg soldier, was brought before
the Grand Jury in New York. 'I testified, told some lies and
was arrested,' he later said. He would cut a deal with the US
Justice Department, secret to this day; at his trial he explained
to the judge that al-Qaeda's objective was to 'attack any
Western target in the Middle East to force the governments of
the Western countries to just pull out of the Middle East'. He
added that the massive bombs in East Africa were 'based on the
Marine [barracks] explosion in Beirut in 1983 and the American
pull-out from Beirut', and that they were designed to force the
United States to leave Saudi Arabia too.

Osama bin Laden's bombers had succeeded in killing hundreds of people, as the Marine barracks bomb did in 1983. But
the victims were not American soldiers; they were innocent
people, mainly African and mainly Muslim. This did not trouble Bin Laden. 'East Africa's bombings were followed by
happiness filling the hearts of the Islamic world,' he said, in a
breathtaking perversion of the truth. 'Thank God our hit was
very strong, it gave them a taste of the atrocities we experienced,' he continued, referring to the massacre of Palestinians
in Lebanon's refugee camps.

His boast contrasted with the cruel reality of what his
bombers had so cynically wrought; not in America, or in Israel
or the occupied territories of the West Bank, but in the streets of
two impoverished African cities. Al-Qaeda knew and exploited

the fact that Kenya and Tanzania were too chaotically governed, too weak to defend their vulnerable population.

In her tranquil African garden, filled with frangipani flowers and hibiscus and protected by gates and guards, Joanne Huskey spoke to me about her work arranging for hospitals in America to send eye surgeons to treat ninety Africans blinded in the blast. She was adamant that not one single American survivor from the embassy had asked to leave; everyone would remain, in solidarity with the Kenyans. 'Now we all seem to be in the firing line – women, children, just because we're American,' she said. 'And the real injustice has been done to the local people, the people who have nothing to do with this, who've been killed and maimed.'

My final hours in the city were spent in the stifling heat of a large tent erected in the park in Nairobi's city centre. The families of African victims had gathered here, in their best clothes, to receive compensation cheques. Moses Rundu accepted his 100,000 Kenyan shillings gratefully, but the money would only keep the family of five surviving children and their mother for four months at most. 'Our dad was the bread-winner and we depended on him for everything,' said Moses. 'We can only trust in God now. He will provide for us.'

7

The Sleeping Giant

'Osama bin Laden and his global network of lieutenants and associates remain the most immediate threat . . . He is capable of planning multiple attacks with little or no warning.'

—George Tenet, Director of the CIA, testimony to the Senate Intelligence Committee, February 2001

Sudan, 1998

'Look, this is amoxycillin suspension – just like you could get in any pharmacy.' We crunched over the broken glass of millions of bottles and vials and picked our way around twisted steel and fallen blocks of concrete. Dr Idris, a pharmacist and once the proud chairman of Sudan's only pharmaceutical and veterinary products factory, was now the custodian of a pile of rubble. In the middle of the night on 20 August, two weeks after the East Africa truck bombs, an American Cruise missile had demolished the al-Shifa factory on the edge of Khartoum, killing a guard. The Clinton administration declared the facility had been involved in the manufacture of chemical weapons and that Bin Laden was linked to what was going on there.

'If America wants to be Lord of the World, why can't it be just and merciful instead of using its power to destroy us?' cried Dr al-Turabi, the Sudanese Islamic scholar and friend of Bin Laden. 'Even if it was linked to chemical weapons, why didn't they go to the UN and get them to inspect us? If we refused then they could say it was suspicious!'

The Sudanese government vehemently denied the accusation that they were developing chemical weapons with al-Qaeda; the CIA let it be known that their agent had dug up a soil sample at the factory which showed the presence of EMPTA, a 'precursor' or substance produced near the completion of the process to synthesise the deadly nerve agent VX. I took a good look at the only earth available in the cracked concrete precinct around the factory, a flowerbed where a single red rose bloomed defiantly among the charred stems left by the missile's passage. No one on the ground seemed in the least bit concerned at what might be lurking around the demolished factory, including Dr Idris, presumably a competent scientist.

To most people outside the White House, the missile strike on the Sudanese factory was a blunder. The press, myself included, were sceptical if not downright critical. As I balanced precariously on top of the demolished factory and delivered my verdict to the camera I said the factory bombing had turned out to be a propaganda coup for the Sudanese government and Bin Laden. A few months later, the Americans quietly dropped their attempts to freeze the international bank accounts of the factory's owner, a prominent Sudanese businessman whom they had hinted was linked to Bin Laden.

Stephen Simon, Clinton's Senior Director for Counter-Terrorism at the NSC, was involved in the decision to target the factory. He still insists the intelligence was good. 'The high level of EMPTA at the site cannot be disregarded,' says Simon. 'Al-Fadl's debriefing, although not yet public, had shown us that he personally knew the al-Qaeda hierarchy and members of the Sudanese military were in the business of trying to get their hands on chemical weapons. The evidence uncovered at al-Shifa, and the attack we launched, should have been taken more seriously.' Given al-Fadl's testimony it seems likely Bin Laden *was* actively trying to obtain chemical weapons, but the

White House failed to make its case publicly and in doing so played right into al-Qaeda's hands.

Afghanistan, 1998–2001

On the same night as al-Shifa was being targeted in the Sudan, the US military launched eighty Cruise missiles at six of Bin Laden's training camps in Afghanistan, hitting five of them; six Arabs, one Turk and around twenty Pakistanis died. Finally, America had struck at the enemy who had plotted against her for at least five years, but the missiles had failed to silence the mastermind himself. A radio soon crackled into life and the voice of Bin Laden was heard praising Allah that he was alive and had again outwitted American intelligence. It had been a close shave, though; Bin Laden had been in one of the camps just hours before the attack. He would rarely use a personal satellite phone again, for he learned that one of al-Qaeda's members near the Pakistan border had provided a 'fix' for the missiles while making a call.

Things were not going well for President Clinton. He was in the midst of the Monica Lewinsky scandal and the press had got hold of the story that just before his solemn announcement of the missile attack Bill Clinton had been watching the satirical film *Wag the Dog*, in which a US President orders a war to distract attention from a domestic scandal. It was too good an opportunity to let pass and the theory that Monicagate was the real driving force behind the strikes became firmly fixed in the minds of many people, especially in the Middle East where contempt for the President increased in proportion to the growing admiration felt by many for Bin Laden and al-Qaeda.

Osama bin Laden had been facing a mutiny within al-Qaeda's ranks from those who questioned his religious authority in ordering the massacre of over two hundred Africans, many of them Muslims. The Prophet Mohamed ordained that, 'To insult a brother Muslim is sinful, to kill him is unbelief,' but al-Qaeda's leader, ever adept at interpreting the Qur'an to his own advantage, announced the unfortunate Kenyans and Tanzanians had been used as a 'shield' by the US. 'When it became apparent it would be impossible to repel these Americans without assaulting them, even if it involved the killing of Muslims, this is permissible under Islam,' he declared. The abortive American attempt to take out Bin Laden silenced his internal critics and began to build a new wave of popular support for al-Qaeda throughout the Muslim world.

I talked to Dr Sa'ad al-Fagih, the Saudi dissident in London, who was monitoring the Arab-language Internet chat rooms on the Web at the time. 'They have made a hero out of him,' he said. 'Thousands of supporters will come now, you will see.'

Bin Laden hardly needed his propaganda arm in London now, so widespread was his fame, or infamy. It was just as well, for since sending out the faxes claiming responsibility for the African bombings Khaled al-Fawwaz had been visited in Dollis Hill at dawn by Special Branch officers. He was bundled into a car, bound for Belmarsh top-security jail where he would languish for years, fighting extradition to America. US investigators had evidence that al-Fawwaz had supplied Bin Laden with the satellite phone used to co-ordinate the East African bombings, and they knew that the London office of the ARC had disseminated al-Qaeda's murderous *fatwas*.

I had been seeking an interview with Bin Laden in the weeks following the African bombings but that was clearly not going to happen now. Not only was the usual route for arranging this disrupted by the arrest of al-Fawwaz; Bin Laden himself had gone to ground since the missile attacks. The Taliban claimed they had put him under house arrest. 'He cannot talk to the press and he cannot conduct any political activity,' said Mullah Omar's spokesman, firmly. For the moment, Bin Laden was muzzled, but no limits were put on his freedom.

Bin Laden's domestic life had always been complicated, but now it became a nightmare as paranoia about his safety

increased. Later his fourth wife, a Yemeni identified only by the
initials A.S., would speak to the Saudi magazine *al-Majella*
about her life at this time with Bin Laden. Her name is Aswar
al-Sardar and she explained that two wives lived in houses in
Kandahar, one in Kabul, and the fourth lived in al-Qaeda's
complex of tunnels in the Tora Bora mountains. Bin Laden
would come to Aswar and her children once a week. 'My house
was a very simple and modest one that looked like an ordinary
village home,' she said. 'As for food, Osama liked bread,
yoghurt, honey and dates. He rarely eats meat.' Aswar learned
not to talk shop with Bin Laden. 'Did you ask him if he was
behind the attacks on the US embassies in Africa?' enquired the
interviewer, Khalid Nasr. 'No, he did not like me to talk about
these issues,' she replied. 'He was angry with me once when I
tried to ask him and told me not to discuss these matters with
him ever again.'

Afghanistan was slipping further into international isolation
as Mullah Omar's Taliban regime denied girls an education
and made women virtual prisoners in their homes. Television
and music were banned and there were public executions in
Kabul's football stadium. UN aid agencies pulled out and
Afghanistan descended into another dark age. America had
been content not to oppose the establishment of the Taliban
regime three years before, in deference to its allies Pakistan
and Saudi Arabia and in the belief that the Taliban would be a
bulwark against Iranian influence and would clamp down on
the drugs trade. Now, as Afghanistan became a pariah state,
America's prime objective was to kill or capture Bin Laden, not
to tackle the wider problem of the failing country which suc-
coured him.

There were more visits from US ambassadors and Saudi
princes in an attempt to persuade Mullah Omar to hand over
Bin Laden. But the reality was that the renegade Saudi dissident was too deeply entrenched, too valuable to the Taliban.
His wife Aswar said, 'He was helping the Taliban, he
bequeathed most of his money to them to spend to make

Afghanistan a strong country.' Al-Qaeda fighters formed the backbone of Taliban units still battling rival Afghan warlords, in the shape of the Northern Alliance, in parts of the country. Bin Laden's money paid for what little infrastructure remained in Afghanistan and he secured financial networks for the lucrative heroin trade that underpinned the Taliban regime. Mullah Omar refused to relinquish Bin Laden or disband al-Qaeda. 'Extraditing Osama bin Laden is . . . tantamount to leaving a pillar of our religion,' he declared.

There were conflicting reports about Osama bin Laden's health; a rumour did the rounds that he had obtained a portable dialysis machine from London's Cromwell Hospital to treat his ailing kidneys. His back was certainly bad; he walked with the aid of a stick, the result of an old war wound, and he was said to be depressed. His health was not improved by at least four attempts to murder him: the latest assassin was caught by the Taliban before he could get to his target. Bin Laden gamely insisted that despite his enemies' best efforts he was thriving. 'I enjoy very good health, praise be to God,' he told al-Jazeera Television. 'We are living in the mountains, we endure this bitter cold, we also endure the summer heat,' he said, adding, on a more upbeat note: 'I continue to practise my favourite hobby, which is horse-riding. Thanks to God I can still ride a horse for seventy kilometres without stopping.' His wife was concerned that his only recreation was to go hunting, which he did every Friday. Aswar also revealed that Bin Laden was concerned with his children's education. Unlike Afghan youngsters – many of whom, including all the girls, were denied the chance to go to school – the Bin Laden offspring had a privileged upbringing. 'They had private tutors who taught them English and the Arabic language, mathematics and sciénces,' said Bin Laden's wife. 'They were also taught how to use the computer.'

With the pressure on him mounting, Bin Laden's rhetoric against the US now increasingly harped on American sponsorship of Israel in its occupation of Palestinian land; his purpose was to illustrate what might happen to other Arab states if they did not fight back. 'The Muslims . . . should learn a lesson from what was inflicted on our brothers in Palestine,' warned Bin Laden. 'The Palestinian people are now displaced and expelled everywhere.' And he referred to US backing for the UN sanctions regime which he claimed was killing children in Iraq. America employed double standards, he argued, punishing Iraq for developing weapons of mass destruction while allowing Israel's nuclear capability to go unchallenged. Bin Laden's core aim remained, as always, to force Americans from the Arabian peninsula, but as support for al-Qaeda grew in the Middle East he was astute enough to broaden his appeal to seek wider support for his *jihad* and more recruits from among young Arabs angry at the plight of the Palestinians, which the US was not prepared to press Israel to resolve.

The Arabic television station al-Jazeera became the new weapon in al-Qaeda's propaganda arsenal. It was set up in 1996 by the Emir of Qatar as an independent Arab-language broadcaster and soon became a powerful voice in the Middle East, where standard television fare was dull and heavily censored. At the beginning of 1999 al-Jazeera broadcast the first detailed profile of Bin Laden, in which he talked about his childhood and his life in exile as well as expounding on his political and religious views – and his desire to obtain a nuclear weapon. It is the nearest to a chat-show, celebrity-style television interview Bin Laden has ever done and it suited al-Qaeda's purpose. At a time when the Director was becoming a hero in the Middle East, people were hungry to know more about the ascetic and distant figure.

Osama bin Laden's name then hit the headlines around the world as the old millennium came to an end. On 14 December 1999, an Algerian called Ahmed Ressam was bringing a car by ferry across a remote Canadian border crossing when a vigilant US Customs inspector, Diana Dean, pulled him over. She had noticed that, despite the freezing temperatures, the man was sweating and his hands were shaking. As well as 130lb of explosives in the boot of his car, a map was discovered in Ressam's apartment with rings drawn around three airports, Los Angeles, Long Beach and Ontario. The Millennium Plot, as it became known, also involved attacks on pilgrims visiting sites in the Holy Land, in Jordan and in Israel. Luckily these plans too were thwarted, but the direction al-Qaeda was moving in was clear: mainland America and 'softer' targets – US citizens and tourists were now in the firing-line. Israel and its Jewish population were also moving up Bin Laden's hit-list. The CIA, monitoring what they called this first 'peak threat' period, warned senior officials in the US administration to expect between five and fifteen attacks both in America and overseas.

Ahmed Ressam represented a new development in al-Qaeda's war of attrition; a more freelance, opportunistic operator who chose his own targets from a general list. A petty criminal who specialised in theft and credit-card fraud in Montreal, Ressam had travelled the well-worn route to Afghanistan and Khaldan, al-Qaeda's premier training camp. There he had followed the normal curriculum, learning about weapons and explosives and building electrical circuits for bombs. But Ressam was also indoctrinated in the black arts of the assassin. One method taught in the camp was the smearing of deadly toxins on door handles where they would be absorbed through the skin of the unsuspecting victim's hand and enter his bloodstream. Al-Qaeda was still determined to use cyanide in the ventilation systems of government buildings, which Ramsi Yousef had tried so spectacularly to do when he bombed the World Trade Center in 1993. In his time at Khaldan, Ressam and his fellow recruits tried experiments on dogs; they injected them with a lethal mixture of cyanide and sulphuric acid and watched them die in agony.

The Senior Director for Counter-Terrorism at the NSC in the Clinton years, Stephen Simon, had a sense of foreboding about Bin Laden's obsession with acquiring chemical, biological and nuclear weapons and where he might deploy such terror devices. 'We knew he had been sitting there for years in Afghanistan, musing about acquiring weapons of mass destruction,' Simon said. 'It was just a question of when he would manage to get hold of something.' With another colleague, Mr Simon wrote a valedictory article for the *New York Times* in January 2000 when he left the White House, warning that al-Qaeda had built cells in more than fifty countries, many of them self-sufficient. According to Simon, 'The article was our parting shot: get ready, guys – it's coming!'

The Yemen, 2000

At the same time as it was hatching the abortive Millennium Plot against 'soft' targets, American airports and tourists in the Holy Land, al-Qaeda was planning a direct assault on US military forces in the Gulf. It would be launched from yet another lawless state, the Yemen, in the south of the Arabian peninsula. Yemenis had been among the original members of al-Qaeda and its fiercest and most capable fighters. They were Wahhabis too, and, like Bin Laden's family, they came from the northern tribal areas bordering Saudi Arabia, where the government has little control. Yemen had always been a Bin Laden stronghold and Osama had taken steps to strengthen further his local ties, in preparation for an attack which might strain his relationship with powerful figures in the Yemen. He took as his fourth wife the Yemeni girl Aswar al-Sardar, paying her father $5,000 through an intermediary to seal the alliance.

The harbour at Aden is one of the finest deep-water ports in the world, strategically placed at the confluence of the Red Sea and the Gulf. A sheet of deep blue water, embraced by two peninsulas at each end of the bay, spreads beneath towering mountains, bleached and blistered in the heat. Steamer Point, on the larger harbour peninsula, was a bustling area full of Chinese restaurants and Indian *dukkas*, stores packed with mysterious spices and glittering saris; testimony to Aden's long history as a naval and trading centre.

By the end of the twentieth century, however, Aden was a crumbling, impoverished place, racked by civil war and dangerous for Westerners. The main source of hard currency seemed to be the kidnap trade, provided unwittingly by intrepid tourists who came to visit the extraordinary white-painted fortresses, the icing-sugar architecture of the Wadi Hadromawt, perhaps appropriately the birthplace of the terrorist leader's father, Mohamed bin Laden. On 30 December 1998, four people from Britain, two of them women, were shot dead during a botched attempt by the Yemeni army to rescue sixteen Westerners held hostage by Islamic militants suspected of ties to al-Qaeda.

Despite the anarchy in the Yemen, that same month the USA reached an agreement with the government of President Ali Abdullah Salih to refuel its warships in the Aden harbour. Ominously, Mohamed al-Owhali, the Nairobi bomber captured in September 1998, had already told the FBI that al-Qaeda's next plan was to attack an American ship in the Yemen.

The first attempt to bomb a US warship, USS *The Sullivans*, had been planned for 3 January 2000, the 'night of power', the holiest day of Ramadan. But al-Qaeda's small boat, laden with explosives, sank as soon as it was launched and the terrorists had to revise their plans. On 10 October, when the USS *Cole* cruised into Aden for a brief visit, a so-called 'gas-and-go' stop, a skiff packed with 500 pounds of C4 plastic explosive slipped its mooring and sped across the harbour. Sailors waved at the two men, suicide bombers, standing in the boat. As they reached the port side of the hull they pressed the detonator, blowing a gaping hole in the warship. Seventeen American sailors died. The only small disappointment for al-Qaeda was that the man told to video the attack for the propaganda unit fell asleep at his observation post on Steamer Point.

The FBI moved into the Yemen in force, as they had done in Kenya. The team was headed by John O'Neill, the New York chief of counter-terrorism. A veteran of al-Qaeda investigations, the blunt O'Neill soon clashed with the Yemeni authorities and the US Ambassador, Barbara Bodine, over the sub-machine guns the FBI insisted on carrying for their safety. 'O'Neill was rude. He was bullying and raised his voice with everyone,' said Bodine. The Yemenis were no pushover, as the Kenyan police had been, and the investigation soon got bogged down in mutual recriminations. None of the main al-Qaeda operatives behind the bombing of the USS *Cole* was apprehended, as they had long since escaped to Afghanistan. After six months the FBI closed down the investigation and left.

Bill Clinton was in the waning weeks of his presidency, pre-occupied with his tarnished place in history and not in the mood to carry out his threat of military retaliation against the Taliban if Bin Laden ever again struck at the US from his base in Afghanistan. Under Clinton's presidency the CIA had suffered budget cuts and a crisis of confidence occasioned by political correctness and an over-emphasis on pen-pushers rather than agents in the field. The Clinton administration had recognised the threat posed by al-Qaeda but lacked the will to counter it even after the African bombings in 1998 when its ineffective missile attacks hardly made a dent in the terror organisation. Al-Qaeda had gained kudos by arousing the ire of a super-power but now, when the military might of the greatest nation in the world was directly challenged by an attack on one of its warships, there was no response at all. Just as the death of the US Rangers in Somalia had been a turning-point, revealing to Bin Laden America's 'weakness' in the face of body bags, so the failure to avenge the USS *Cole* attack was another key moment. America would come to bitterly regret its inaction. Clinton's successor would have to deal with a fanatical organisation further emboldened by what it interpreted as its enemy's weakness and lack of appetite for a battle.

By February 2001 US intelligence officials were convinced that Bin Laden was behind the attack on the warship but the new President, George W. Bush, and his National Security

Advisor, Condoleezza Rice, decided against any immediate military response. The threat, however, had not diminished; it had in fact increased. And over the period of Ramadan, that winter, the CIA later admitted there was a second 'peak of threat reporting'. Terror cells planning attacks against Americans in the Persian Gulf region were broken up, and weapons, including anti-aircraft missiles, were seized. These operations also netted proof that Islamic charitable organisations had either been hijacked or specially created to provide support to terrorists in other countries.

Bin Laden and his top advisers may have been physically remote, cut off from the rest of the world in the medieval and mountainous state of Afghanistan, but as Osama himself later scornfully remarked, they were fully plugged in to the age of television and the Internet. They watched and listened as the trials of the East African bombers began in New York in the spring of 2001. Jamal al-Fadl, the defector; Ali Mohamed, the former US soldier; the Nairobi bombers Mohamed al-Owhali and Mohamed Odeh; and Bin Laden's former secretary, Wadih al-Hage, all took the stand. There was revelation after revelation about al-Qaeda's extensive network and its deadly purpose. It had been more than two years since these men had first started to spill the beans about their organisation to FBI investigators and intelligence agencies. Bin Laden and his inner circle knew that some of al-Qaeda's methods and the location of their main logistical bases, in East Africa for example, would have been compromised. They were already one step ahead, becoming more cellular in structure; fewer individuals, even at the topmost levels, were now in the loop in the planning stage of terror operations. Europe was becoming the new staging-ground where Muslim communities provided cover and support for small groups of activists sheltering under the al-Qaeda umbrella. These activists were mainly Egyptian and North African militants from Algeria, Morocco and Tunisia.

In February 2001, in Operation Odin, British police arrested a group of men in London and Leicester suspected of links to an al-Qaeda cell in Frankfurt. The Frankfurt cell had been exposed in December just days before the traditional Strasbourg Christmas market which attracts tourists from all over Europe. Al-Qaeda had planned to bomb it. Telephone taps revealed that al-Qaeda sleepers in Italy were also involved. Indications of a Europe-wide al-Qaeda network were building, but there was no evidence which would stand up in a British court. The men arrested in the UK were released, to the frustration of the British security service, MI5, which had tipped off the Germans to the existence of the Frankfurt cell.

That same month, February, the CIA's Director, George Tenet, gave testimony before the Senate Committee on Intelligence: 'Osama bin Laden and his global network of lieutenants and associates remain the most immediate and serious threat,' Tenet stated. 'He is capable of planning multiple attacks with little or no warning.' The CIA Director also warned that 'softer' targets which presented opportunities for mass casualties were the kind of targets that terrorists were increasingly seeking out.

During the summer of 2001 the warning signals reached an almost deafening crescendo, but the intelligence community claimed the net effect was one of garbled radio traffic and insisted there had been no clear message about al-Qaeda's plans. There were rumours that the US embassies in Delhi and in Aden were being cased for a terror attack. American forces in the Gulf, on land and at sea, were put on 'ThreatCon Delta' – the highest alert; intelligence had been received that they were actively being targeted.

During that summer there was a third 'peak threat' detected by America's intelligence agencies. Plots were uncovered in the Yemen, Saudi Arabia and Europe as the CIA launched what they later described as a wide-ranging disruption effort against Bin Laden's organisation to drive up his security concerns and lead his organisation to delay or cancel its attacks. George Tenet later admitted to Congress that 'our collection sources lit up during this tense period' and revealed that spies had indicated that 'multiple spectacular attacks were planned and some of them were in their final stages'. Inside the CIA some thought that al-Qaeda might be trying to feed them disinformation, to create panic, but most analysts concluded the threat was real. The reporting they were studying was maddeningly short on detail but there were ominous hints of something significant in the pipeline. The suggestion was that the targets were American but, as Tenet later admitted, 'We never acquired the level of detail that allowed us to translate our strategic targets into something we could act on.' Condoleezza Rice, the woman responsible for co-ordinating all the intelligence and advising the President, later described 'a great deal of chatter in the system' at this time.

In the face of these half-understood terror threats the US once more put the Taliban on notice. In June they warned Mullah Omar that America had the right to defend itself and would hold the regime responsible for attacks against US citizens by terrorists sheltering in Afghanistan.

One month later, in July, a smartly dressed man passing through Dubai airport was stopped and questioned by Emirates authorities. By chance they had apprehended an important figure in al-Qaeda's European network; a man the French and British authorities had been watching. His name was Djame Beghal, an Algerian who operated out of London and the Midlands and who also had contacts in Paris and Brussels. Beghal was on his way back from Afghanistan, where he had been called for a meeting with al-Qaeda's head of recruitment, the Palestinian, Abu Zubaydah. A bomb attack was being planned on the US Embassy in Paris and Beghal was to co-ordinate it.

Under interrogation in Dubai, Djame Beghal broke down and confessed; the Emirates authorities said that Islamic scholars had been brought to his prison cell to convince him that Bin Laden's interpretation of *jihad* was wrong. The sceptics thought more heavy-handed local techniques had done the trick. By the beginning of September, Beghal had been extradited secretly to France and raids on al-Qaeda suspects in Europe were about to get the green light. 'It was a close shave,' according to a source in Whitehall. 'We thought we had stopped al-Qaeda in their tracks before they hit a major target in the heart of a European city.'

A few days later, on 9 September, a disturbing piece of news shattered the uneasy calm which had descended on MI6 head-quarters, the enigmatic, brooding building whose green glass windows stare at the Thames by Vauxhall Bridge. Ahmed Shah Masoud, the leader of the Northern Alliance and the man long backed by the British as the best alternative to the Taliban regime, had been killed – by a bomb hidden in a television camera. Two Arabs posing as television journalists had been given false letters of accreditation by the Islamic Observation Centre in London in order to get access to Masoud. The direc-tor of the Centre, Yasser al-Siri, a man wanted for terrorist offences in Cairo, had long been suspected by Egyptian and British intelligence of being a member of Islamic Jihad, part of al-Qaeda. 'The assassination of Masoud was a *quid pro quo*,' I was later told. 'The Taliban must have known that they would be in US sights after September 11 for supporting Bin Laden. They wanted to get rid of the one person they feared might seize power in the coming battle for Afghanistan – Masoud. Bin Laden did the dirty deed for them – and for himself.' It was an ominous signal that Bin Laden's power was almost at its zenith; he was planning to shape the political future of Afghanistan following his ultimate act of terror two days after Masoud's death.

Bin Laden's wife, Aswar, later recalled these last fraught days as her husband and the Taliban finalised their high-risk political strategy: 'He was constantly worried, tired and exhausted due to lack of sleep and he was taking medicine and sleeping pills to help him get to sleep,' she said. 'He used to come to me once a week but then it was only every two to three weeks and he would say he was busy, had problems and was in constant meetings with Mullah Omar and the Taliban leaders. Even when he wanted to travel to another area he didn't tell his wives – contrary to the past, when he would take one of us with him.'

That summer the growing megalomania of al-Qaeda's Director had been openly on display for even the lowliest intelligence agent or laziest journalist to see. In the bazaars of the Middle East, the religious *madrassas* of Pakistan, anonymous mosques in German cities and damp, terraced streets in northern British towns, young Muslim men were watching a clandestine and fuzzy video. It was al-Qaeda's latest offering: a recruitment advertisement and a call to arms. For the first time it was also produced in DVD format so it could be widely disseminated via the Internet. Having failed to film the humiliation of the USS *Cole* themselves, Bin Laden's propaganda unit had spliced together American television pictures of the damaged warship, limping out to sea, with a victorious show of al-Qaeda's strength. On the video masked rebels in a training camp chant, 'We thank Allah for granting us victory the day we destroyed the *Cole* in the water.' A gathering of white-robed figures, al-Qaeda's top hierarchy, resembles a scene from a James Bond movie, a SMERSH-like coalition with Bin Laden in the middle, grinning satanically. This parody of an evil empire would be amusing – if it were not so deadly serious.

Then the tall slim figure of Bin Laden, his long, thick beard now showing streaks of grey, is seen reading a poem at the wedding of his son, Mohamed, to the daughter of one of his top lieutenants, Mohamed Atef, the head of al-Qaeda's military committee. 'In Aden our brothers rose and destroyed the mighty destroyer, a ship so powerful it spreads fear wherever it sails,' intones Bin Laden. 'The victory of the Yemen will continue.'

He promises an intensified holy war that will draw in the whole Muslim nation; in his appeal for aid to the Palestinians fighting Israel he shifts his emphasis away from the usual refrain of the occupation of the Holy Places. The images are of dead Palestinian children, women being beaten on the West Bank, a small boy under a hail of Israeli bullets in Gaza. The message is blatant and effective: give me support in the violence I am about to unleash on the real power behind the injustice inflicted on Muslims. The Director of al-Qaeda ends with this warning: 'To all the *mujahideen*, your brothers in Palestine are waiting for you; it is time to penetrate America and Israel and hit them where it hurts the most.'

Part II

ANATOMY OF MURDER

8

September 11

'Oh my God, the crew has been killed, a flight attendant has been stabbed – we've been hijacked!'

—Flight attendant aboard United Airlines Flight 175

The morning of 11 September 2001 was clear and sunny with a hint of the autumn to come in the woods around Boston when, at 8:00 A.M., American Airlines Flight 11 pushed back from Gate 26 at Logan airport. The captain, 52-year-old John Ogonowski, and his ten crew members anticipated a quiet run to Los Angeles with only eighty-one passengers aboard the Boeing 767. After take-off, at 8:13 A.M., the pilot received instructions from the control tower to turn twenty degrees to the right. 'Twenty right AA-11,' responded Ogonowski. He was then told to climb to 35,000 feet, the plane's cruising altitude. There was no response to this instruction.

The next transmission came ten minutes later, not from the captain but from a man speaking in heavily accented English: 'We have some planes, just stay quiet and you will be okay,' said the voice. The speaker thought he had only keyed the plane's public-address system, but one of the two pilots had surreptitiously pressed the microphone button on the plane's control stick, so controllers on the ground could hear the announcement. A whispered mobile-phone call was received by a ground worker from Madeline Sweeney, a flight attendant, to say that four hijackers were aboard the plane. 'A hijacker cut the throat of a business-class passenger and he appears to be dead,' she relayed back. Four hijackers had stormed the front of the plane and 'had just gained access to the cockpit'. Sweeney tried to call the cockpit but got no response.

Almost immediately the plane changed direction, turning south towards New York City, and began to descend. The transponder stopped transmitting its signal indicating the plane's flight number and altitude. Someone on board must have known to switch it off, making it harder to track the plane's progress. Someone had also known how to get into the locked cockpit with the special 'Boeing key'; perhaps grabbing it off a wounded flight attendant or forcing a crew-member at knifepoint to open the door. Radio and text messages sent from the ground went unanswered. Another attendant, Betty Ong, punched the number 8 of a seatback GTE Airphone and got through to an airlines reservation agent. 'She said two flight attendants had been stabbed and a passenger had had his throat slashed,' the agent reported. Ong passed on the information that four hijackers who seemed to be Middle Eastern had come from first-class seats 2A, 2B, 9A and 9B. There were in fact five hijackers, led by a man who at 8:33 A.M. made another announcement, calmly and politely, to the passengers and the controllers below. 'Nobody move, please. We are going back to the airport. Do not try to make any stupid moves.'

Madeline Sweeney's voice on the mobile phone was now a scream. 'I see water and buildings – oh my God, oh my God!' Minutes later Flight 11 sliced into the North Tower of the World Trade Center on the tip of Manhattan. A documentary-maker, filming with the New York Fire Brigade in the street below, raised his camera instinctively as he heard the plane roar overhead. He recorded the moment of impact as the huge machine

crashed at five hundred miles an hour into the wall of glass and
steel, mushrooming out in a cloud of fire.

Thousands of miles south, in Florida, the President of the
United States was arriving at a school in Sarasota to take part in
a reading session with the children. A senior aide brought
George W. Bush news of what seemed to be an accident involving a small twin-engined plane. 'This is pilot error,' the
President recalled saying. 'The guy must have had a heart
attack.'

Four minutes before Flight 11 hit the World Trade Center, a
pilot on a second plane out of Boston, United Airlines Flight
175 to Los Angeles, had radioed the control tower in response
to an enquiry if he knew Flight 11 was in trouble. Captain
Victor Saracini, Flight 175's pilot, confirmed that he had heard
something which indicated a problem with the earlier plane.
'We heard a suspicious transmission on our departure from
Bos [Boston],' said the captain. 'Sounds like someone keyed
the mike and said, "Everyone stay in your seats."'

Within ninety seconds Flight 175 itself, with nine crew and
fifty-six passengers aboard, suddenly veered from its course
over northern New Jersey, moving south before making a
U-turn to the north, towards New York City. Again the
transponder was shut off.

At 8:50 the manager of United Airlines' systems operations
centre in Chicago received a call from a maintenance mechanic.
He had been called by a woman, who screamed, 'Oh my God,
the crew has been killed, a female flight attendant has been
stabbed – we've been hijacked!' before the line went dead.

Across the water from the World Trade Center, a couple in an
apartment had set up their video camera to film the smoking
North Tower. At 9:03 the camera caught Flight 175 heading
swiftly and unerringly, like a dart, for the second skyscraper,
the South Tower. On the audio track the screams of the woman
sear that moment in the memory: 'Oh my God, oh my God, oh

Holy Jesus . . .' repeated over and over as the spray of burning
aviation fuel and debris rain from the sky.

Sitting on a stool amid the schoolchildren in Sarasota, a camera
also caught the face of George W. Bush as he was told about the
second plane. The President's features froze into a mask, but
his eyes showed the disbelief and the horror as the White
House Chief of Staff whispered in his ear, 'A second plane hit
the second tower; America is under attack.' Bush later recalled
clearly what went through his mind in that instant: 'They had
declared war on us and I made up my mind at that moment
that we were going to war,' he told the *Washington Post*. 'Really
good,' the President said to the children still reading around
him as he excused himself and left the room. At 9:30 he
appeared before the television cameras outside to announce
'terrorism will not stand', an echo of the words used by his
father eleven years before. 'This will not stand,' George Bush
senior had said when Iraq invaded Kuwait in 1990. It was a
supreme irony that these words prompted the deployment of
US forces to the Gulf, an act which Osama bin Laden would use
to justify his reign of terror against America.

In Washington George Tenet, the Director of the CIA, was
breakfasting at the St Regis hotel with an old friend, ex-Senator
David Boren. The 'chatter' in the intelligence system over the
summer, the sense that something big was about to happen, at
last made sense. 'This has Bin Laden all over it. I've got to go,'
Tenet said to Boren. 'I wonder if this has anything to do with
that guy taking pilot training,' the CIA Director mused, referring to a French–Moroccan, Zacharias Moussaoui, who had
been detained just weeks before after attracting attention at a
Minnesota jet training facility.

Ten minutes before Flight 175 hit the World Trade Center
another plane, American Airlines Flight 77, bound from Dulles
airport near Washington to Los Angeles, also stopped

responding to radio calls. At 8:56 A.M. the Boeing 757, with six crew and fifty-eight passengers aboard, had its flight transponder turned off and no one could raise the pilot, Charles Burlingame. Among the people on board was Barbara Olson, a frequent commentator on CNN and the wife of Theodore Olson, the US Solicitor General. Mr Olson was in his office when his secretary told him his wife was on the phone. 'She said the hijackers had box-cutters and knives – they rounded up the passengers and the two pilots at the back of the plane,' said Theodore Olson. He told his wife about the Trade Center crashes. 'What should I tell the pilot?' his wife asked. She was cut off and her husband alerted the Justice Department command centre to the hijacking. Mrs Olson called back and said the plane was circling, then moving north-east.

Secret Service agents burst into the West Wing office of the White House, startling the Vice-President, Dick Cheney, starting work at his desk. 'Sir, we have to leave immediately,' said one of the agents. Radar showed an aeroplane making for the centre of Washington DC.

The ground controllers were finding it hard to track Flight 77 without the transponder but had picked up the aircraft as it crossed the Pentagon building on the edge of the city. They thought it was on autopilot and heading for the White House, but the plane suddenly made a sweeping circle to the right, dropping down low over a traffic-jammed highway. Skimming the roofs of the cars, Flight 77 slammed into the western face of the Pentagon shortly after 9:40 A.M.

In the bunker below the White House the instruction went out to the Federal Aviation Administration to land all the 4,546 aircraft that were in the skies above the United States that morning. Fighter planes were scrambled as both combat patrols and to provide an escort for Air Force One, bringing the President to a secure USAF base. The nation was put on 'DefCon 3', the highest level of offensive readiness. Bush and Cheney conferred on a secure line and the order was given to shoot down any civilian airliner known to be in the control of hijackers. 'I had the television pictures of the World Trade Center before me and a clear understanding that once the plane was hijacked, it was a weapon,' said the Vice-President.

United Airlines Flight 93 was forty minutes late that morning leaving Newark airport to fly to San Francisco. It took off at 8:42 instead of at 8:00, as it should have done to play its assigned role in the deadly aerial ballet. The captain was Jason Dahl and there were six other crew members and thirty-seven passengers aboard the Boeing 757. As it flew west into northern Ohio, United Airlines ground control transmitted a system-wide message warning all its pilots of a potential 'cockpit intrusion' following the hijacking of Flight 77. The crew on Flight 93 replied by pushing a button that read out 'confirmed' to show they had received the message.

On board, passengers began receiving mobile-phone calls from relatives and friends alerting them to the seizure and crashing of the earlier flights. Suddenly, at 9:25, there were two short radio bursts from Flight 93 and ground controllers heard garbled shouting, distorted by the frequency of the signal: 'Get out of here, get out of here!' It was followed by a scuffling sound and then an accented voice speaking rapidly.

'Hi, this is the captain,' a man said. 'We'd like you all to remain seated. There is a bomb on board and we are going to turn back to the airport.'

As the radio message was logged on the ground the US military were informed. In the bunker an aide approached the Vice-President: 'There is a plane eighty miles out,' he said. 'There is a fighter in the area, should we engage?'

'Yes,' replied Cheney, without hesitation. Later he would tell the *Washington Post* the decision had seemed 'painful but nonetheless clear-cut – I didn't agonise over it'.

The cockpit recorder on Flight 93 picked up the sound of someone being choked, then voices in Arabic reassuring each other, 'Everything is fine.' One of the passengers, Tom Burnett, called his wife Deena, who was giving their three children breakfast in San Francisco: 'I'm on Flight 93 and we've been hijacked. They've knifed a guy and there's a bomb on board – call the authorities.'

In New Jersey Lyzbeth Glick received a call from her husband Jeremy on board Flight 93. He described Middle Eastern-looking men wearing red bandannas round their heads. 'I love you,' the couple said to each other over and over again. Jeremy asked if it was true what other passengers had heard – that planes had crashed into the World Trade Center. He wondered if that was where Flight 93 was headed. Herded into the back, the passengers were beginning to whisper among themselves. They were thinking of 'rushing the hijackers', Glick, a former judo champion, said on the phone to his wife. Did she think it was a good idea? 'Go for it,' Lyz replied.

Meanwhile flight attendant Sandy Bradshaw called her husband and said there was talk of doing something – she was filling coffee pots with boiling water in readiness. Another passenger, Todd Beamer, was patched through to an Airphone supervisor in Illinois, Lisa Jefferson. He told her two pilots were lying dead or gravely wounded on the floor in the first-class cabin.

Deena Burnett called her husband, Tom, sobbing as she told him another plane had crashed, this time into the Pentagon. 'My God,' was all he could say. 'They seem to be taking planes and driving them into designated landmarks all over the East Coast,' said his wife. 'It's as if hell has been unleashed.'

At 9:36 Flight 93 made a U-turn and started heading back to Washington. As the plane lurched Todd Beamer became agitated and told the phone supervisor they were flying erratically. 'We're going down, we're coming back up. We're turning around and going back north,' said Beamer. He asked Lisa Jefferson to recite the Lord's Prayer with him. He said he and the others had formed a plan to hit back. 'I thought it was pretty dangerous. I asked was he sure he wanted to do that?'

said Jefferson. 'Todd said at that point he thought that was what he had to do.'

Also on board Flight 93 was Donald Greene, an executive of Flight Instrument Corporation and a qualified pilot. The other passengers probably knew of his skills, and felt confident they could get the plane down safely after overpowering the terrorists.

'Are you ready? Let's roll,' said Beamer before laying down his phone. Jeremy Glick put his phone to one side too, after telling his wife to take care of their new baby daughter Emmy. 'Hang on, I'll be back,' he told Lyz. She handed the phone to her father, unable to listen any longer.

The air-traffic controllers kept calling the cockpit, but in vain. Relatives kept vigil by their telephones – the lines were still open, but all they heard was a crackling sound and then silence. At 10:03 Flight 93 crashed in a field south-east of Pittsburgh; a crater forty feet deep bloomed around the wreckage.

On Air Force One President Bush anxiously asked, 'Did we shoot it down or did it crash?' Two hours later came the confirmation: the plane had not been shot down by fighter aircraft. 'I think an act of heroism occurred on board that plane,' Dick Cheney said quietly. The crashing of four American planes and the murder of the 245 innocent people in them was just the beginning of the death and destruction visited on the United States that day.

9

The Egyptian

'With my blood and my sword I will defend Islam. May America be destroyed – her armies and the Pentagon.'

—Egyptian worshippers at al-Azzar mosque,
October 2001

The angry crowd swirled on the floor of the mighty al-Azzar mosque in the centre of Cairo. It was a Friday, 12 October, the day after the US bombing of Afghanistan began in retaliation for the terror attack of September 11. Our camera crew was somewhere down there in the press of male bodies. Worshippers climbed on each other's shoulders to denounce America – the Great Satan, the enemy of Islam. Suddenly, somewhat the worse for wear, our colleagues were spewed out of the mêlée into the lines of black-clad riot police ringing the courtyard.

Such protests, such cries of hate against America, have been heard here many times before from a population angry at its leaders' compliance with the foreign superpower. From Anwar Sadat, who made peace with Israel through the Camp David Accords, to Hosni Mubarak, who supported the American-led coalition against Iraq during the Gulf War, the Arab street has been at odds with its rulers. To the average resident of Cairo, America's influence in Egypt has long been seen as the latest colonial boot placed on the neck of a great and ancient civilisation. The al-Azzar mosque has become the scene of ritualised protest against America; protest ignored and often firmly suppressed by the government. But this time it was more personal. The crowd's enemy was the United States, and America's enemy, Bin Laden, was its hero. He had chosen one of them to be his instrument of war.

Cairo was home to the young Egyptian who masterminded and executed the most daring terror attack ever carried out in the West, the simultaneous hijacking of four aeroplanes and the destruction of great edifices symbolising the economic and military might of America. Mohamed Atta's face stared out from every newspaper and television screen across the world, unmistakably Egyptian with its chiselled, Pharaonic features. His arrogance and fanaticism were betrayed by the cold, staring eyes.

That day a lonely, grey-haired figure sat drinking tea at a table in the Cairo Shooting Club, a colonial building set behind high security gates surrounded by dusty lawns and ringed by shabby concrete blocks. Mohamed al-Amir Awad al-Sayed Atta was reflecting on his infamous son, Mohamed, who used the last of his family names in the passport he handed to the American Airlines staff as he boarded Flight 11 on September 11. In a rambling, two-hour conversation with *Panorama*, al-Amir refused to acknowledge that his son was guilty of the massacre. Mohamed was 'missing', but he expected to hear from him – it was all a terrible mistake. 'He can't even fly a kite. He used to get stomach pains whenever he travelled by plane. His sister used to have to get him medication for it.'

Instead, Mohamed al-Amir had two themes he wanted to expound upon: the Israelis' responsibility for the Palestinian problem and the evils wrought by America, the Jewish state's great protector. 'America is responsible for planting the seed of terrorism in the world. They killed ninety million Indians, they shackled African youths and made them slaves,' he charged.

Like most of his countrymen, al-Amir was incensed by America's support of Israel. 'The pulse of the Arab street says that America is a filthy thug who wants to hit the Islamic nations,' he shouted. 'America wants to kill the Palestinians. Israelis are filthy racists – what about the massacre of Sabra and Chatila – why didn't America make a move then?' These were the beliefs al-Amir's son learned at his knee.

Although Mohamed al-Amir spurned America's culture and railed against its tolerance of adultery and homosexuality, he nevertheless recognised the power of its currency. He demanded $25,000 from us for an exclusive televised interview. The money would go to the Palestinian cause, he said. We declined to pay him but there was no stopping the stream of words from this embittered man.

The journey that Mohamed Atta made was certainly influenced in some respects by his father. It was to end in the inferno of the World Trade Center, inspired and orchestrated by Bin Laden from Afghanistan. The journey began in an apartment in Cairo in Abdin, just a stone's throw from the balcony where President Nasser, the great Arab nationalist leader, acknowledged responsibility for his country's defeat in the Six-Day War against Israel. It was a moment of despair felt across the whole of the Middle East, the death of Arab hopes of re-establishing Palestine.

It was to Abdin that an ambitious young lawyer came with his family in 1978. He had struggled to break free from his roots in the farming village of Kafr el-Sheikh on the Nile delta and establish himself as a successful professional. Mohamed al-Amir brought with him his wife Bouthayna, two daughters, Mona and Azza, and his only son, Mohamed, then ten years old. Al-Amir had sympathies with the Muslim Brotherhood, an organisation founded in 1928 with the aim of establishing a strict Islamic regime, although in recent years it had tempered its radicalism.

The family were devout Muslims, but modern in outlook. Mohamed's mother and sisters dressed fashionably, their heads uncovered. For Atta's father, an austere and strict man, the key to advancement was academic success and he pushed his children relentlessly. Mohamed is remembered here as a shy boy who was never allowed to play football with the other children. His father would anxiously call him inside to study.

Hassan Attiya, a friend at high school, recalled Mohamed as a boy set apart from his playmates from the beginning. 'I think he wanted to play with the rest of us boys but his father wanted him to perform excellently at school,' Attiya said. He described Mohamed as an effeminate child, 'delicate, even virginal, but a very nice person'. Mohamed senior declared his son's 'virginal' qualities to be admirable. He acknowledged 'he has always been a loner, just like me'.

Family photographs show a serious child, tight-lipped, with a disconcertingly direct gaze. Mohamed was close to his mother, Bouthayna – too close, his father grumbled. 'I used to tell her she is raising him as a girl and that I have three girls, but she never stopped pampering him,' he complained. The only picture in which the boy seems animated is one in which his attractive mother presses her face adoringly to his. Mohamed smiles, sheepishly, at the camera.

Mohamed al-Amir was not popular locally. He was regarded as overbearing and snobbish – a man with a Mercedes outside the door who was vocal about the way the elite of Cairo prospered as some in Egypt reaped the benefits of cordial relations with America. The aid that it brought, he complained, did little to alter the lives of the poor.

By the time Mohamed was seventeen the family had moved to a better address, a top-floor flat in a modern block in Pyramid Street, with a view of the monuments, symbols of Egypt's glorious past. His older sisters had obtained excellent degrees from Cairo University, and good jobs as a doctor and a zoologist. Mohamed was in their shadow, expected as the only boy to do even better. A photo taken on the beach shows two beautiful young women, one with an arm protectively round him, the other with a hand placed reassuringly on his knee. Mohamed, between them, looks anxious.

Mohamed Atta was living through turbulent years, both in Egypt and more widely in the Middle East. President Sadat had been assassinated by a group of Islamic extremists within the army. In Iran, mullahs had set up a theocracy and were exporting their religious revolution. Israel invaded the Lebanon in pursuit of the PLO and in Beirut a new and deadly weapon began to be deployed, the suicide bomber. In October 1983 Hizbollah blew up the US Marine barracks, killing 241 American and French soldiers. In the eyes of the Islamic world, the power of the 'martyr' was proved when Washington pulled its forces out of Beirut.

Mohamed Atta enrolled at Cairo University in 1985, joining the Faculty of Engineering to study architecture. The Syndicate, or Trades Union of Engineers, had always been a stronghold of the Muslim Brotherhood, but there is no outward sign that Atta developed any political leanings at university despite the turmoil all around him in the Middle East.

'He was average, he followed the crowd, he just wasn't a leader,' remembers Wael Sabry, who studied with Atta at university. 'He was very serious, his assignments were always in on time – he was devout and he prayed regularly, but that's not unusual, many of us do.' A photograph taken on a graduation trip down the Nile shows a different youngster from the one in family pictures, relaxed in a sports shirt, a bag slung round his shoulders, grinning broadly. He was still seen as innocent, with no sign of girlfriends. But this too was not unusual in the social and religious setting of university life in Cairo.

In 1990, Atta was graduating just as American troops and tanks were moving into Saudi Arabia, site of the Holy Places of Islam, to defend the kingdom against Saddam Hussein. His father already had plans for him far beyond Egypt. He had enrolled Mohamed at the Goethe Institute in Cairo to learn German, 'the language of engineers', as he put it. Al-Amir insisted his son obtain a Ph.D. as his sisters had done, and he was to get it abroad. 'I need to hear the word "doctor" in front of your name,' said his father. 'Your sisters are doctors, and their husbands are doctors, and you are the man of the family.'

On 24 July 1992, Atta arrived in the city of Hamburg in Germany. Prosperous and bourgeois, the former jewel of the Hanseatic League bestrode the river Elbe, enjoying the new economic boom brought on by the collapse of Communism to the east. Hamburg had another side too, brash, neon-lit and seedy, centred around the infamous Reeperbahn sex district. It was an alien environment for a 22-year-old devout Muslim who was far from home and embarking on a new and uncertain phase of his life. Atta was soon homesick and lonely. There was a significant Turkish population in the city but they were more secular Muslims who had been guest workers in Germany for many years. There were few Arabs from a similar background to the young Egyptian.

Mohamed Atta had been sponsored by a German couple, teachers who had met his father in Egypt, and he stayed in a room in their house in Hamburg. Like all foreign students he had to pass an exam showing his proficiency in German before his tourist visa would be converted into a student's visa for an extended stay. Atta got off on the wrong foot, his father interfering even now in his son's new life. When Mohamed was refused his first-choice place, to study architecture at the University of Applied Science, his father took out legal action on the grounds of alleged racial discrimination. The university agreed to accept him but by then Mohamed had found a new course, in town planning at the Hamburg–Harburg Technical University in the industrial suburb of Harburg.

The technical university is a model of German modernist architecture, efficiency and state support. Wandering through the spotless plaza, the buildings curved harmoniously on either side of me, broken by glass towers, huge half-empty lecture theatres and a bustling canteen with hearty and heavily subsidised meals. Students here are destined to become the backbone of an industrial society, soberly dressed, conservative, embarking on the first rung of certain ascent to the corporate heights of BMW or Siemens.

The university employs a tireless and charming public relations man. Anyone else would have reacted to the enormous pressure from the media investigating Mohamed Atta's alma mater by simply shutting his door and disconnecting his phone, but Reudiger Bendlin is all smiles and helpfulness. The university, he explained to me, prides itself on its multicultural intake, with nationalities from Asia and the Middle East and all over Europe represented. Like all foreign students here, Mohamed Atta received free tuition courtesy of the German state.

Beyond the modern buildings of concrete and steel, across a small walkway, an old German chalet-style house remains, somewhat incongruously. Behind a small dormer window in the attic lies the orderly domain of the man who, more than any other, knew Mohamed Atta during his years in Germany. Professor Dittmar Machule is the Head of the Urban Planning Department, a courteous, scholarly man with an academic reputation as an expert on ancient Syrian cities. In his study, filled with artefacts from archaeological digs, I spent hours discussing his infamous pupil.

From the start, the new Egyptian student impressed and intrigued his teacher. 'He was somehow special, quiet, reserved, polite and very intellectual,' Professor Machule told me, 'but the notable thing about him was that he was very, very religious. However, he never came across as someone extreme, unstable or narrow-minded. It was the combination of his religious beliefs and the interest and curiosity he had in pursuing a modern study, like town planning, in all its dimensions, that made him exciting to teach.' The two men shared a mutual passion for the old cities of the Middle East; Machule would later admit that he may have been blinded to the dark side, the austere and unforgiving nature of Atta's personality.

In Hamburg Atta, with his hitherto virginal outlook on life, was forced to adjust to a Western society, with its permissive, sexually open atmosphere. He would cover his eyes when semi-naked women appeared on television. When his landlady walked around the apartment with her arms bare or wearing a dressing-gown, she felt he was uncomfortable and disapproving. Mohamed Atta told friends back in Egypt that is why he moved out, into student accommodation in Harburg, after six months. He aggravated his new room-mates with his messy habits and his selfish behaviour, however. They found him gloomy, reluctant to enjoy himself.

'Germany and the Western world were a strange place for Mohamed, he was very much an Egyptian,' Volcker Hauth told me late one night as he pored over his draughtsman's board. One of only two German students who became friends with the reserved Egyptian, Hauth today practises as an architect in Hamburg. A tall, earnest, bespectacled man, he lives in a small and orderly flat, its contents perfectly designed and meticulously placed. 'Mohamed was definitely not part of the fun generation,' laughed Hauth, whose own deeply-held Protestant faith recognised a kindred religious spirit in Atta. 'He was not interested in cars, or money – or even women,' Hauth went on. What interested Atta was how to gain knowledge of Western ways of planning and to learn lessons from them to apply in an Islamic context, in the old cities of the Arab world.

Atta took a part-time job in Hamburg as a draughtsman with a design consultancy called Plankantor. Jörg Lewin was to employ him for five years. 'Mohamed's strength lay in his ability to draw extremely precisely; he was very meticulous, even pedantic. He never opened up as a person. He wasn't especially liked by the others but he was perfectly pleasant.' From the start, Atta's strict adherence to his religion was remarked on. 'He would get his prayer mat out five times a day. During that time he was utterly absorbed – he wouldn't hear you if you spoke to him. We accepted it, although it was unusual for us. After all, some people take five minutes out for smoking – well, Mohamed would take five minutes for praying,' explained Lewin. Atta fasted at Ramadan and was careful never to breach the dietary laws of Islam. 'When we all sat down for coffee and cake he wouldn't eat any of the icing on top in case it contained gelatine, pork products,' said Lewin. 'He would examine the packaging of biscuits minutely to see what the ingredients were.'

Two years after he came to Hamburg, Mohamed Atta embarked on a series of trips back to the Middle East, to Syria, Saudi Arabia and home to Cairo. These journeys marked a watershed in his life and set him on the path towards al-Qaeda and the terror attack of September 11.

In 1994 Atta went on study tours to Istanbul in Turkey and to Aleppo in Syria, both ancient cities in once great Islamic empires. The Egyptian student now had a chance to show his knowledge of his own culture, and a teacher remembers him in Istanbul passionately lecturing his German college mates on the superiority of the Islamic way of planning and building cities. There was no discussion to be had with him, he was dogmatic, his mind closed on the subject. Others found it increasingly hard to communicate with him.

Atta was fascinated by the city of Aleppo, and it would become the subject of his academic thesis. The man who had seemed so dislocated in Hamburg was suddenly different, more assertive, more at ease. 'He was a fish back in water once he got to a familiar Arab country,' recalls Hauth. 'He could laugh and joke, it was clear this is where he felt at home.' There were rumours of a romantic entanglement. Atta confided to Hauth he had met a young Palestinian woman in Syria. She was beautiful and he admired her. She would tease him and call him her 'little Pharaoh'. Marriage, however, was out of the question, he decided. The girl was too independent, too worldly, not well-connected enough. His family wanted him to marry an Egyptian, the daughter of an ambassador.

The next year, 1995, Atta travelled to Saudi Arabia to make the pilgrimage to Mecca, the *Haj*, which every devout Muslim is expected to undertake at least once. He went alone. The *Haj* is where agents of Bin Laden often take the opportunity to seek out devout young men susceptible to their message. It is believed that Mecca may have been the first place where direct contact was established between al-Qaeda and Mohamed Atta. He grew a beard, a sign of devotion.

He sent a postcard back to the Plankantor office. It was the first occasion in five years they had received any message, card or greeting from him, according to Jörg Lewin. 'It was the only time he ever expressed something personal. He said what a great experience he had had in Mecca.' It is clear now that this experience marked a turning-point in his life. When he returned to the university in Hamburg Mohamed Atta did not shave off the beard.

Soon he returned to the Middle East, this time home to Cairo. It was another study trip, to look at the old quarter, known as the Islamic City, a medieval jumble of markets and old workshops which the government wanted to develop for tourism. With Volcker Hauth and another German student, Ralph Bodenstein, Atta was there to analyse the effects of re-development on the social and economic fabric of this poor area.

Today Ralph Bodenstein teaches in the American University in Beirut. A slim, attractive man, an expert in Islamic studies, he remembers the strength of the political views Atta expressed on that trip to Cairo. It was as if he was seeing his home country with more critical insight. 'He was a calm man but when he was upset, he became passionate. And he got really upset and extreme in his judgements when it came to politics,' recalls Bodenstein.

Atta realised that the Egyptian authorities wanted to demolish old buildings and clean up the area for tourists regardless of the consequences for local people. 'He had a very strong sense of social justice and he thought the officials were just interested in their own careers and financial enrichment,' says Bodenstein. 'He was very critical of the planning decisions, the nepotism.' His friends noted that Atta expanded his criticism to encompass the 'Americanisation' of Egypt, which threatened to turn the old city into an Islamic Disneyland. He railed against the undue influence of the US on Mubarak's government and the alienation of the Westernised Egyptian elite, 'fat cats' he called them, from the man in the street. Egypt, he said, had opened up to Western influence and market capitalism regardless of the real needs of the people. 'He told me it was grotesque that strawberries were being grown in the Nile delta for the European market, luxury goods, while the poor could not afford to buy wheat imported from America,' remembers Ralph Bodenstein.

It was not only American political influence in Cairo which incensed Atta. He saw the USA as leader of the international community failing to help the Muslim population in the Bosnian war. And he considered the Oslo Accords between the PLO and Israel, America's ally, to have sold out the Palestinian cause. Why did the US lead bombing sorties against Iraq and yet refuse to prevent Israeli attacks on Palestinians, he demanded. 'I could sense a frustration and rage, especially in his political critiques about what was going on in the world and the biased politics against Muslims, as he regarded it,' concludes Bodenstein.

This kind of talk was dangerous in Cairo at this time. Following a wave of terror attacks, the trials of a number of members of the extremist group, Islamic Jihad, were taking place. There were accusations of unfair proceedings, torture, the fear of execution. To Atta it seemed as if a street war was in progress. Heavily-armed troops stormed parts of the city and there were summary arrests of political activists, many of whom had also taken care of the social needs of the poor.

Atta was angry and afraid. He had always intended to return to his country and use his degree to get a prestigious job in Cairo, using his skills for the good of his people. He told Volcker Hauth of his fears: 'He felt his beard, his social and political beliefs, marked him out as a criminal. He wanted to live in Egypt and work in Egypt but he was afraid he would be arrested. He was sad and depressed about his professional future.'

Atta's emotions were torn and confused. He wanted to live in Egypt but feared he had no future there. He was homesick in Germany and longed for his domineering father to allow him to return. He had been staying at home during the study trip, though his German friends had only met his father fleetingly. Now Mohamed senior was adamant his son had to complete his degree. He told his mother that he had had enough and that he wanted to stay at home. He told her he missed the family. She told him, 'Daddy wants you to go, you mustn't upset your father. He has spent a great deal of money on you and you must finish your education.'

Mohamed Atta returned, with a heavy heart, to Hamburg in the spring of 1996.

10

Between Two Worlds

*'I want my family and everyone that reads this will to fear
Almighty God and not to be deceived by what happens in life.
Fear God and follow his prophets if you are a real believer.'*

—Mohamed Atta's will, written 11 April 1996

Once back in the cold climes of northern Germany, Mohamed
Atta began to drift apart from Volcker Hauth and Ralph
Bodenstein. Their studies were taking them in different direc-
tions and the Germans sensed that Atta was drawing back from
his Western friends. Hauth recalls: 'Mohamed's bitterness
increased, it was a gradual thing.' Bodenstein believes that the
trip to Cairo had reinforced Mohamed's conviction that he
could never feel at home in the West. And yet he was con-
demned, by his father's ambition and his own fears about
Egypt, to live in Germany. 'Mohamed was so religious, so conservative, he found it difficult to communicate with people in
Hamburg, they just weren't interested in the same issues. He
suffered because of it and he became increasingly alienated,'
according to Ralph Bodenstein.

Mohamed Atta, confused, angry and lonely, was emotionally
vulnerable. He needed a refuge, a place where he could find
like-minded people. He found that refuge in seedy Steindamm
street, near the main train station, the haunt of prostitutes and

drug-dealers. The al-Quds mosque occupies the top floor of a blank-faced modern building, squeezed between a body-building gym and a Vietnamese supermarket. Al-Quds is the Arabic name for Jerusalem, site of the third holiest shrine in Islam, the al-Aqsa mosque on the Haram al-Sharif. Since the occupation of East Jerusalem by the Israeli army in 1967, 'al-Quds' has become a rallying-cry for the Palestinian cause in the Arab world. The mosque was already known to German intelligence as a place where Islamic militants congregated.

The al-Quds mosque is a simple room which holds at most just over a hundred people. The white walls have Qur'anic verses painted on them. Outside, groups of nervous but tough-looking young men in leather jackets loiter on Friday mornings. When I visited in October 2001 a man on the staircase leading up to the mosque advised us, 'It would be better for you if you were to go.'

Atta became a regular at the mosque in 1996, and both German intelligence and American investigators believe it was here that the Egyptian became drawn inexorably into the al-Qaeda network. His radicalisation and growing political awakening had begun with his trip to Mecca, a Bin Laden recruiting-ground, the previous year. It had opened his eyes to the political reality of life in Egypt. And back in Hamburg Atta began to play a more active role. He came into contact with a German–Syrian named Mohamed Haidar Zammer, a known extremist and Bin Laden associate who had fought in the old days in Afghanistan and then in Bosnia. He operated through the al-Quds mosque, the medium for his contacts with young men developing similar extremist views. They formed a small, distinct group among the other worshippers, not sanctioned or organised in any way by the mosque officials.

It is a pattern that has become all too familiar to the German intelligence services. For six years Dr Herbert Müller, a schol-arly Arabist and the foremost Islamic expert for the domestic intelligence service, the BKA, has been investigating extremist Islamic movements in German cities. 'There are definitely some mosques where the isolation experienced by some students suffering culture shock is exploited,' Dr Müller told me. 'There are indications of small groups in one or two mosques who are the representatives of fundamentalist Islam. They have terrorist aims and they seek out more capable people from among their fellow believers and get them involved in their activities.'

A former member of an extremist Islamic organisation which is part of al-Qaeda explained how the organisation's recruiters operate on susceptible young men. 'Someone approached me in the mosque as I was praying, and started to talk to me about injustice in the Middle East, the poverty, our impotence in the face of Israel,' this man told *Panorama*. 'He made me want to listen to him – to find a solution. At first these people don't talk about violence. They concentrate on how much injustice America has caused in the world and how to get rid of this unfairness. They mention Palestine, they call on you to uphold your national dignity, to defend your people, and suggest for that you must sacrifice yourself. Then your people will live after you and will always remember you.' The young man, himself an Egyptian, speaking in the privacy of a quiet courtyard in Cairo, believed this was the way Mohamed Atta was approached.

At the al-Quds mosque Atta became friendly with men from other Muslim countries, many of them Moroccans. Some became fellow students at the technical university in Harburg. Saïd Bahaji, a Moroccan with German citizenship, signed up there for an electrical engineering course. Mounir al-Moutassadeq, another electronics student, began his course in October 1995, with Atta helping him find a flat. Two students from other colleges in Hamburg joined the group of young North African and Arab men coalescing around Mohamed Atta: a Yemeni called Ramsi bin al-Shibh and another Moroccan, Zacharias Essebar.

On 11 April 1996 Mohamed Atta wrote his will, witnessed by al-Moutassadeq and another friend from the mosque. Drawing up a will is not unusual in itself; in the Muslim world it often

indicates the person is about to embark on his travels. But Atta
had just returned from his trip to Cairo and had no plans to
leave Germany. Why did he draw up this document at the
Hamburg mosque, instead of at home, in Egypt, where family
members could have witnessed it?

The instructions in his will carry two clear messages: not to
mourn his passing and not to be deceived by what life has to
offer. Death, according to Atta, is a glorious destiny. 'I don't
want anyone to weep and cry or to rip their clothes or slap
their face because this is an ignorant thing to do,' he ordered.
No women should be allowed at his grave and specific instructions, verging on the obsessive, were given as to the washing
and dressing of his body.

Dr Herbert Müller read Atta's will for me, with interest. 'I
believe it formed part of the circumstances by which he was led
into a situation from which he could no longer escape. He was
readying himself ideologically for a final act; he probably
wanted to make it known that by writing this he was going to
commit an act in which he himself would die.' The conclusion
Dr Müller drew from reading the will was clear: 'It's a sort of
psychological preparation, carried out by someone committing
suicide against the background of being a *mujahid*, a warrior
following the way of God.'

Ralph Bodenstein, from his knowledge of Mohamed Atta's
political views, believes that the date of the will is significant.
The 11th of April 1996 was shortly after the Israelis bombed a
UN refugee camp in southern Lebanon, killing several hundred Palestinian civilians. The Israeli operation was called 'The
Grapes of Wrath', but the wrath was largely in the Arab world,
where people were incensed at the muted criticism of Israel in
the West. Ralph Bodenstein thinks it may well have been this
event that caused Atta to begin his personal *jihad*.

The will reveals Atta's obsessive fears about women and
sexual purity. Although a common theme in the Islamic world
it is also one which has left its imprint deep in the testaments
left by young male suicide bombers. 'I don't want women to

come to my house, to apologise for my death . . . I don't want any women to go to my grave at all during my funeral, or any occasion thereafter,' Atta sternly commands. 'The person who will wash my body near my genitals must wear gloves on his hand, so he won't touch my genitals,' he instructs the reader. Mohamed Atta would return to the theme of sex and death five years later in his final instructions to the hijackers on the night of 10 September. But then it would be to entice them with the vision of seventy virgins when they reached heaven, the *houris* promised by the religious texts to Islamic martyrs, eternally beautiful and compliant.

There has been much speculation about Mohamed Atta's sexuality. 'Terrorist Mohamed Atta and Several of His Bloody Henchmen Led Secret Gay Lives!' screamed the *National Enquirer* on 22 October 2001. More earnest and scholarly journals have also explored themes of homo-eroticism and narcissism in Atta's personality, and that of his mentor, Bin Laden.

The truth is probably much simpler: not gay, but certainly repressed and confused. Anyone who has lived or travelled widely in Muslim countries knows how considerable the tension is between libido and repression, the obsession that exists with sex and the need to control it. Women's sexuality is a major threat to male supremacy. Not only touching a woman but even looking at a female outside the family is forbidden. It has been a constant struggle for me, reporting from the Middle East, to persuade male interviewees to look me in the eye when the camera is running.

Muslims maintain that their society respects women, that they need protection and are worthy of veneration. But it is hard for Westerners to see the way many Muslim women are treated, as the possessions of their menfolk, as anything other than misogynistic.

Mohamed Atta came from a devout but a modern family. His mother and sisters did not wear the veil, the two girls went on to attain Ph.D.s and have high-flying careers. His father has commented on his son's modesty, his virginal qualities – even his femininity, which his mother encouraged. There was never any hint of a girlfriend in his university years, only the fleeting friendship with the Palestinian student in Syria. This was not unusual in an Islamic society where women are unavailable until marriage, a society where men sometimes turn to other men, temporarily, to fill that gap.

The more time he spent in the West, the more authoritarian Atta became in his attitudes to women. Bodenstein and Hauth teased him, saying women could look provocative in the way they wore the *hejab*, the Islamic head covering, with just their eyes showing. He responded angrily, denouncing women for wearing headscarves that were too colourful, too rakishly arranged. He criticised young Egyptian women for wearing jeans. Atta was caught in the classic trap experienced by the young Muslim male: women were desirable but off-limits. They were dangerous and therefore to be feared. He was now twenty-eight but when asked about marriage brushed the questions aside. His will showed his fears that thoughts about women and sex were polluting and would not be allowed to distract an ascetic Islamic warrior.

Outwardly, Atta still looked the same. He was always well-groomed and nattily dressed. He never wore jeans, the sign of American cultural imperialism, but always neatly pressed trousers and his signature leather jacket. He still worked diligently at the Plankantor design agency, nineteen hours a week. The rest of the time he spent on his course at the university.

Professor Machule had been teaching him for four years now and marvelled at the way Atta held on to his Islamic faith in such a secular environment. Of all the students he had ever taught from Muslim countries, Mohamed was the only one who did not alter his way of life in response to Western influence, never missing the call to prayer five times a day.

Atta's will was written as he was establishing himself in a circle of young, like-minded Muslims through the al-Quds mosque. Investigators now believe that all these men, most of whom were from North African countries, were adherents of an extremist Islamic sect known as *Takfir wal Hijra*, which means 'Unbelief and Migration'. Dr Azzam Temimi, the Director of the UK Institute of Islamic Political Thought, describes *takfir* as an ultra-radical trend within Islamic fundamentalism, particularly in the countries of the Maghreb. Others have simply labelled *takfir* as Islamic fascism.

The movement had its roots in Egypt in the 1960s as a splinter group from the followers of Sayyid Qutb, the revolutionary thinker who has been most influential on Bin Laden and the whole *jihad* movement. This offshoot, led by an agricultural engineer, Shukri Mustafa, believed that the secular world must be fought against, that contemporary society as a whole was no longer Muslim but in a state of disbelief or *takfir*. Only migration, a withdrawal from society, as the Prophet himself did when he withdrew from Mecca to Medina, could ensure Islamic purity. The sect, many of them science and engineering students in Egyptian universities, formed communities in the desert with the emphasis on discipline and military training. Errant members were excommunicated and punished severely.

The ideology is particularly dangerous because it provides a religious justification for slaughtering unbelievers, both Muslim and non-Muslim. *Takfiris* believe it is permissible to kill those who disagree with you, even though they are Muslim, because they are *takfir*, unbelievers. Their families, women and children, can be disposed of as well, as they are related to those who have sinned. This belief was the driving force behind the horrendous massacres in recent years in Algeria. Ayman al-Zawahiri, Bin Laden's Egyptian deputy, is believed to be one of the chief *takfiri* ideologues, according to Dr Temimi. Bin Laden may have learned to harness and exploit this violent offshoot when his compound in the Sudan was attacked in 1995 by gunmen believed to be *takfiris*. 'These people have been frustrated in their attempts to bring about pure Islamic states in their own countries, Egypt and Saudi

Arabia. As a result they hit the country that thwarts their plan, the United States,' says Temimi.

French intelligence officials have warned that the goal of the sect is to blend into corrupt societies as a means of plotting attacks against them, even if that means drinking alcohol, dressing in a Western style and being seen with women. Roland Jacquard, a French scholar of Islam, has called *takfiris* 'the hardcore of the hardcore' of Islamic militants.

Two new recruits were about to join the inner *takfiri* circle at the al-Quds mosque. They were both from the Middle East and they would become Mohamed Atta's closest confidants. With him, they would pilot three of the hijacked planes on September 11.

11

The Shadow and the Playboy

'He was a normal young man until he went to Germany, where it seems he met these fanatics, who have a very different understanding of Islam than we do.'

—HRH Sheikh Abdullah bin Zayed, UAE Minister,
October 2001

The dawn spread pink along the desert each side of the empty highway. It was six in the morning and we had already seen camels on their early morning gallops racing on the horizon. Young boys, Bangladeshi camel-jockeys, bounced on their backs in a strange slow-motion dance, touching, ridiculous. I had come to the Emirates, to Dubai, a city of glittering towers, its extravagant pastiche of Arab architecture hiding anonymous shopping malls and a plethora of international banks.

I was heading north to Ras al-Khaimah, one of the smallest and poorest of the Emirates, to the home of the man who piloted United Flight 175 into the South Tower of the World Trade Center. I studied a photo of Marwan al-Shehhi, pudgy-faced with glasses and the first shadow of a moustache. He was just eighteen years old, serious with only a hint of a smile, dressed in a traditional Gulf robe and head-dress. The picture was taken for his school yearbook just before he left the Emirates to study in Germany.

Ras al-Khaimah is one of the most conservative of the

Emirates, its inhabitants descendants of the Shooh tribe, Bedouin people. Shopkeepers lower their shutters to the rhythm of the mosque. The streets empty as each call to prayer echoes through the town. The local university is funded by Saudi Arabia and espouses the same strict Wahhabi doctrine.

Marwan al-Shehhi was the son of a local imam, a deeply religious child who would switch on the prayer tape at the mosque for his father. Marwan won a place to study at the al-Ain University, a prestigious and religiously conservative Emirates college.

Al-Shehhi is a very common name among the Shooh tribe but eventually we found the imam's mosque, small, white-washed and deserted, by the gates of the local hospital. A surly taxi driver, lounging outside, regarded us with suspicion and disclaimed all knowledge of the whereabouts of Marwan al-Shehhi's home. It was five weeks after the September attacks and no journalist had yet managed to find the family or speak to them about their son. We had already had difficulties in getting anyone local to agree to come to Ras al-Khaimah to help us.

Despite the generally pro-Western stance of the Emirates and its desire to welcome investment, inside the velvet glove lurks the iron fist of an omnipresent security apparatus. Al-Shehhi's suicide mission brought shame on a staunch ally of America and the West which has staked its future on becoming a centre for international banking and tourism. Although the government was quick to condemn the terror attacks there was nervousness about dissent within the population where, as in other Gulf States, there is considerable sympathy for Bin Laden's aims. The best policy for officialdom was to keep the whole thing quiet, to downplay the part played in the deaths of thousands of Americans by a young citizen of the Emirates.

A teenager outside a coffee bar eventually offered to help and took us to a comfortable single-storey villa, newly tiled and painted. A man was just disappearing inside. I hammered on the door but the frightened Filipino maid who answered was not giving anything away. Helpful neighbours, passing by, volunteered various explanations – the family didn't live here, they did but they had gone away, they'd be back in an hour, a day, maybe never. Finally a very old woman emerged, bent over, crying. She squatted on the doorstep and when I asked her about al-Shehhi she started keening and swaying. 'The son of the house is gone to a place from which he will never return – shame is on us,' she cried, over and over again.

I had been told that Marwan's mother had refused to leave her bedroom since the tragedy but before I could find out if the family knew why their 22-year-old son had become *shaheed*, a martyr, a smart black jeep screeched up in a cloud of dust. A policeman in military fatigues jumped out and clapped his hand over our camera lens. The surly taxi driver had done his civil duty and informed the authorities of our presence. This was the start of the obligatory afternoon in the local police station, which is the bane of so many television reporters' lives when working in the Middle East. This particular occasion was relatively painless – many cups of cardamom-flavoured coffee were drunk while interminable phone calls were made to Dubai to establish our *bona fides*. Our paperwork was photocopied and endlessly stamped. There was no question of returning to interview anyone about the renegade al-Shehhi. The day ended with us being courteously, but firmly, escorted by the police to the boundaries of the Emirate of Ras al-Khaimah and seen on our way, with a friendly warning not to return. At least we managed to keep the video footage we had shot.

Later I found out more about Marwan and his family. After his father's death, a half-brother, Mohamed, had become head of the family. Marwan, devastated by the loss of his father, fell out with his half-brother, who insisted he marry a local girl named Fawzeya. Marwan decided to travel to Germany to study in August 1996 and was sponsored by the Emirates government, as frequently happens. The official story of Marwan al-Shehhi would be relayed to us by the Minister for Information, one of the sons of the ruler of Abu Dhabi.

I was summoned to the opulent surroundings of the Burg al-Arab, the spectacular sail-shaped edifice which claims to be the only seven-star hotel in the world. In an overpowering suite boasting his-and-hers bathrooms in pink and purple marble, leopardskin banquettes, and three different drawing rooms, I met HRH Sheikh Abdullah bin Zayed. Hardly older than al-Shehhi himself, the prince, educated in the West, was relaxed and very open. He was determined to emphasise that what the hijackers had done was completely unacceptable to Islam.

'They have misunderstood their religion, their culture, heritage and history,' said Sheikh Abdullah, speaking quietly but with great force. 'This is a great religion and it has always asked for tolerance. I can't think of anything which has affected our religion more than what these people have done, harming innocents. There is no justification at all, in Islam, for these attacks.'

Like so many of the hijackers, Marwan al-Shehhi had no obvious lurking demons, no family history of religious fanaticism. He was on the threshold of a good career, generously underwritten by a wealthy state. 'He was paid $4,000 a month in government sponsorship for his studies,' Sheikh Abdullah confirmed. 'His father had died, but there did not seem to be any big problems between him and his family. He was a normal young man until he went to Germany, where it seems he met these fanatics, who have a very different understanding of Islam than we do.'

Marwan al-Shehhi enrolled at a language school in Bonn to get a grounding in German before embarking on a university course in the language at the city's university. He was friendly but lazy and failed his first semester. A photograph shows Marwan at this time, his beard thicker now, grinning happily in the middle of a group of students of different nationalities; they are all about to sit down at a table groaning with German cheeses, bread and meat. By all accounts Marwan spent his time aimlessly, half-heartedly studying and hardly bothering to show up for lectures. He was easy prey for other, stronger characters who would give his life a purpose.

That year, 1997, another young student from the Middle East had begun his studies in Hamburg. Ziad Samir Jarrah was a very different character from Marwan al-Shehhi or Mohamed Atta, without the conservative background and the smouldering political resentments. However, this young man, despite no detectable deeply-held convictions, would also be converted into a suicidal foot-soldier in a holy war. He would pilot United Airlines Flight 93, the fourth plane to be hijacked.

Fun-loving, handsome and charming, his family in the Lebanon doted on Ziad. His uncle Jamal Jarrah told the BBC, 'He was the beloved boy of the family, always having fun, charming and able to fit in anywhere.' The son of a local government official and a schoolteacher from the green and fertile Beka'a valley, Ziad loved sports, especially swimming and basketball. He was adored by his two sisters Dania and Nisren. The family was prosperous and secular in outlook. Although they were Muslim, Ziad Jarrah was sent to a series of exclusive Christian schools in Beirut. He never seemed to have any interest in religion or politics. Jarrah was a playboy who loved to party and he even drank alcohol in the form of an occasional beer. He had one burning ambition only – to be an aircraft engineer.

Jarrah's closest friend was his cousin, Salim, just three months younger than him. At the age of twenty they left the Lebanon in search of an education overseas, and a good time. A photograph shows the two sitting on the plane travelling westward, laughing together at the adventure that lay ahead. They went to the northern town of Greifswald to perfect their German. There Ziad Jarrah met Aysel Senguen, a Turkish–German girl, studying to be a doctor. A photograph shows them together – Jarrah boyishly handsome, with stylish, horn-rimmed spectacles; his girlfriend a very attractive, chic young woman wearing red lipstick, her dark bobbed hair swinging as she leans towards him.

The couple started living together at weekends, a move not altogether approved of by his family back home. 'He was living with his girlfriend, something unthinkable for an Islamic fundamentalist, unthinkable even for a normal Muslim,' his uncle explained, still deeply puzzled and angry. 'We loved the girl, she is very nice. She loved Ziad too much.' The local imam at the Greifswald mosque remembers Jarrah and his cousin Salim as 'weak Muslims', wayward members of the local community who did not attend Friday prayers.

Ziad Jarrah moved to Hamburg after winning a place to study aircraft engineering at the prestigious Applied Sciences University, half an hour's drive from the Technical University where Mohamed Atta was studying. Jarrah's girlfriend, Aysel, moved to Bochum near Dortmund to continue her studies but the two continued seeing each other at weekends.

In a gracious white stuccoed house in Hamburg, set back from the leafy street, eighty-year-old Rosemarie Canel showed me her delicate flower paintings: baskets of roses, a waxy camellia done in oils. This forceful old lady was Ziad Jarrah's landlady for nearly three years. 'He was a very nice boy, we used to sit together with a cup of tea and have a chat,' she remembered. 'He wanted to get his degree and return to Beirut and open his own engineering business.' For the first year he spent most of the time in his room watching television or studying. His girlfriend would visit him and confided to Rosemarie that the couple wanted to get married, but her father did not really approve of Ziad. Rosemarie Canel tartly advised her to visit the Lebanon for herself, to see how women were treated, before she committed to marry him and move there. 'He really loved the girl,' Rosemarie said emphatically.

Ziad Jarrah's academic career appeared undistinguished. He worked hard but his professors said he was not one of their brightest engineers. Dr Müller of the BKA's Islamic Unit has established a pattern to the recruitment of young Muslims in Germany. From studying al-Qaeda's operations in the West he believes that Bin Laden's organisation targets young students of a particular kind. 'At certain universities in our country Islamic activists are interested in acquiring an education with a practical bias,' said Dr Müller. 'They avoid the humanities, which tend to expose them to Western philosophy, Western thought. The focus is on technical skills, and, as the attacks in America made clear, well-educated people, from technical faculties, were able to inflict maximum damage.'

During 1997 the group at the al-Quds mosque – Mohamed Atta, the expert in modern building techniques, Saïd Bahaji, Zacharias Essebar and Mounir al-Moutassadeq, all engineers – had been joined by a new worshipper. Marwan al-Shehhi, still struggling with his language exams, had asked to be transferred from Bonn to the Harburg Technical University attended by Atta. His request was granted but the authorities at Harburg would later confirm that al-Shehhi, although technically on their books, hardly ever appeared on the campus. No one knows exactly when and where Marwan al-Shehhi met Mohamed Atta, but the younger man was to become the Egyptian's shadow, first in Germany and then through America and finally in the skies above New York, smashing his plane into the second World Trade Center tower just minutes after Atta had flown into the first.

In the summer of 1997 Mohamed Atta abruptly and without explanation terminated his five-year stint at the design consultancy, Plankantor. He was to disappear from Hamburg for over a year. He was vague when he went to see Professor Machule about his destination and his reasons for going. 'He told me there were problems back home and, when I enquired further, he made it clear by his expression and his manner that I should not ask any more questions but just accept his explanation,' said Machule. In the liberal tradition of a German academic institution, no one seemed to question Atta seriously about why he was going or how long he would be away.

Atta took the well-trodden route of the al-Qaeda volunteer, organised by Mohamed Haidar Zammer, al-Qaeda's recruiter in Hamburg. He travelled to Pakistan and on to a guesthouse in Kandahar, in southern Afghanistan, the stronghold of the Taliban. Atta was enrolled at Khaldan, the most hardcore of al-Qaeda's dozen training centres, a spartan, mountainside encampment near the town of Khost. Between fifty and a hundred foreign students were billeted here at one time; there was even a hospitality section for processing the new arrivals.

It was at Khaldan that Atta completed the basic fifty-day course undergone by all al-Qaeda recruits, learning about weaponry and explosives. The quiet Egyptian was soon recognised as a valuable asset for the terror network: he was highly educated; he had a good cover already established in an important European country; and he spoke flawless German. Atta was picked out for his potential leadership qualities and then began a second round of more intensive training, this time with a strong psychological emphasis to build his mental stamina and instil in him the group's ideas of martyrdom and *jihad*. Western intelligence believes that Abu Zubaydah, al-Qaeda's top recruiter and the commander of Khaldan camp at the time, earmarked Mohamed Atta as a suitable candidate to lead an important mission. He was given the chance to volunteer for a suicide attack and given time to think about it before accepting.

The propaganda videos of the camps made by al-Qaeda's industrious and professional public-relations arm have the air of an army recruiting film about them, for that is what they are, and that is why they circulate clandestinely among Muslim communities in the Middle East and in the West. The videos show masked men, in black Special Forces-style uniforms, engaged in feats of physical endurance, emerging silently from fox-holes, stealthy and menacing. They run along poles and burst into ruined buildings, flattening themselves against walls as they fire wildly around them. In the middle of the mayhem

a tall figure in white robes appears, smiling calmly and enigmatically. He is persuaded by the respectful crowd around him
to raise his Kalashnikov and prove the accuracy of his shot. He
is Osama bin Laden, the *emir,* the Director.

The reality of life in the training camp was more mundane,
with lectures about bomb-making and basic chemistry, com-
puting and lessons in European languages. Food was simple:
staples like rice and lentil stew. But Bin Laden himself would
appear at each camp, usually twice weekly, to give lectures,
urging the recruits to fight to drive American and other infidel
forces from the land of the Holy Places. A painted map
recovered from an al-Qaeda building shows Saudi Arabia
surrounded by small American, British and French flags, rep-
resenting foreign bases and ships. Above the map was written
'Occupation of the Holy Land by the Crusaders'.

Intelligence agencies and prosecutors have based their
assessment of al-Qaeda's training methods and its ethos, at the
time Mohamed Atta was in the camps, on a manual seized by
police in Manchester in 1998. It was found in the flat of Anas
al-Liby, an al-Qaeda operative who had been involved in reconnaissance of the US Embassy in Nairobi before the truck
bombing. He had sought political asylum in the UK but fled
before the apartment was raided. The book's ornate cover is
inscribed with delicate embossing and embroidered flowers,
along with the title, *Declaration of Jihad Against the Country's
Tyrants: Military Series.* On the first page, a drawing of the globe
emphasises the Middle East and Africa. A sword is plunged
through the axis, a hand gripping the base.

Any doubts about the interpretation of Islam which Bin
Laden espouses is dispelled by the first page, which sets the
tone for the whole volume:

Islamic governments have never and never will be
established through peaceful solutions and co-operative
councils. They are established as they have always
been – by pen and gun, by word and bullet, by tongue

and teeth. The confrontation we are calling for with the
apostate regimes does not know Socratic debates . . . but
it knows the dialogue of bullets, the ideals of
assassination, bombing and destruction.

The hundred-odd pages set out the principles of the military
organisation of al-Qaeda, ranging from a history of the movement and its beliefs, to the practical requirements of Soldiers for
Allah, operating undercover on terrorist missions. Their aim is
summed up as 'the overthrow of godless regimes and their
replacement with an Islamic regime'. The whole manual is an
incongruous combination of medieval barbarity, with its chap-
ters on 'Assassination Using Cold Steel' and 'Guidelines for
Beating and Killing Hostages', and modern practicality. There
are detailed sections on ciphers and codes, how to establish
safe houses and the surveillance of targets. The manual extols
the tradecraft of famous undercover agents from the times of
the Roman Empire to spies who sold British naval secrets to the
Nazis. Mossad, the Israeli intelligence service, comes in for
praise for its professionalism, as does the Russian KGB for its
skill at dissembling.

Mohamed Atta scored highly on all the indices set out as
qualifications for advancement within the organisation – matu-
rity, religious devotion, physical fitness, patience and calmness,
intelligence and insight, and above all, the acceptance of sacrifice. '[The recruit] has to be willing to do the work and undergo
martyrdom for the purpose of achieving the goal and establishing the religion of majestic Allah on earth,' states the
manual.

The time that Mohamed Atta spent in Afghanistan in 1998
was a period of ambitious reach for Osama bin Laden, the year
al-Qaeda effectively went global in its organisation and in its
targets. As we have seen, it was in February of that year that al-
Qaeda, in a parody of corporate practice of the time, formally
merged with other like-minded terror organisations. As an
Egyptian, Mohamed Atta was welcomed into the ranks of the

Islamic Jihad fighters, some of the most hardened and fanatical al-Qaeda affiliates, followers of Ayman al-Zawahiri. After the September 11 attacks, Osama bin Laden would affectionately and admiringly refer to 'Mohamed of the Egyptian family' as the leader of the mission.

That spring the planning for the attacks on the East African embassies was in its final phase. While Atta was in training at Khaldan, the Liverpool-born Palestinian, Mohamed al-Owhali, was completing his stint in the same camp. He confirmed to a court in New York during his trial that it was at this time he approached his 'Sheikh', Bin Laden, and asked him for the mission that led him to the gates of the US Embassy compound in Nairobi.

The last event witnessed by Mohamed Atta in the al-Qaeda camps could only have stiffened his resolve and increased his hatred for America, already honed during his time in the camp. In August, following the embassy bombings, eighty-two US Cruise missiles were launched against Bin Laden's training compounds. They missed their target, the Director, but killed a few of his Pakistani followers in another camp near Khost. It was a propaganda coup for Bin Laden, as thousands of young Muslims flocked to join the man who had provoked a superpower to unleash its military might on al-Qaeda. The *jihad* against the infidel which Bin Laden had threatened for so long had begun in earnest. In a statement to an Italian newspaper, little noticed at the time, the leader of al-Qaeda warned: 'The International Front announces that the war has begun. All the Islamic world has mobilised to strike a prominent American or Israeli strategic objective, to blow up their aeroplanes and to seize them.'

Emboldened in the aftermath of the Cruise strikes by his growing support in the Middle East, Bin Laden and his top lieutenants, Ayman al-Zawahiri, Mohamed Atef and Abu Zubaydah, sanctioned Mohamed Atta to return to Germany. He may not have known it yet but the concept of the September 11 attacks was forming in the minds of Bin Laden and a very small circle of his most trusted aides. Mohamed Atta would soon become involved in actively planning al-Qaeda's most ambitious attack to date, involving prominent American strategic objectives and aeroplanes.

12

The Hamburg Cell

'My life and my death and my sacrifice belong to Allah, the Lord of all the Worlds.'

—Dedication on Mohamed Atta's thesis, October 1999

Professor Machule sighed and scratched his head with his pencil. 'Maybe, if I look back now, I should have made more of the changes I saw in Mohamed when he returned to the university,' he admitted. 'He didn't smile any more, he looked serious and worked continuously, as if he was driving himself to finish his studies. A student who knew him told me he didn't even sleep at night because he wanted to finish his thesis.' At the time, Dittmar Machule did not question the change that had come over his star pupil, after his long and unexplained absence abroad, or why he now seemed to be working to a deadline.

The professor's assistant, however, an elegant and observant woman in her sixties, did find his behaviour odd. Chrilla Wendt was one of the few people – almost all of them women – who noticed Atta's increasingly arrogant and misogynistic behaviour. It rankled with Western women, while most men tended to make politically correct excuses about male-dominated Arab culture.

Chrilla Wendt was assigned by Professor Machule to help Mohamed Atta turn his final thesis into polished German. As the weeks went by she found the Egyptian's attitude towards her increasingly strained. He seemed afraid of getting too close to her, physically at the desk where they sat, and emotionally too, in his dependence on her help. In the end he refused to attend any more sessions with her. 'I had the feeling he was scared, we were getting too close just sitting there together and working. He had been bright and friendly when he first came here. But now he was uptight, arrogant and not friendly at all.' A photograph taken at this time shows a fit-looking, bearded Atta, in heavy leather jacket, squatting by the river at Harburg. His right arm is round another man's shoulder, a friend whose face is out of the picture. Mohamed stares straight at the camera, his features stern and determined.

Outside the university, Atta's life was apparently a closed book. But the quiet Egyptian was slowly becoming the commander of an al-Qaeda terror cell whose members were recruited through the al-Quds mosque. The training manual found in the UK sets out the commander's first duty – to rent a safe place for the group to gather and plan.

Number 54 Marienstrasse is a small, cream-coloured apartment block in Harburg, just a short walk from the Technical University. The district is quiet and anonymous, full of Turkish guest workers, none of them likely to enquire into the background of new arrivals or their purpose. 'It is preferable to rent apartments in newly developed areas,' advises the manual, 'where people do not know each other, rather than in older quarters where people know each other and strangers are readily identified.' The landlord, Thorsten Albrecht, noticed nothing unusual about the three Arab students who came to see him at his office in October 1998 to enquire about renting the first-floor apartment. They were smartly dressed and spoke good German. He noticed that all three had beards.

Herr Albrecht took me round the two-bedroomed apartment – a small kitchen, two rooms and a bathroom, all painted white. He showed me the lease which was signed by Mohamed Atta using his family name, al-Amir, and by Saïd Bahaji and Ramsi bin al-Shibh, two friends from the al-Quds mosque, in December 1998. Bahaji, as a German citizen, took responsibility as the main lessee. The rent was always paid promptly. 'It is necessary to have at hand documents supporting the undercover member, government permits, etc.,' says the manual. Indeed, Albrecht pointed out that 'all the paperwork, their visas and student credentials were in order', and they were undemanding in their requirements. 'The only specific request they made was for two high-speed lines to connect their computers, although as students this didn't seem that unusual,' said the landlord.

Neighbours noticed plenty of comings and goings; the group of men, glimpsed through an open door, seemed to be reading from the Qur'an. Glancing out of her window across the street, a woman noticed they had pinned what looked like diagrams and drawings to the wall. These were quickly removed once the occupants of Number 54 realised their neighbours could see in. One local man was told by one of the occupants of the flat that they came from Afghanistan.

Saïd Bahaji was the quartermaster of the cell. A 22-year-old Moroccan, he had served in the German army in a tank unit and was completing his engineering course at the Technical University. He had a German mother and he was courting a Turkish girl with German citizenship. He was least likely to raise suspicions as an outsider or a likely radical. Bahaji was a computer junkie: on his personal webpage he listed his interests as 'spending time on the PC with games and Internet programs'. He also had less innocuous interests – he was, for example, a regular visitor to the websites of Azzam Publications, a company operating out of a post-box address in London, named after Bin Laden's early mentor Dr Abdullah Azzam. The websites specialised in 'providing authentic news about Jihad and the Foreign Mujahideen', and advertising the 'suitability' of suicide missions. 'There is no other technique which strikes as much terror into their hearts and which shatters their spirit as much,' opined Azzam Publications. Saïd Bahaji's name also appeared on the mailing list for their underground website 'Qoqaz', dedicated to recruiting for the cause of holy war in Chechnya. The site features gruesome images of mangled bodies and inflammatory language, set in graphic borders of dripping blood.

Ramsi bin al-Shibh, the third man whose name appears on the Marienstrasse lease, was the key logistics organiser for the cell. A Yemeni from the Hadromawt, the wild tribal area where Bin Laden's own father had been born, Bin al-Shibh is believed to have been an important al-Qaeda operative before he turned up in Germany in 1995, seeking political asylum. He pretended to be a Sudanese student but had in fact worked as a clerk in the International Bank of the Yemen, and may have been sent to Germany to establish a foothold there for al-Qaeda. He applied for asylum and moved into a camp just north of Hamburg. A year later his application was rejected but, anticipating this, Bin al-Shibh had already returned to the Yemen and applied in his own name for a student visa for Germany, which was granted, enabling him to return to Hamburg. Ramsi bin al-Shibh, like the others who would become involved in the plot, recognised and exploited Europe's open borders and was adept at working the system – trying first the asylum route and, when that failed, falling back on the country's welcoming stance towards foreign students.

Bin al-Shibh met Mohamed Atta soon after he first arrived in Hamburg in 1995. The Yemeni was an intensely religious young man who quickly gravitated towards the al-Quds mosque, where he would help others to interpret the Qur'an. He was crucial in focusing the Islamist beliefs of the Hamburg circle on al-Qaeda's philosophy. Bin al-Shibh would use his financial skills and knowledge of the international banking system to become the conduit for money to support the September 11 plot, and he would also attempt to become one of the pilots. Later, one of the architects of the attacks would call Ramsi bin al-Shibh 'the co-ordinator of Holy Tuesday'.

Marwan al-Shehhi, the young man from the Emirates now living in Hamburg, frequently stayed at 54 Marienstrasse. And the 24-year-old Moroccan, Zacharias Essebar, was by now also a member of the cell. Videos of the preaching of an extremist cleric in Britain, Abu Qatada, urging participation in *jihad*, would be found in Essebar's flat after the September attacks. Qatada was the religious authority whose *fatwas* Bin Laden had used to condone al-Qaeda's violent actions since the days in the Sudan.

That summer of 1998, Ziad Jarrah took a part-time job at the same car company as Zacharias Essebar and began attending the al-Quds mosque. Rosemarie Canel noticed a subtle physical and mental difference in her tenant. She was painting a portrait of him, a gift for his parents in the Lebanon, who had sent her presents through Ziad. Rosemarie showed me a photograph she had kept of the portrait, an arresting image of a handsome young man against a green background, the colour sacred to Islam. Sporting a new beard, slim-faced and serious for once, Jarrah's eyes without his glasses are large and luminous, almost other-worldly.

'He had started spending nights out, and weekends away, with new friends in Hamburg,' Rosemarie remembered. 'As well as the beard he had a prayer mat in his room which I had never seen before. I used to tease him about it.' Aysel Senguen noticed a difference too. She was still dating Ziad but now she complained to Rosemarie that he seemed jealous of even the smallest attention paid to her by other men; he was more touchy and critical. But he never mentioned Mohamed Atta or any of the others to her. Ziad Jarrah's name now appeared too on the mailing list for the Qoqaz website. The fun-loving

24-year-old Lebanese had also become a recruit to the Marienstrasse terror cell.

As Mohamed Atta neared the end of his thesis he made a request to the accommodating head of his department, Professor Machule. He wanted a special prayer room where Arab students could pray in private. Machule, who regarded Atta's ability to combine religious fervour with the modern requirements of an urban planner as 'somehow unusual and beautiful', was eager to help. A room in a portable cabin on the campus was set aside. Unknown to Machule, Atta and Bahaji then formed an 'Islamic society', installing a computer and a phone line in what had now become their private office. The Students' Union, which was supposed to monitor the facility, had no idea the computer was there until the German police came calling the day after Atta was identified as the pilot of hijacked Flight 11.

Sitting in the canteen with me, nervously drinking coffee, a young member of the Students' Union explained how since September 11 he had spent long hours being grilled by the police. 'No one at the Union really knew what went on in the prayer room with this Islamic society, or who attended,' he told me. 'The only records that exist in the files are of grants paid to Mohamed Atta to purchase religious books and tapes, but we didn't check out the literature. The first we knew of there being a computer there was in the mayhem after the terror attacks. The press were banging on our door and we thought we had better go and unlock the prayer room and see what was there.' It was then that the phone and computer were found. The BKA is still studying the computer's content and the phone records. Once again the Technical University had proved how helpful and how unquestioning it could be in fostering an open, multicultural environment of which the terror cell could take advantage.

The university was not alone in being oblivious to the developing cell of Islamic extremists. More qualified, professional intelligence-gatherers also failed to pick up traces of

Mohamed Atta and his group, although they came tantalisingly close to identifying the network operating out of Marienstrasse.

Earlier in the summer of 1998, one of Bin Laden's top financial lieutenants had been arrested near Munich. Mamduh Mahmoud Salim was the biggest fish in the organisation to be hooked at that time. He was known to have run Bin Laden companies in Sudan and to be on al-Qaeda's ruling council or *shura*. He was also suspected of trying to purchase nuclear material for the terror organisation. The CIA had placed Salim on a watch-list, and were waiting for him to leave Dubai, where he lived, to seize the opportunity to arrest him. They got their chance when he visited Bavaria.

Salim protested that he had only come to Germany to purchase a second-hand Mercedes – and to find a more attractive German bride than the Arab one he already had. 'She has nothing in terms of femininity that could attract a man,' Salim rather ungallantly stated in his testimony to the police. His trip was part of a pattern of visits he was making to various parts of Germany, which in the light of September 11, and the activities of the Hamburg cell, now suggest he was visiting members of the al-Qaeda network in Germany.

Salim was quickly extradited to America by a tight-lipped FBI team which did not wish to brief their German counterparts too fully on what they knew about him and al-Qaeda's network. Concerned about what a senior member of Bin Laden's organisation was really doing in Germany, Bavarian officials started a full-scale investigation into Salim's contacts that autumn. High on their list of suspects was a Syrian-born trader, Mamoun Darkanzali, whose import–export business in Hamburg generated no visible activity. Salim's mobile phone had Darkanzali's number programmed into it and a financial probe discovered that since 1996 Darkanzali had had power of attorney over Salim's Deutsche Bank account, indicating Darkanzali controlled the distribution of al-Qaeda funds.

Darkanzali was put under surveillance and officers of the domestic intelligence service began tailing him round the city. It was soon discovered that he was a regular attendee at the al-Quds mosque. He spent time with one man in particular, Saïd Bahaji. It was exactly at this moment, December 1998, that Bahaji began living at 54 Marienstrasse with Atta and Bin al-Shibh, along with their regular guest Marwan al-Shehhi.

However, the surveillance operation took little notice of the students and what they were doing in Marienstrasse. They seemed too ordinary, and, as an official admitted to me, 'We were not sure exactly what we were looking for at the time.' No one approached the university to check out the students. If they had done so they might have established that the men were religious to a fanatical degree, or had recently taken long trips to undisclosed destinations in the Middle East. They might have discovered the common thread which linked them through the al-Quds mosque, extended also to the newly acquired 'prayer room' on the campus. That room was always locked and only Atta and Bahaji had a key.

The German intelligence and investigatory apparatus proved, like its American, British and European counterparts, to be no match for Bin Laden's insidious network. Whether by accident, or more probably design, the choice of Hamburg as a base for al-Qaeda's operations had been fortuitous. The German internal intelligence service, the Verfassungsschutz, is based on a federal system. Hamburg as a city-state only had 100 staff in the entire service, a far smaller group of investigators than bigger provinces like Bavaria or Baden-Württemberg. The priority was seen as monitoring the growing right-wing threat from German fascists and only a couple of officers could be spared for the Islamic watch. Neither of them spoke Arabic.

Indeed, there were only four Islamic experts in service at that time in the whole of Germany. The patterns – radical groups within mosques, unprofitable businesses owned by individuals who seemed to have plenty of money, Arabs with German wives – had been duly noted, but investigators were not yet clear how al-Qaeda actually operated. What intelligence the FBI was gathering through its investigations into the Nairobi bombings was not being shared with the Germans. Some German officers believe that the Americans still mistrusted them, a legacy of the Second World War.

Another legacy of the reaction to the racism and repression of the Nazi era was the law which forbade the wiretapping of suspects unless there was hard evidence of an offence being committed on German territory against the state itself. Instead, the emphasis was on religious freedom and tolerance. 'We allowed extremists to come here and fight their religious wars within our community, with no state limitations on what they could do,' one German intelligence operative told me bitterly. 'It's a scandal that we turned a blind eye all those years.' As in Britain and France, Germany proved more accommodating, more protective of those expressing religious hatred, than the countries they came from where such views were harshly repressed.

In the autumn of 1999, Mohamed Atta submitted his thesis on applying modern planning and building techniques to enhance the ancient Islamic city of Aleppo. Since the September attacks Professor Machule has kept it under lock and key, refusing to let outsiders rifle through the pages looking for clues. But the professor decided to show me the thesis, late on a winter's afternoon, in his attic study as the lights went on in the campus below. It is thorough and detailed, expressed in neutral terms, full of meticulous coloured plans and diagrams of street layouts and traffic-calming schemes. According to the professor, it was one of the best theses he ever marked and he awarded it 1.7, a Distinction. 'Mohamed's work was factually sound, uncoloured by any ideology, completely unemotional and clear, but there was one thing about the thesis we had never encountered before,' said Machule. He showed me a dedication on the front, in German, an inscription from the Qur'an. 'My life and my death and my sacrifice belong to Allah, the Lord of all the Worlds,' the professor translated. At the time he had thought nothing of it.

But Mohamed Atta's behaviour at his oral exam, in which he gained the highest possible mark, shocked two of Machule's colleagues who were present, Chrilla Wendt and another woman examiner. Professor Machule shook Atta's hand and congratulated him and the woman examiner extended her hand too. Atta ostentatiously refused to take it, an embarrassing moment which was again glossed over. It is only now that the dedication of his thesis to his 'sacrifice' and his attitude to women have aroused comment and soul-searching within the university Department of Urban Planning.

As 1999 came to an end, so too Atta's life in Germany was drawing to a close. That winter he returned to Afghanistan along with Marwan al-Shehhi, Ziad Jarrah and Ramsi bin al-Shibh. Each of the four men took a different route there to avoid being associated with the others. The CIA believes it was at this time that the four were chosen by Mohamed Atef, Bin Laden's military commander, to take part in a high-profile suicide mission. They were selected for their abilities, their clean records and the solid cover stories they had already established in Hamburg which would enable them to get the vital US visas. As men with no record of affiliation to al-Qaeda there was no need for false identities with all the attendant risks.

The four co-conspirators returned to Europe by separate routes and on different dates and immediately began preparing for their mission. Atta, al-Shehhi and Jarrah all applied for new passports – Atta and Jarrah told the Egyptian and Lebanese consulates in Hamburg they had lost their documents, and al-Shehhi obtained a new passport through his home country, the UAE.

The Emirates authorities have long been familiar with the well-worn trail that leads back from Afghanistan to Pakistan and then through Dubai, the Middle Eastern gateway for the cities of Europe and America. The tell-tale sign of the *mujahid*, the Islamic warrior, is the stamps inscribed in his passport. HRH Sheikh Abdullah, the Emirates Minister, told me, 'It is hardly coincidence that not only Marwan al-Shehhi but others too got new passports around the same time. They didn't want the authorities to know they had been to Pakistan and Afghanistan when they applied for US visas. They wanted to start with a clean sheet.'

For one hour, a kind of valedictory moment, on 9 October 1999 the members of al-Qaeda's terror network in Germany congregated in the place which had brought them together. A video taken at Saïd Bahaji's wedding at the al-Quds mosque in Hamburg does not show even a glimpse of his veiled German bride, but the camera moves around Bahaji's circle of friends, sitting at a table. Ziad Jarrah is there, Marwan al-Shehhi, Ramsi bin al-Shibh and Zacharias Essebar – all members of the Hamburg cell. Bahaji and Bin al-Shibh would remain in Hamburg, the vital link to al-Qaeda in Afghanistan, supporting members of the cell who would shortly disperse further westwards.

There were no public farewells at the Technical University. Mohamed Atta had not celebrated his successful graduation like the other students, with champagne and kisses. Dittmar Machule remembers only a fleeting moment, at the end of the year, when he caught a glimpse of Mohamed hovering at his open study door – as if about to say something. The professor was busy and asked his pupil to wait a moment. Atta hesitated briefly, then disappeared down the corridor. Now, Professor Machule wonders if he had come to say goodbye. Machule's scholarly reserve cracks when I ask him how he felt when he learned what his star pupil had done on

September 11. 'It has torn me apart . . . The man in whom I had invested so much energy and enthusiasm – a town planner, a creator, turns out to be a destroyer.' The professor was on the verge of tears. 'What can you possibly think when you hear that this man is a killer?'

13

Deadly Lessons

'Atta had no passion for flying. He approached a plane as if it was a means to an end . . . I couldn't help being suspicious as to why he was there.'

—Ann Greaves, student at Huffman Aviation,
summer 2001

The first sight that greets the traveller arriving at Newark airport in New Jersey is a poster of the Twin Towers on the wall behind the immigration booths. 'Welcome to America' is emblazoned across it in English, ironically in German too. This was Mohamed Atta's first glimpse of the United States and the iconic buildings of the World Trade Center, symbols of the economic might and cultural power of America in the twentieth century.

Atta arrived at Newark from Europe on 3 June 2000. Marwan al-Shehhi had arrived at the same airport a few days before. Their families, in Egypt and the Emirates, had no idea they had gone to the United States. Ziad Jarrah would land in Atlanta later that month. The most ambitious terror plot ever hatched against the West had begun its research and planning phase. The trio made their way, separately, south. They were heading for Florida, the sunshine state, where people can learn to fly cheaply and quickly, thanks to the benign weather.

Venice in Florida, like its European namesake, is on the water. A curve of pastel motels, the green of perpetually watered lawns stretches beneath regimented and stately palms. The tempo here is slow, the residents retirement-age. But on the edge of town a racier set has established their own small patch of territory, an airstrip hosting a string of small flying schools, among them Huffman Aviation and the Florida Flight Training Center. Small planes buzz continuously overhead; the odd executive jet calls in to airlift geriatric emergencies to the nearest hospital; and affluent businessmen pilot in their Cessnas to take their families to lunch at Sharkey's beach bar.

Mohamed Atta and Marwan al-Shehhi showed up at Huffman Aviation in June 2000, enquiring about flying lessons. They had tourist visas, not the student visas which, strictly speaking, they should have had to take a course, and they had made no prior booking. The boss of Huffman, a bluff Dutchman, Rudi Dekkers, nevertheless took them on. 'They just walked through the front door. We have no obligations whatsoever to do a background check on them. If it's a foreigner we want to see a passport and that's what we did.'

Atta claimed he already had a private pilot's licence, but this is unlikely as he had only arrived in the States less than a month before. Al-Shehhi said he had a few hours' flying experience. Both men had a plausible cover story: they maintained they were not happy with the flying school they had been to and wanted to work towards a commercial pilot's licence to get a job with airlines back home. No one at Huffman seemed sure exactly where it was in the Middle East the two men came from.

I spent a few days hanging out at Huffman – it's that kind of place, best described as Florida-relaxed, friendly, a bit chaotic with constant comings and goings. I got the impression that the bottom line was what counted at Huffman and that not too many questions were asked. 'Look, we're a business, we're trying to make money. That's difficult in aviation,' acknowledged Dekkers. 'Someone walks in here with an okay form of identification then I have no reason not to do business.'

Dan Pearson, the former student co-ordinator at Huffman, turned up to meet me sporting regulation aviator shades and a shirt printed with Florida pineapples. 'The two Arabs were always well dressed in sports shirts and well-pressed trousers,' said Pearson. They looked just like Americans and gave no hint of being religious. Unlike in Germany, no one ever saw them praying. 'Al-Shehhi was a friendly, outgoing sort of guy, but if he ever started chatting to anyone, Atta would come over and draw him away.'

Mohamed Atta struggled from the start to hide his true feelings about Americans in line with the *takfiri* creed, which exhorted its adherents to mask their true purpose even if it meant breaching strict Islamic rules.

'He had an attitude problem – it came up constantly with the instructors,' Dan Pearson admitted. Atta's stand-off with one instructor in particular, an old-school ex-Navy pilot, was well known around Huffman. 'The "attitude" word came up with Eric – they clashed because Atta was not taking instruction and Eric refused to sign him off on one of his grades,' said Pearson. Rudi Dekkers, who rather more bluntly described Atta to me as 'a son of a bitch', threatened him with expulsion if his attitude did not improve. Only then did Atta swallow his pride and buckle down to work.

Ziad Jarrah, by contrast, was a model student and everyone's friend. I drove a few hundred yards down the airstrip from Huffman to the Florida Flight Training Center, where the Lebanese student enrolled that summer. Another Dutchman, Arne Kruithof, owned this small and struggling school which had clearly not had Huffman's commercial success. Tall and rangy, good-looking in chinos and a leather flying jacket, Kruithof had refused to talk to the press before. He was depressed and angry, his business broken in the wake of the September attack, his confidence in human nature destroyed. He had genuinely liked Ziad Jarrah, who fitted in well with the small and tight-knit group of eight students. They had come from all over the world, and most of them were destined to become professional commercial pilots.

'He was basically a pussycat, the kind of guy who wanted to be loved. He would even offer to put out the trash cans at night, which no one else did,' mused Kruithof. 'I remember him bringing me a six-pack of beer at home when I hurt my knee one time and sitting for hours on my sofa chatting.'

Jarrah had plenty of money and a car which he let the other students borrow. His family in the Lebanon knew he was learning to fly and regularly wired money for the fees, and generous pocket money too. Jarrah had the air of a poor little rich kid, eager to make himself popular. He rented his own flat in Venice; he needed privacy, he said. However, he never seemed to use it, spending most of the time sleeping on a sofa in the apartment the other students shared.

He often cooked for his flatmates. A photograph shows a grinning Jarrah, surrounded by his friends, knife poised to carve a glistening Thanksgiving turkey in celebration of the most American of festivals. Kruithof noticed that Jarrah would drink the odd beer and, unlike other students from the Middle East, he never seemed uncomfortable or disapproving of the school's receptionists, clad in tiny T-shirts and skimpy skirts.

No one would ever have imagined that, just five months before, Ziad Jarrah had been secretly to Afghanistan, to Bin Laden's camps to train in terror techniques. He had been indoctrinated as a *jihadi*, a potential martyr for Islam, before going to the States to begin his preparations. Jarrah's girlfriend, Aysel Senguen, later admitted she suspected he had gone to Afghanistan but had no inkling he had joined al-Qaeda. He would return again during his time in America.

The pictures of a Jarrah family celebration in happier times are, in true wedding-video tradition, wobbly, over-long and faintly embarrassing. The Arab pop music is insistent, the beat repetitive. Stout ladies in modest dresses, arms slightly raised, sway their hips decorously. In the midst of this display the eye is drawn to one slender figure, a youth in black, moving sinuously, his fingers snapping the air. Ziad Jarrah is handsome, the focus of attention – and he knows it. Yet this was the man who had come to Beirut for a family wedding on his way back from al-Qaeda's camps. His relatives had no idea of the journey he had made.

His uncle is emphatic: there was no outward sign of Jarrah's conversion into a religious extremist. 'We didn't notice any change in his behaviour, his thoughts, his beliefs, nothing. He was the same Ziad we knew as a child right up until the last time we saw him,' said Jamal Jarrah. 'The way he was dancing and socialising with us at the wedding. It just doesn't fit with what we know about Osama bin Laden and his beliefs – a man who so clearly turned his back on his family and made such a dramatic change in his life.'

It does, however, fit with the sect-like *takfiri* precepts which the terror cell in Hamburg are believed to have followed: hiding the true nature of your extreme beliefs, adopting Western ways the better to strike at the infidel. Drinking, even breaching rules of sexual purity, to hide your true intent. It seems that Ziad Jarrah was the most successful of the group in his dissembling, better than Mohamed Atta in hiding his true face from his family, his friends and even his fiancée.

A German student, Thorsten Bierman, became Jarrah's closest friend at the flying school. He found that the cheerful, easy-going Lebanese had a different attitude once he was in the air. He became single-minded, completely focused and strangely selfish. He was not interested in sharing tasks or deferring to his co-pilot's wishes. On a trip to Fort Lauderdale, Bierman took the pilot's seat and Jarrah shared the navigation and radio duties. On the way back, when the roles were reversed, Jarrah cut him out. 'He wanted to do everything single-handed – he wouldn't listen to my protests. It wasn't safe and I decided not to fly with him again after that experience,' said Bierman.

One of the other students at Huffman that summer was Ann Greaves, a feisty grandmother from Kent who was fulfilling a life-long dream by learning to fly. Like Chrilla Wendt, the female teacher at the Technical University in Hamburg, Ann Greaves was suspicious of Mohamed Atta from the start. Her dislike of Atta was partly instinct but also heightened by his offensive attitude towards women, whom he clearly regarded as inferior. 'His bearing was of someone very much in command, arrogant, with his head held high, and the striking feature were his eyes – they were extremely cold and they never wavered,' Ann told me.

Mohamed Atta let it be known around the flying school that he was a member of the Saudi royal family and that Marwan al-Shehhi was his bodyguard. Ann Greaves did not believe this although she could see that al-Shehhi was subservient to Atta. Acting as his shadow he would sit behind him in the plane, observing his movements at the controls. Marwan even protected Mohamed from the physical contact with women he so obviously feared. 'Once I tried to take a seat cushion from the plane away from under Atta's arm, but as I put my hand out al-Shehhi literally lunged forward and put himself protectively between me and Atta. I couldn't understand why his response was so over-protective,' complained Ann Greaves. 'It was an incident that left a nasty taste behind.'

Mrs Greaves found herself wondering what the two men were doing at Huffman and why they wanted to learn to fly. It was clear that Atta had absolutely no enthusiasm for what he was learning, in contrast to most would-be aviators. 'Atta had no passion for flying. He approached a plane as if it was just a means to an end. And that sparkle just wasn't there. I couldn't help being suspicious as to why he was there.' Ann Greaves concluded they were drug-runners who needed to fly small planes.

The only time that their fellow student saw any enthusiasm was one day in the computer room at Huffman, three months into their flying course. Atta and al-Shehhi tended to hog the computers, surfing the Net for information, collecting e-mails for hours on end. Greaves came in, unobserved, and caught them in a rare moment of celebration.

'I couldn't see the computer screen but the two men were hugging each other with joy, almost dancing and I thought, wow, there must be some life in them after all. I cannot pinpoint the date exactly but it was some time in the middle of October,' she remembered. The American warship USS *Cole* was attacked by al-Qaeda in Aden harbour on 12 October 2000.

It was a beautiful Florida evening, golden and calm. At Sharkey's beach bar people were congregating to watch the sun set over the ocean. I drove slowly along the road running parallel with the Venice airstrip, searching along the row of identical and anonymous apartments, thin-walled, their windows blank. It was one of these that Ziad Jarrah had rented, 150 East Airport Avenue.

I was not surprised to find it positioned exactly equidistant from the entrances to the two flight schools, a perfect meeting-place for the three conspirators from Hamburg. It seems incredible that in such a small place, where Arab faces were unusual, no one ever observed them together.

They needed to communicate because that summer the planning began to go awry. Ramsi bin al-Shibh, the al-Qaeda man back in Hamburg, was meant to have joined them for flight training in order to become the fourth pilot. He had applied, back in May in Germany, for a US visa. It had been turned down. In August, Ziad Jarrah approached Arne Kruithof with a request for help. 'He told me this guy was a really nice guy and I said I would try to help sponsor his visa. He even made a down-payment of $2,200 on the course,' said Arne.

Again the application was turned down. Desperate by now, Bin al-Shibh went home to the Yemen and tried to get a visa there. He failed a third time. His timing was ill-judged: the attack on the *Cole* occurred while he was in the Yemen. He hastily returned to Germany and made a final, fruitless, attempt to get a visa on 25 October.

So why did Ramsi bin al-Shibh arouse US suspicion and why did that suspicion not lead investigators to the Florida flight schools and the activities of the cell from Hamburg? After September 11, FBI agents let slip to Arne Kruithof that Bin al-Shibh was suspected of involvement in the al-Qaeda plot to bomb the *Cole*. But three of his visa applications were made and refused *before* the Aden attack. It seems his Yemeni nationality alone was enough cause for the US State Department to refuse his visa. There were fears that once in the USA Bin al-Shibh was the type who would overstay his visa and just disappear. There was, however, no direct evidence tying him to al-Qaeda and so his efforts to join the Florida Flight Training Center, which had sponsored one of his visa applications, did not ring any alarm bells or prompt investigation of his friend, Ziad Jarrah.

The Hamburg cell did not give up their plans to bring a fourth pilot from Europe to America for training. Zacharias Essebar, another member of the group, tried his luck at getting a visa but was also turned down. Ramsi bin al-Shibh's reaction to this new setback was to fly to London for a meeting with someone else recommended by his bosses, a young French–Moroccan student.

Zacharias Moussaoui rented a flat in Brixton, south London, and appeared on the surface to be an ambitious student who wanted to become a businessman. But he had a secret life. In 1998 he had trained at Khaldan, the same al-Qaeda camp in Afghanistan as Mohamed Atta attended, at exactly the same time.

Bin al-Shibh flew to London in the first week of December 2000 to meet Moussaoui. Later it would emerge that Bin al-Shibh had reservations about Moussaoui's suitability after meeting him, but time was marching on and a fourth pilot was needed for the plan. Just days later Moussaoui set off for

Pakistan, en route again for Bin Laden's camps. Moussaoui had already e-mailed an aviation school in Norman, Oklahoma, enquiring about flying courses, an indication that he already knew he might be called upon to join the group. He had even set up a phoney background reference, a letter from a Malaysian company called Infocus Tech appointing him as 'marketing consultant' in the US, UK and Europe. It stated he would receive a monthly fee of $2,500. Now he set off for Afghanistan for further instructions from the leadership and further training for his mission.

By the end of the year 2000 three of the four pilots who would navigate the planes on September 11 – Mohamed Atta, Marwan al-Shehhi and Ziad Jarrah – had qualified as light-aircraft commercial pilots. An ambition that Bin Laden and his military planners had nurtured for years, to use al-Qaeda pilots to turn planes into weapons against the infidel, was one step nearer.

After the bombing of Afghanistan scattered al-Qaeda's forces in October 2001, evidence of the organisation's efforts to gain flying skills was found in the wreckage of the terrorists' safe houses. A page torn from an aviation magazine listing flight schools in Florida and the paperwork from a Microsoft Flight Simulator '98 computer game were found by a reporter from the *New York Times*.

Until September 11 there had only been spectacular near-misses when it came to terror plots involving using planes as missiles. The light aircraft which crash-landed on the White House lawn in 1994 had led the US Secret Service to estimate that, with a large enough explosive charge, it could have damaged the White House and even killed the President.

Ramsi Yousef's plot to blow up a dozen US airliners over the Pacific had been uncovered in 1995, before he could execute the bombings. But a key figure in the terror plot involving those passenger planes, Yousef's uncle, Khalid Sheikh Mohamed, had escaped and still harboured ambitions for an aviation spectacular. And the conversation that one of the co-conspirators, Abdul Hakim Murad, had with the Philippines intelligence service revealed that Murad had trained as a commercial pilot in American flying schools, in Albany near New York, Richmond in Virginia and San Antonio, Texas.

Murad made it clear that as early as 1994 fanatical extremists like Yousef's group, linked to al-Qaeda, had already begun to think of using a plane as a weapon of mass destruction.

'He will hijack the aircraft, control its cockpit and dive it at CIA headquarters,' read the intelligence report of the Murad debriefing. 'There will be no bomb or any explosive that he will use in its execution. It is simply a suicide mission that he is willing to execute . . . The subject was observed to be very angry at Americans and the United States government.'

The CIA later learned that in 1996 Mohamed Atef, Bin Laden's military commander, drew up a study on the feasibility of hijacking US planes and destroying them in flight. It was influenced by Ramsi Yousef and Khalid Sheikh Mohamed's unrealised plans. The CIA's analysis of the September 11 attacks put together ten months later concluded that Khalid Sheikh Mohamed was, if not the architect, one of the chief planners of the terror that day. Osama bin Laden himself was involved in deciding how to create the greatest death toll. When the proposal to employ small planes packed with explosives was discussed, it was Bin Laden who reportedly suggested using even larger planes.

An incident which European intelligence believe also influenced Bin Laden and shaped his planning was the abortive attempt of the Algerian terror group, the Groupe Islamique Armé (GIA), to inflict punishment on France for its assistance to the Algerian government. In December 1994 Air France Flight 8969 was hijacked in Algiers and the French pilot told to head to Paris. He deceived the terrorists by claiming he did not have enough fuel and diverted the plane to Marseilles. There the GIA's intention was revealed. They wanted to crash the fully-fuelled plane into the Eiffel Tower and demanded three times the amount of fuel actually needed to get to Paris. An elite French paramilitary force stormed the plane, killing all 4 terrorists and rescuing 161 hostages and crew. This taught Bin Laden that only by having his own pilot aboard a hijacked plane could he be sure of the aircraft reaching its target.

The CIA now believes that the crashing of Egypt Air Flight 990 in October 1999 off the coast of Newfoundland may have been another trigger. The cause of the disaster is still unknown but there was speculation in the press that the plane was crashed deliberately by a fanatical Egyptian airline pilot. It encouraged Bin Laden to believe that passenger planes flying from US airports could be vulnerable.

After the September 2001 attacks the intelligence community in the United States would admit to a 'failure of imagination' in not preparing for a massive domestic terror attack using aeroplanes. Two years earlier, however, in 1999, a report prepared for the National Intelligence Council, a think-tank affiliated to the CIA, warned that terrorists associated with Bin Laden might hijack an aircraft and crash it into an American government building. 'Suicide bombers belonging to al-Qaeda's Martyrdom Battalion could crash-land an aircraft packed with high explosives (C4 and Semtex) into the Pentagon, the headquarters of the Central Intelligence Agency or the White House,' the paper read. Someone had imagined the scenario but no one would take action to prevent it.

By the end of 2000 the three members of the Hamburg cell had their pilot's licences but their only experience was in flying small, twin-engined planes. That winter Atta had already paid a visit to a store used by professional pilots, choosing a shop thousands of miles away from Florida, in Ohio, to avoid being recognised. He bought flight-deck videos for a Boeing 747 Model 200 and a Boeing 757 Model 200. Then he returned in December, ten days before taking his exams, to purchase videos of the Boeing 767 Model 300 and the Airbus A320 Model 200.

Just five days after getting their licences, on 26 December, the newly qualified Atta and al-Shehhi took an intriguing trip which could have alerted the authorities they were up to something suspicious. Dan Pearson, Huffman's student co-ordinator, remembers it because it was the day after Christmas and he was having dinner with his family when he received a phone call. It was Mohamed Atta, saying he had flown one of Huffman's planes to Miami International airport and was stuck there because the aircraft would not start.

'I was amazed that they should have taken a small plane into an international airport of that magnitude, at the busiest season of the year – it just didn't make sense. What were they playing at?' Pearson wondered.

The incident escalated when an angry official from the FAA, the Federal Aviation Administration, called to say Atta and al-Shehhi had literally abandoned the plane, just off the busy main runway, and had walked across the apron, a restricted area. They had blocked a large jet's access but seemed totally unconcerned. They dumped the plane and hired a car to get home.

'I told Atta what he'd done was insane, but the impression I got was that he just didn't care,' said Pearson. It is likely that the two Arabs were testing the security of Miami airport or observing the movements of the big jets using the runway. Whatever they were up to, official inquiries went no further. After September 11 there were tough questions as to why the FAA had not investigated further or even filed a report on the incident. Students back at Huffman wondered why the two newly-qualified pilots had not been grounded for their violation of airport security.

Three days later, on 29 December, Atta and al-Shehhi were on another mission to further their knowledge of big jets. They flew to Opa Locka in Florida and enrolled for six hours of training on an advanced jet simulator.

In a darkened hangar on the airfield, the brightly lit runway rushes up to meet you. The angle and pitch of the jet's turns,

1. Ramsi Yousef, the Islamic extremist with links to al-Qaeda, convicted of bombing the World Trade Center in 1993.

2. The Egyptian 'blind Sheikh', Omar Abdel Rahman, convicted of plotting to blow up New York landmarks in 1995.

3. Dr Hassan al-Turabi, Osama bin Laden's Sudanese friend and mentor.

4. Osama bin Laden, sporting his Kalashnikov, in a still from an al-Qaeda propaganda video.

5. Bin Laden with Dr Ayman al-Zawahiri, his Egyptian deputy (left) and Mohamed Atef, al-Qaeda's military commander, who was killed by an American airstrike in November 2001.

6. The scene of destruction around the US Embassy in Nairobi, after al-Qaeda detonated a truck bomb in August 1998.

7. The Egyptian: Mohamed Atta, leader of the Hamburg cell and field commander of the September 11 attacks.

8. Mohamed Atta as a boy in Cairo with his father, Mohamed, and his (adored) mother, Bouthayna.

9. Marwan al-Shehhi, the young man from the Emirates who would follow Atta like a shadow, crashing the second plane into the World Trade Center.

10. Ziad Jarrah, the playboy Lebanese student who hijacked Flight 93 before it crashed into a field near Pittsburgh on September 11.

11. Ramsi bin al-Shibh, the Yemeni member of the Hamburg cell, who escaped before the September attacks and remains one of the world's most wanted men.

12. Zacharias Moussaoui, the French–Moroccan student who lived in Brixton, London, and is suspected of being the 'twentieth hijacker'.

13. The fuzzy passport photograph of Mustafa Ahmed al-Hawsawi, Bin Laden's money man, who masterminded the funding of the September attacks.

14. 'The Last Night' document, an exhortation to the nineteen hijackers, believed to have been written by Mohamed Atta.

15. Just hours before the hijackings a CCTV camera at a bank in Portland, Maine captures the face of Abdulaziz al-Omari, a watchful Mohamed Atta behind him.

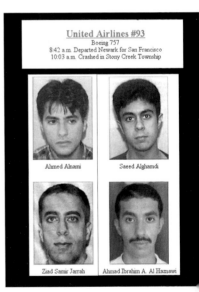

16. The four groups of al-Qaeda hijackers who seized the planes on September 11, as featured on the FBI's website.

17. President George W. Bush on the morning of September 11, receiving the news that a second plane has crashed into the World Trade Center.

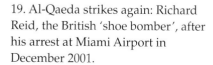

18. Ground Zero, New York City.

19. Al-Qaeda strikes again: Richard Reid, the British 'shoe bomber', after his arrest at Miami Airport in December 2001.

20. Afghan troops at the siege of Tora Bora, al-Qaeda's hideout, December 2001.

21. US 101st Airborne troops scrambling out of a Chinook during Operation Anaconda, exhausted after the firefight which claimed the lives of seven Americans.

22. The author outside an al-Qaeda cave above the valley of Shah-i-Kot Paktia province.

viewed from the captain's seat inside the cockpit, is so realistic it makes you feel queasy. This is the domain of Henry George, instructor at a flight facility which can take a pilot through a jet transition course to the most advanced level possible.

'These two men were interested in flying a full-motion simulator that would replicate a jet aircraft,' George remembered. 'They said they were going to be interviewed for a job with a major airline in their country and needed exposure to jet aircraft.' Atta and al-Shehhi paid $1,500 in cash and spent three hours each practising turns.

In his laconic style Henry George confirmed that what they were aiming to do was surprisingly easy, and much of it could be picked up from computer games. 'It doesn't take much to learn to do what they ended up achieving – to fly a plane at a building, or make a turn into a skyscraper. Hitting a specific floor would require more precision flying,' he explained. 'They were actually over-trained for the task they performed. They already had about 300 hours' flying time. What they got out of us was exposure to a 727 – the ability to feel the performance of the plane.' Like others, George noticed the two Arab students' approach to the task had been low-key, workmanlike: 'I think they were just making sure that when they got into that jet they could complete the task successfully. I did not sense there was a passion for flying – they were just preparing to perform a job.'

The year of the millennium was in its final hours when Atta and al-Shehhi turned their backs on Huffman Aviation, their task there accomplished. Ann Greaves, who had still to qualify, felt a twinge of jealousy when she last saw the man she so instinctively disliked. 'I can remember watching him take off, fly round and come down again, and I was envious as he was more experienced,' she remembers. 'I saw him take a steep turn in the circuit and those are my last memories of Atta, flying his twin-engined plane, coming out of the turn.'

On September 11 Ann Greaves was watching television back home in England, mesmerised by the sight of the smoking North Tower of the Trade Center. Then she saw a plane heading towards the South Tower. 'I saw the second aircraft make a steep banking manoeuvre and head directly for the building. "My God!" I said to my husband, "I hope this has nothing to do with those two Arabs at Huffman."' No one had yet made public the names of Atta and al-Shehhi but Mrs Greaves immediately picked up the phone and called the FBI.

14

Below the Radar

'We had not been attacked in our homeland since Pearl Harbor and we didn't feel that America itself was the target of terrorist activities. There were serious breakdowns in our systems – and they had a fatal impact.'

—Senator Bob Graham, Chair, Senate Intelligence
Committee, November 2001

I had spent hours poring over the computer screen at Huffman Aviation. Each flight made by Mohamed Atta and Marwan al-Shehhi was carefully logged – the aircraft number, the flying hours and also the cost of each lesson. Alongside was a column showing the two men paid for their courses in instalments, $1,070 at a time, nearly $19,000 each in total. In the pleasant Venice suburb of Nokomis I found the local branch of the Florida SunTrust Bank, next-door to branches of Dunkin' Donuts and KFC. Like the fast-food outlets it had a drive-thru dispenser, where the two men would collect their dollars, a little at a time, each week.

Probing the money trail which led, over two years, from Bin Laden himself in the mountains of Afghanistan to the American travel agencies where business-class tickets were purchased days before the fated flights, provides many insights into the terror organisation's rules of good financial house-keeping. It reveals how al-Qaeda kept below the radar screen of the world's banking institutions, despite their much-vaunted claims to be able to detect the ill-gotten gains of organised crime.

The money to fund the Twin Tower attacks was coming through the United Arab Emirates, one of the world's most successful and anonymous banking centres. In Abu Dhabi, the capital of the Emirates, I waited for an audience with the Governor of the Central Bank, His Excellency Sultan Nasser al-Suwaidi. The Governor was finishing off some papers, his calm demeanour masking the political turmoil his government was facing. His staff were beavering away elsewhere in the vast marble building where extensive computer systems were churning and cogitating. The UAE was under intense pressure from the West to investigate several dozen names on two US and UK Treasury black-lists. Many of the individuals and dubious financial institutions on the roll-call were suspected of having used the Emirates as a conduit to finance terror. At stake, the Governor knew full well, was the reputation and long-term stability of the Emirates' banking sector, already suffering losses in the wake of the September 11 attacks.

The Governor confided that four money transfers had been made from the Emirates to Marwan al-Shehhi's bank account in America. 'It was seen as normal. After all, he's a UAE citizen. The transfers totalled about $100,000 and with a UAE student it's normal to have a large transfer to buy a car or something,' he explained.

'Wasn't that still a lot of money for a student?' I asked, conscious that the sums that oil-rich Abu Dhabi might consider 'normal' to lavish on its overseas students might be rather high.

'Well, it was a total of about $100,000, but in four transfers,' replied al-Suwaidi. 'Only one of those, for about $70,000, was above the amount that might register a Suspicious Transaction Report, or STR, in the USA, where the money was going.'

And did it raise an STR? 'It should have raised an STR,' the Governor drily replied, 'and if it wasn't noted in the States, where they have stringent anti-money-laundering laws, it's very difficult to expect our financial institutions to provide that kind of preventative action.'

The truth is that most of the sums transferred by al-Qaeda to Marwan al-Shehhi's account were deliberately kept at a level which would not trigger alarm bells. Around $10,000 was moved on the first two occasions, and $20,000 in the third transaction. Only the final tranche, in September 2000, was the substantial sum of nearly $70,000. That payment, it later transpired, had registered at SunTrust, which raised an automatic STR to the US Treasury's Financial Crimes Enforcement Network (FINCEN). But, like most of the 150,000 similar reports sent each year, it went unnoticed until investigators started probing in the wake of September 11. That missed report of the $70,000 was a small piece of the jigsaw, but nonetheless a distinct clue that could have put investigators on the trail of the al-Qaeda plotters.

The prime suspect behind the UAE transactions, a man ranked number four on the wanted list behind Osama bin Laden and his two top henchmen, was literally a shadowy figure. I scanned the blurry coloured photograph, discreetly provided by a source in Dubai, a passport picture which looked deliberately out of focus. It featured a youngish bearded man in traditional Gulf attire, long white robe and traditional headdress. The photocopied pages of his passport revealed it to have been issued in Saudi Arabia, and to belong to a Mustafa Ahmed al-Hawsawi, whose passport stamps show he travelled widely in and around the Gulf region, to Qatar, the Emirates and Saudi Arabia in the months leading up to September 11.

Mustafa Ahmed, alias Shayk Saïd, Bin Laden's chief financial lieutenant in recent years, was the money man behind the September 11 attacks. Sometimes directly and sometimes in concert with others in the al-Qaeda hierarchy, he was the conduit for the cash to finance the hijackings. He also had links with the Saudi-backed charity, the Islamic Relief Agency, suspected of financing the Nairobi cell in the East African bombings.

The SunTrust account in Florida was jointly held in the name of Marwan al-Shehhi and Mohamed Atta, enabling both to draw out money and to use credit cards issued on the same account. It became the seed fund for the terror operation, providing the cash for the flight training, living expenses and long-distance shopping trips to buy various items they would need.

While the three members of the Hamburg cell were learning to fly in Florida in the second half of 2000, a second al-Qaeda group was also at work in the United States. This time the group was based on the west coast, in California – like Florida, a state noted for its aviation industry and its plethora of small flying schools.

Khalid al-Midhar and Nawaf al-Hazmi, both Saudis, had established a base in the large, vibrant port city of San Diego where there is a large Muslim population. Both men were already veteran al-Qaeda operatives who had taken the oath of allegiance to Bin Laden. They began their flying lessons at Sorbi's flying school, with noticeably less application and success than Atta's group in Florida. They had told the school they wanted to fly Boeings but were advised to begin with a less ambitious programme. Their instructor, Rick Garcia, described al-Midhar and al-Hazmi as 'dumb and dumber' when they took their introductory flights with him. One of them even started praying loudly as his friend approached the landing strip at the controls of the Cessna aircraft. It was clear they were not going to make the grade as pilots, however hard they tried.

Like Atta and al-Shehhi, the two Saudis were always seen together. And there were other parallels: one was more communicative, more friendly; the other quieter and brooding. Khalid al-Midhar was the more distant of the San Diego pair. His photo shows a hard, muscular face with an arrogant tilt and beetling brows. By contrast Nawaf al-Hazmi appears younger, jollier with his rounded, softer face and thick black hair.

Both men mingled with local Muslims at the Islamic Center of San Diego where they bought the blue Toyota Corolla car which they would ultimately drive across the States and park at Dulles airport on September 11 before boarding American Airlines Flight 77.

Al-Hazmi moved into the home of a retired professor of English, Abdusattar Shaik, who described his lodger as 'a homebody' who had no friends except al-Midhar and seemed to have nothing to do, although he claimed he had enrolled for English-language lessons. He read religious texts and followed a strict Muslim diet. Following the pattern of so many al-Qaeda operatives who preferred non-Arab wives who could give them good cover, and perhaps a good time too, al-Hazmi told the professor he wanted to find a Mexican bride. He posted an advert on a lonely-hearts website, advertising himself as a 'Saudi businessman looking for a partner to live in Saudi and the USA'. The only replies he received were from Egyptian women. A picture emerges of a lonely, troubled young man, ripe for a suicide mission when his marital ambitions came to nothing.

The third member of the California chapter of al-Qaeda was another disappointed and frustrated young man. Hani Hanjour, the son of a wealthy family from Taif, a resort town in Saudi Arabia, had drifted between his home and various flying schools in America for five years. He hoped his good English would help him get a job as a pilot with Saudi Arabian Airlines, but twice the company turned him down. He had poor college grades, had failed his medical and was struggling to pass his commercial pilot's licence. Hani's photo shows a fine-boned face, sad-eyed, sensitive and weak.

Hanjour had been converted to militant Islam, according to his brother, not in Saudi but during his years in America. On his return to Taif in 1998, he spent his time reading religious books and riding horses on the farm he had bought with inherited money. He left a year later, telling his family he had got a job as a commercial pilot in the Emirates. In May 2000, Hani

Hanjour turned up at Sorbi's flying school in San Diego, with Nawaf al-Hazmi.

Hanjour would spend the next year trying to perfect his flying skills, first in San Diego and then in Phoenix, Arizona. He seemed typical of the many wealthy young Saudis who had chosen to escape to the laid-back west coast of America from their strict Islamic country. A sharp-eyed FBI agent at the Bureau's Phoenix office, Ken Williams, noticed that a number of Islamic militants in his patch were signing up for flying courses that summer, at the Embry-Riddle Aeronautical University. He knew some of them were members of a British extremist organisation, al-Muhajiroun, which had links to Bin Laden. One Saudi even had contacts with Abu Zubaydah, the master recruiter of al-Qaeda. Williams' suspicions were fuelled still further when he learned that some of the men were enquiring about airport security. Visiting the apartment of one of the Middle Eastern students, Williams had seen a poster of Bin Laden on the wall; it prompted him to mention the al-Qaeda leader's name in his subsequent memo. The FBI agent's alarm was heightened when the student admitted he considered the US a 'legitimate target' for Muslim fundamentalists.

Williams' boss at the Phoenix office had worked on the Osama bin Laden specialist unit within the FBI's international terrorism section and he fired off a five-page memo on 10 July suggesting the monitoring of 'civil aviation universities/colleges around the country'. The memo specifically raised the possibility that Osama bin Laden could be using US flight schools to infiltrate the country's civil aviation system. It suggested that local FBI field officers liaise with the flight schools about suspicious individuals and bring in the CIA to add any information they might have on those students.

The memo went to FBI headquarters in Washington and to New York, where the Bin Laden unit was based. But it went no further up the chain, languishing instead in countless e-mail inboxes and filing trays. Its suggestion smacked of 'racial profiling' and it was quietly buried without being shown to the

CIA. The Williams memo might have raised too many awkward questions about intrusive government, civil liberties and the role of the FBI in intelligence-gathering – the preserve of the CIA – rather than the Bureau's traditional duties of law-enforcement. It might have ruffled feathers but in the process it might also have led to a nationwide sweep of flying schools. Williams said later that he felt 'out on an island' as he diligently pursued his research with no intelligence information made available to him from either the FBI's specialist unit or the CIA. Although Hani Hanjour had already left Phoenix he was a friend of the radical student who had prompted Williams to write his memo. A joint FBI/CIA trawl of recent Middle Eastern students might have led to some connections being made and might even have prevented four Islamic militants, newly qualified pilots, taking off on September 11.

Apart from their dubious flying skills there was nothing else about the three Saudis in California that summer that jarred. The manager of the Parkwood Apartments, Holly Ratchford, who had briefly rented a unit to al-Hazmi before he found permanent lodgings, described him as 'a polite man who paid his rent on time – he just didn't stick out'. Those words were to be echoed time and again throughout America in the days following September 11. The greatest skill of the hijackers would be their ability to go about their business unnoticed in the many communities in which they lived – to hide in plain sight.

There were, however, valuable clues as to the real identity of al-Hazmi and al-Midhar, right in front of the noses of the security services of at least two countries for at least eighteen months before the September attacks. Those clues were missed through a combination of incomplete intelligence, bureaucracy, delay and a lack of co-ordination – all the elements which had hampered Western attempts to fight al-Qaeda's growing network right from the start.

In late 1999 the CIA learned that two suspected Bin Laden operatives, 'Nawaf' and 'Khalid', were preparing to meet in Malaysia, but the agency did not know the men's full identities.

However, in the first week in January US intelligence had obtained a copy of the passport belonging to 'Khalid'; they discovered his full name was Khalid al-Midhar and he had a multiple-entry visa to the US. On 5 January al-Midhar and his sidekick Nawaf al-Hazmi slipped into Kuala Lumpur for the important meeting. It had been called by 'Khallad', the *nom de guerre* of one of Bin Laden's most important associates, Tawfiq bin Atash, to co-ordinate the upcoming attack on an American warship in the Yemen.

Also present at the meeting was Ramsi bin al-Shibh, Atta's flatmate from Hamburg. His presence along with al-Midhar and al-Hazmi suggests that the purpose of the meeting was to discuss not only the attack on the USS *Cole* but the September 11 project as well. The CIA was not aware of the purpose of the meeting or of the identities of all the individuals there – including Bin al-Shibh. But they did know that the man who had called the meeting was an important al-Qaeda operative. Unknown to the terrorists the Americans tipped off the Malaysian security service to video the meeting, but it would be months before the tape found its way to America to provide a photographic record of the men present that day.

Khalid al-Midhar and Nawaf al-Hazmi both re-entered the US ten days later, on 15 January. The CIA failed to alert the Immigration Service that al-Midhar had a US visa, despite the fact they knew he had just attended a meeting with a known associate of Bin Laden's. The two Saudis were able to stay in America with absolutely no attempt to find them or to discover what they were up to.

Nine months later, after the bombing of the USS *Cole* in October 2000, attention focused again on the mysterious meeting in Malaysia. By now 'Nawaf' was known to be al-Hazmi and a source had told the CIA that both he and al-Midhar were linked to the master planner of the *Cole* bombing. Yet still nothing was done.

It was not until 23 August 2001 that all the CIA's information on various suspect individuals was reviewed and al-Midhar and al-Hazmi were finally put on a 'watch-list' at ports of entry around the US. It was too late; al-Hazmi had been back in the US for eighteen months and by now al-Midhar had left the US and returned a second time. FBI agents would still be searching for the men when the planes hit their targets less than three weeks later.

Florida Senator Bob Graham, a pilot himself and the man who heads the Senate Intelligence Committee, was incredulous when I talked to him in Washington, just weeks after the September attacks, and asked him about Khalid al-Midhar and the watch-list.

'It was a breakdown in the hand-off of information from the intelligence agencies to the domestic law-enforcement agencies,' Graham said bluntly. 'Several of these people had been tracked by intelligence until they got inside the United States and then they were lost in our own country.' Graham was gearing up for Senate hearings to inquire into the intelligence failings that allowed September 11 to happen. The hearings would conclude that the al-Midhar episode was a serious intelligence failure – the most serious of all the blunders committed by various US agencies. The Director of the CIA admitted, 'There were opportunities, both at headquarters and in the field, to act on developing information. The fact that did not happen pointed out that a whole new system, rather than a fix at any single point in the system, was needed.'

The American authorities had other chances as well to question the would-be terrorists just after they had completed their flight training in Florida. Both Mohamed Atta and Ziad Jarrah left and re-entered the States, their journeys showing up on the radar screens of at least two American government agencies in January 2001.

Ziad Jarrah left Florida at Christmas, newly qualified as a pilot. Arne Kruithof was sad to see him go. The next time he would hear of Jarrah was on September 11 when agents from the FBI turned up on his doorstep and moved into his office to question staff and systematically scan the flight school's files.

His receptionist was in tears – she had helped Jarrah search for a flat – and Kruithof angrily insisted the FBI had made a big mistake. After several nights of sleeping on the floor as the agents worked around the clock, Kruithof was told bluntly by one of the FBI men, 'You've got to face the facts: Jarrah was a terrorist – that's all there is to it.' Kruithof has still not come to terms with his betrayal by the Lebanese student whom everybody loved.

Jarrah headed from Florida to Afghanistan, via Pakistan. It was his second trip to Bin Laden's camps. It gave him a chance to report back to the leadership on the success of the flight training and to bring back new instructions. Someone in the CIA, most likely in Islamabad, must have had their suspicions about the young Lebanese traveller who came back through Pakistan and took a flight to Dubai en route for Hamburg, on 30 January. Jarrah's travel pattern, at the very least, had raised suspicions about his contacts. Western intelligence agencies are alert to the movements of young militants using Pakistan as a stopover on their way to the training camps of Afghanistan.

The Americans cabled the authorities in the Emirates to ask them to question Jarrah on his stopover. A source in the Emirates revealed this unusual request to me, late one night in a hotel in Dubai. His voice was lowered but emphatic: 'It was at the request of the Americans and it was specifically because of Jarrah's links with Islamic extremists, his contacts with terrorist organisations. That was the extent of what we were told.'

Ziad Jarrah was his usual friendly, smiling self when challenged at the airport. He admitted he had spent two months in Afghanistan. When asked about the US visa in his passport he replied that he was a pilot and would be returning to the United States. The information was relayed back to Washington but no more instructions were forthcoming. And so Jarrah was allowed to proceed and boarded his KLM flight to Amsterdam and on to Hamburg. The Americans knew he had links with extremists, they were told he was on his way to America and, crucially, that he was a pilot. Yet nothing was done and no checks were made on him when he returned to America.

In the wake of the September attacks there were clearly bruised feelings as Western fingers were pointed at the Emirates for its allegedly lax financial procedures and its diplomatic links with the Taliban regime. With the Jarrah incident, plus the $70,000 transfer to al-Shehhi's account that triggered a Suspicious Transaction Report that was never investigated, the Emirates had some cause to lob the ball neatly back into the American court.

I enquired of the FBI why Ziad Jarrah's name was never put on a US watch-list at ports of entry, despite the fact that another US government agency, the CIA, had been so wary of him. I was told flatly that the agency never commented on 'current investigations'. The Senate Hearings, probing the intelligence failures in Washington's corridors of power, had another mystery to add to their list.

Two weeks before Jarrah was stopped in Dubai, Mohamed Atta had tested the weak points in another American front-line agency in the fight against terror, the Immigration and Naturalization Service (INS). He was taking a calculated risk, coming back into Miami on 10 January from a week's trip to Europe. His visa, the one he had used to come to America six months earlier, had expired. Would the INS notice, and if so, what action would they take? A sharp-eyed female inspector did notice and directed Atta to a special room for further questioning.

There was, if she had but realised it, a curious parallel here with the case of Ramsi Yousef, the 1993 World Trade Center bomber, whose papers had not passed muster when he arrived in New York eight years previously. He had nonetheless bluffed his way through.

The INS allowed me to visit what they called a 'hard secondary' area, like the one where Atta had been detained. Here visitors who have aroused suspicions that they may be illegal immigrants are given a verbal grilling. A line of burly officers, trained in tough interrogation techniques, stand commandingly on a dais raised above the supplicants below.

I watched as weary and luckless individuals pulled out of the immigration lines tried to make their case for entry into the United States. A French-speaking man attempted to convince a sceptical officer he was just a visiting tourist. Forced to produce holiday snaps from his wallet to justify his claim, he struggled to explain what he was doing posing in full chef's garb outside an American restaurant where he was clearly illegally employed. He found himself back on the next plane to France. 'Hard secondary' was clearly not a place for the faint-hearted.

Mohamed Atta, however, remained cool under fire during an hour of intensive questioning. He displayed the classic character requirements of 'tranquillity and unflappability ... patience for enduring afflictions' as laid down in the al-Qaeda training manual.

Atta insisted that he had applied for a student visa in September 2000, before his visitor's visa expired, but had not yet received the papers. Without the necessary computerised records of visa applications to check this, there was no way of instantly verifying his claims. Under a strict reading of the law, Atta should have been deported at this point, but he knew that in practice individual officers had discretion over and above the rules. Atta finally persuaded the officer in 'hard secondary' to waive the student visa requirement and let him in with an extension stamp to his expired visa. The INS even agreed to forget the fine of $170.

Emboldened by his success, Atta was to leave and re-enter America again at least twice, in April and July, just two months before the attacks. By this time his extended visa had again run out. But he was not even challenged by immigration officers.

'There isn't a question in my mind that the al-Qaeda guys knew that border security was lax. They knew it for years, everybody knows it. Certainly everybody in my business knows it!' Bob Blitzer, the FBI's former head of counter-terrorism, was clearly angry when I spoke to him about INS controls.

The INS spokesman, Russ Bergeron, later admitted that Atta 'took advantage of the system' – a system already creaking at the seams, according to the INS officers I spoke to. Some half a billion people pass annually through the air and sea ports and the land borders of this vast country, as many as 8 million of them illegal immigrants. In the national recriminations that erupted in the wake of the attacks, the INS became a convenient whipping-boy.

Senator Bob Graham told me, 'The fact that Atta was able, repeatedly, to enter America with an expired visa is an atrocious commentary on our system, on the INS at the front line of our borders and on the State Department responsible for issuing the visa and seeing the terms of it are complied with.'

The woes of the INS were compounded when, six months to the day after September 11, Huffman Aviation received INS forms clearing Atta and al-Shehhi for take-off. They were copies of their M1 student visas approved for flying lessons, the proper visas the two men needed and had applied for while at the flight school. Although now dead and internationally infamous, Mohamed Atta and Marwan al-Shehhi were, it seemed, still raising no alarm bells in the INS system. Calls for the resignation of the Director of the INS reached a deafening crescendo and President Bush announced an inquiry into the creaking bureaucracy.

In the final analysis the INS emerged bloodied but with some real gains from the débâcle of Atta's visa revelations. There was an injection of new funds and, more significantly, proper investigatory powers for INS officers to chase up illegal immigrants beyond the airport gates. But that was only after September 11, the day America lost its traditional openness of spirit towards the huddled masses fleeing economic and political persecution. Afterwards, America became a sadder and a wiser place.

15

Targets

BIN LADEN: *'Not everybody knew about the operation.
Mohamed from the Egyptian family was in charge of the
group.'*

UNIDENTIFIED SAUDI SHEIKH: *'This was a great job. He was
one of the pious men in the organisation. He became a
martyr. Allah bless his soul!'*

—Taken from video recording of al-Qaeda meeting,
November 2001

How far did Mohamed Atta plan the devastating attacks of
September 11 by himself? That is the question no one has yet
answered satisfactorily, even with the discovery of a videotape
of Osama bin Laden chatting with a visiting Saudi sheikh after
the cataclysmic events. The grainy footage, shot in a guesthouse in Jalalabad sometime in November, illustrates perfectly
the banality of evil. The two men, a fanatic and a sycophant,
discuss dreams and portents while almost chuckling over the
deaths of thousands in the terror attacks. The fate of their own
al-Qaeda hijackers hardly seems to concern them.

It is almost certain that of the group in America only Atta,
the commander who led them, knew all the details of the plot.
'The brothers who conducted the [attacks], all they knew was
that they have a martyrdom mission and we asked each of
them to go to America. But they didn't know anything about
the operation,' confirmed Bin Laden in the video, adding that
even most of the top members of al-Qaeda's ruling council
knew nothing of his plans.

From the moment Mohamed Atta passed his commercial pilot's exams on 21 December 2000, his movements show that the commander of the Hamburg cell had now become the leader of an al-Qaeda group forming inside America to carry out the attacks. The mission was still in its research and planning phase and the exact targets may not yet have been settled, even in the spring of 2001. It was clearly to be an aerial terror attack, but where exactly should they strike?

Atta began to make a series of wide-ranging trips across America and back to Europe, to Madrid and Hamburg, crisscrossing the Atlantic, sometimes for only a few days, suggesting his journeys had an urgent and specific purpose. Intelligence and law-enforcement agencies believe Atta was liaising with al-Qaeda back in Europe, passing on information and receiving instructions for the next phase of the planning which would involve expanding the team inside America. The al-Qaeda training manual recommends that operatives arrange face-to-face meetings where messages can be passed on via couriers, rather than using telephones, faxes or e-mail to communicate.

'They said, "Never mind the money – just go to Hamburg."' The thick-set taxi driver took his large hands off the steering wheel of his cream Mercedes, waving them dismissively. He was describing the three men he had picked up at a bus stop at 7:00 A.M. on 20 April 2001. 'I couldn't believe it – a fare of 1,200 marks, just like that. It must have been urgent or they would have got a train,' said Karl-Heinz Horst as he drove me along the grey shoreline where Hamburg meets the Baltic Sea. It was winter, six weeks after the Twin Towers attacks, and the trees were bare and black. They had been bursting with green life in April, when Karl-Heinz last came here bringing three mysterious Arab passengers all the way from Furth, a small town in Bavaria.

Karl-Heinz Horst lives and works in the far south of Germany, near the Czech border. He had a feeling that his passengers had come across that border just before he picked them up. Two spoke no German or English and seemed unfriendly as they sat in the back of the cab, hunched down in their seats as if to escape the driver's eyes in the rear-view mirror. The third man, who sat alongside Horst, was more chatty and spoke some English.

As they passed Würzberg they saw the aftermath of a serious road accident on the autobahn. The man in the passenger seat suddenly volunteered some information. 'He told me he had seen a lot of dead bodies where he came from,' Karl-Heinz recounted. 'I asked where that was and he said he had been a soldier in Afghanistan.' The other two interjected angrily – it seemed they were cautioning their companion not to talk any more. The rest of the long journey passed in silence.

Once in Hamburg, Karl-Heinz Horst was instructed to call the number of a mobile phone to get an address to take them to. But the individual who answered said he would meet them at the main railway station. At the bustling station taxi-rank, just a few hundred yards from the al-Quds mosque, Horst noticed that his passengers jumped out and embraced the man waiting for them, as if they knew him well. There was a brief altercation when the Hamburg resident refused to pay the agreed fare, an event which imprinted his face on Horst's memory.

Five months later the taxi driver was glued to his television in Bavaria as the horrifying events of September 11 unfolded when he briefly saw a picture of the man who had paid the taxi fare. 'It was Mohamed Atta, I am positive of that. I contacted the police and picked out more photographs of him,' Horst declared. Bavarian investigators are still trying to find out who the three men were and if they are still in Germany. Horst's experience fits the evidence that intelligence agencies have gathered over the years, that al-Qaeda missions are often coordinated through a series of couriers carrying instructions sent from their military commanders. But to this day no one has identified Mohamed Atta's important and secretive visitors, at least one of whom was from Afghanistan.

Atta is known to have been in Hamburg that spring. He cleared out of the flat at 54 Marienstrasse and handed over the key to the German terror cell's quartermaster, Saïd Bahaji. He also ventured further afield in Europe, making two visits to Spain, in January and again in July. The Spanish police chief, Juan Cotino, has indicated that Atta met a man known as Abu Dhadah, whom the Spanish authorities accuse of being an Islamic extremist and a 'sleeper' in Bin Laden's extensive network in that country. Dhadah's telephone number was later found in Atta's belongings. But exactly what the Egyptian was doing in Madrid has not yet been established.

Mohamed Atta's second visit to Spain in July, just two months before September 11, coincided with a trip that Ramsi bin al-Shibh, the Hamburg cell's logistics man, made at the same time. Both men made their way to Salou, a small coastal town on the Mediterranean coast. Spanish intelligence officials say the 'strong presumption' is that the two men met in the tourist resort. They both avoided known Islamic radicals in Salou but there are indications that three other individuals were in town to make contact, perhaps to hand over instructions, money and discuss last-minute details.

When I spoke to the US Attorney General, John Ashcroft, at the US Embassy in London in December 2001, he was on his way to Spain and Belgium to publicly bolster the efforts of local law-enforcement agencies to arrest members of al-Qaeda's network. Ashcroft was convinced the timing and the range of Mohamed Atta's travels across Europe were significant, if still largely a mystery. 'We are still working on developing a full understanding of these trips and the variety of his destinations. It's not all intelligible to us yet.' He added drily, 'Obviously, we don't just think they were random opportunities to accumulate frequent flier miles.' Ironically it would later turn out that Mohamed Atta *had* registered for free mileage awards with American Airlines, the very airline whose Flight 11 he would later fly into the World Trade Center.

Tracing the journeys that Mohamed Atta made in the spring

of 2001, not only to Europe, but within America itself, has become a race against time. For his travels may well hold clues as to where future al-Qaeda cells are planning to attack and what exactly they aim to do.

That February, Atta visited Norfolk, Virginia, the site of a huge US Navy base. He returned again in April and it is believed that he was scouting out the aircraft-carriers. That same month he and al-Shehhi rented a light aircraft from a flying school in Atlanta, Georgia, presumably for aerial reconnaissance and further flying practice.

Scanning a map of this area, I found that just a hundred miles due north of the Atlanta airfield there is a massive nuclear power complex, at Watts Bar in Tennessee, at the foot of the Appalachian mountains. Interestingly, Atta was spotted in a small town nearby asking strange questions. He wanted to know about the local water reservoir behind the massive Watts Bar dam and whether it connected with the river flowing by the two nuclear power plants.

Could Atta have been planning either to breach the dam and threaten the nuclear power station, or to smash a plane directly into Watts Bar, causing a massive radiation leak? This would be one version, on an apocalyptic scale, of the so-called 'dirty bomb': a terror attack using a suitcase full of radioactive waste in the middle of a city. Breaching the protective shield of a nuclear reactor, especially using a large plane as a missile, could precipitate nuclear fallout over a large area.

On 30 January 2002 a little-noticed government warning to American industry highlighted the discovery, presumably in Afghanistan, of computer software in the possession of an unnamed individual with links to Bin Laden. The sophisticated Australian software is used for structural engineering, in particular for 'dams and water-retaining structures'. The bulletin concluded these programmes demonstrated 'terrorist interest' in water supply systems and dam construction and quietly drew the attention of the security departments of the relevant industries to this.

'Atta was very active scoping things out,' Bob Blitzer, the former FBI head of counter-terrorism told me. 'There is tremendous pre-operational planning that goes into this, and these people spend a lot of time watching and researching various scenarios. In my view he was ordered to go and see what was out there, as the man on the spot in the US, to look at them for future planning purposes.'

Another aspect of Atta's research has raised a further spectre to add to the fears of al-Qaeda's exploration of nuclear contamination as a terror weapon.

James Lester is the kind of man who wastes no words and speaks his mind. 'He was just a butt-hole, that's what he was,' is his considered verdict of Mohamed Atta. Lester, a grizzled, taciturn man in checked shirt and dungarees, was puzzled and annoyed by the three Arabs who had flown into the small airstrip in Belle Glade, Florida on a Saturday morning in February 2001 when he was trying to finish refuelling the planes in time to be at his sister's birthday lunch. The small planes belonged to a crop-dusting company and were used to spray agricultural chemicals over large open fields.

One of the men spoke good English but was clearly contemptuous of the black worker he encountered on the deserted airstrip, in the same way he had been dismissive of the women who crossed his path. He demanded to be allowed to get into the cockpit to see if he could start the plane and kept asking questions about fuel capacity and range. Lester had to push him away, he was so determined. When the FBI came calling a week after September 11 with a photo album, Lester had no hesitation in picking out the man he almost came to blows with. It was Atta. 'I said hey, you gotta go, and I just pushed him and he walked off with the other guys,' Lester remembered. It turned out that Atta had made several trips to other crop-dusting companies in south Florida between February and April 2001.

It has long been the ultimate terror scenario: a chemical or biological attack on a major city by fanatics using a small plane to spray poison. John Ashcroft told me: 'We know that in the camps instruction was given in certain kinds of warfare, including the potential of chemical and biological warfare. The al-Qaeda manuals we have submitted in previous trials tell us that.' Indeed, Lesson 16 in the manual found in the house in Manchester in 1998 contains details on how to isolate the lethal chemicals ricin and abrin, from 'castor-oil plants' and 'precatory beans'. The crop-dusting enquiries made by Atta seemed to signal Bin Laden's ambitions to spread chemical poisons and biological agents, using small planes, over heavily populated areas. The very same month that Atta was researching chemical spraying, a New York court hearing evidence in the Nairobi bombing trial took a statement from L'Houssaine Kerchtou, the veteran of the Afghan *jihad* who had since become Bin Laden's personal pilot. 'They wanted to have someone who already has a license and can fly crop-dusters,' he told the court, explaining that he had been trained at a Kenyan flight school. Kerchtou claimed his crop-spraying skills were needed on al-Qaeda's Sudanese farms. Those farms also doubled as terror training camps.

Bob Blitzer has no doubt that Atta was actively researching some kind of chemical attack on an American target. 'You have to figure out, with crop-dusting planes, he wants to spray some kind of agent on people and do a lot of damage. There's no other logical conclusion you can reach. It may have been to report back to people higher up, some kind of intelligence-gathering for the future, but it's very significant.'

The story of the would-be twentieth hijacker, which took me from a run-down street in Brixton, south London, to a grim prison block near Minnesota, provides the most alarming evidence of al-Qaeda's interest in finding ways to spread deadly poisons.

'Urgent! I am arriving tomorrow to your school. Zuluman Tangotango.' Up popped the e-mail on Brenda Keene's computer screen in Norman, Oklahoma on 22 February 2001. Brenda, the administrator of the Airman school, an attractive brunette with long curly hair and carefully painted lips, sighed. The mysterious Zuluman Tangotango had been e-mailing her on and off for five months enquiring about a commercial pilot's course and trying to negotiate a better rate. 'What happens if I fail the check ride or my written exams? Do I have to pay more money? I've never failed anything in my life, but there's always a first time,' another e-mail read.

When Zuluman Tangotango turned up at the flying school the next day he seemed pleasant enough, a black man in his early twenties, round-faced and burly. His head was shaved and so were his cheeks but he had a small, neat goatee beard. His real name was Zacharias Moussaoui, the French–Moroccan student who had been living in London for the past three years until Ramsi bin al-Shibh visited him in a panic, unable to get a US visa himself to train as a pilot.

Instead of the normal twenty minutes it took to process his application Zacharias spent two and a half hours with 'Miss Brenda', as he called Keene, pedantically reviewing every detail on the form and trying to beat down the price. Finally he elected to sign up for and pay $5,000 for the first part of the course only, the private pilot's licence. Keene noted that Moussaoui had chosen to come on a tourist visa and not the normal student's visa that pupils would obtain. If she had looked closely she would have seen that the US visa was issued in Islamabad, Pakistan.

Moussaoui was not short of money despite his haggling. He had declared $35,000 cash on his customs form when he arrived at Chicago airport and he opened a bank account in Norman, depositing $32,000 into it.

Moussaoui kept himself to himself at the flight school and took lodgings in the town with two other local Muslim students. He attended the local mosque and joined a gym to improve his fitness. The al-Qaeda manual advises: 'Avoid visiting mosques, do not get involved in advocating good and

denouncing evil in order not to attract attention to yourself.'
The other trainee pilots were careful not to be seen as religious
in any way. But Zacharias, it seemed, ignored these instructions.

'He was very dogmatic,' Suhaib Webb, an imam at the
Oklahoma City mosque, complained. 'People did not like him.
He was angry with the Muslims, saying we weren't religious
enough.' And things were not going well at Airman too. Brenda
Keene explained: 'Normally a student would solo in ten to fifteen hours. He had fifty-seven hours of flight with us and never
made it. The instructor felt Moussaoui wasn't competent to fly
solo and wouldn't sign him off.'

It would later emerge that Airman flying school was on an
al-Qaeda 'approved' list. As early as 1993, Ihab Ali Nawawi,
another member of the organisation who played a minor role in
the Nairobi embassy bombing, had trained there. The summer
before Moussaoui's arrival, Brenda Keene had shown two other
Arabs round Airman, but they had decided in the end to sign
up at a school in Florida. Their names were Mohamed Atta
and Marwan al-Shehhi.

Effectively grounded, Zacharias Moussaoui disappeared
from the Airman school in May 2001 but stayed in Norman
and kept himself very busy. In June he bought flight-deck
videos from the very same store in Ohio that Atta used. They
showed the configuration of the Model 200 and 400 Boeing 747.
That same month, according to US court documents, he made
'enquiries about starting a crop-dusting company'. A month
later he was calling Ramsi bin al-Shibh, back in Hamburg,
asking for money. On the first day of August, using a false
name, Bin al-Shibh wired $14,000 from train stations in
Hamburg and Düsseldorf to Oklahoma. Undeterred by his difficulties at the Norman flight school, Moussaoui was still
proceeding with the original plan.

A thousand miles north of Norman, just off the freeway that
runs into Minneapolis, Minnesota, a security fence surrounds a
giant complex sitting in acres of manicured grass, beside a lake.

This is the Pan Am International Flight Academy where pilots from all the major airlines train. As I approached the massive buildings, with brown mirrored windows hiding everything within, I could not help but marvel at Zacharias Moussaoui's sheer bravado. On 13 August the man who failed to qualify to pilot a tiny prop plane coolly walked in here and registered to train in the simulator of a massive 747 Boeing jet.

For over a year, all over the States, in Florida, in California, in Arizona and in Oklahoma, small aviation schools had been giving a group of Arab men lessons, all of whom showed no enthusiasm and little aptitude for flying. In a competitive business relying on foreign students, none of those schools had questioned what the men would do with the skills they were learning. But al-Qaeda ran out of luck in Minnesota, when Zacharias Moussaoui came up against the big boys of aviation.

An instructor became suspicious of the man who paid fees of almost $9,000 in cash and was singularly lacking in flying skills or even basic experience. Moussaoui's eagerness rang alarm bells when he said he would 'love' to fly a 747 from Heathrow to New York's JFK airport on the simulator. It was 'an ego-boosting thing', he enthused, and he seemed suspiciously interested in the door-locking mechanism and the plane's control panel. Moussaoui became belligerent and evasive when questioned about his background. He said he was from the Middle East and refused to speak French, even though his passport showed he was born in France. Alarmed, Pan Am officials tried to contact the local FBI and only succeeded in getting the attention of an agent when they warned that a big jet of the type Moussaoui was seeking to learn to fly could be used as a missile.

An urban myth that did the rounds after September 11 had it that Moussaoui aroused suspicion when he only wanted to learn how to steer once airborne and showed no interest in taking off or landing. Pan Am deny this. That makes the sixth sense of the instructor, who feared he was dealing with a potential hijacker, even more remarkably prescient.

The local FBI office in Minneapolis acted immediately, seizing Moussaoui at the nearby motel where he was staying. They held him on a visa-violation charge at the local jail, where he refused to talk. A variety of aviation equipment was found in his luggage, a radio, the Boeing videos and other items, all things which a flying-school student might legitimately have. The detainee's computer was the one piece of luggage the agents were really interested in.

It was just three and a half weeks before the September 11 attacks. The FBI did not know it but they were up against the clock to discover who Moussaoui really was and what he was up to. Brenda Keene received a visit from two FBI agents bearing a photograph of Zacharias. 'They were tight-lipped, and would only say he'd done something bad,' said Keene. 'They took away all of his training records.' The FBI had discovered from another Arab student that Moussaoui was a 'fundamentalist' and now they put out a 'trace', a request to friendly governments for information, which prompted a cable from French intelligence revealing that Moussaoui had been associated with Islamic extremists and was known to have travelled to Afghanistan. Critically, the French reporting did not tie him specifically to al-Qaeda or any other terrorist group. A bureaucratic nightmare now ensued which would enmesh the investigation in red tape, bringing it to a halt at the very moment when finding out more about Moussaoui's activities might have averted the September attacks by putting America on alert for airborne terror.

Two FBI agents in the Minneapolis office asked headquarters in Washington for a warrant to search the computer and Moussaoui's phone records. But lawyers at the FBI, after looking at the flight school information and the French intelligence cable, refused to take the request further up the chain to the Justice Department because it did not specify that Moussaoui was operating at the behest of an identifiable overseas terror group. The frustrated local agents tried a different tack, seeking to open an investigation into Moussaoui under broader laws than anti-terrorism legislation, but were again rebuffed by Washington.

One of the agents, Coleen Rowley, would later write in her account of those fraught days: 'When, in a desperate measure to bypass the FBI HQ roadblock, the Minneapolis division undertook to directly notify the CIA's counter-terrorist center, FBI HQ personnel chastised the Minneapolis agents for making the direct notification without their approval.'

Just one month earlier in Phoenix, alert local FBI agents had worried about Islamic extremists taking flying lessons, but their bosses had not listened. Despite the concerns of field staff in Minnesota investigating another suspicious would-be pilot, the FBI bureaucracy neither recollected the earlier memo nor circulated it to Minneapolis, where Moussaoui was being held. And yet it was the very same unit at FBI headquarters, the Radical Fundamentalist Unit, which had handled – or failed to handle – the Phoenix memo which was now being contacted by the Minneapolis agents who were in a frenzy about what the French–Moroccan student was up to. One of them even speculated in case notes that Zacharias was the type who might be interested in flying a plane into the World Trade Center. But Minneapolis was accused by headquarters of just getting people 'all spun up about Moussaoui'. The middle reaches of the FBI seemed more interested in following correct legal procedure and fending off encroachment on their turf by the CIA than solving the mystery of what Moussaoui was really doing.

After September 11 there was harsh criticism of the Justice Department and their investigatory arm, the FBI, as being too hidebound, too focused on obtaining a successful prosecution by sticking to the rules. The meticulous approach of these organisations in constructing the cases against al-Qaeda's East African bombers, and the successful outcome of those trials, had ironically only strengthened this blinkered approach.

Senator Graham, a vocal critic of the FBI, told me: 'The FBI's orientation is to find out who committed a crime after the fact, then bring him to justice. They've not been oriented towards *preventing* crime. They've had a culture of restricting access to the information they gather because they did not want it to be downgraded in terms of its potential use in a criminal trial.' The end result of that, according to Graham, was the kind of tragic near-miss that the case of Moussaoui represented. 'That FBI mentality has caused a mismatch between our domestic security and the kind of information our intelligence agencies have been gathering abroad,' concluded Graham.

The case of Khalid al-Midhar, the al-Qaeda suspect preparing for the September 11 attacks in San Diego who should have been on a watch-list, showed the lack of flow of CIA foreign-based intelligence into US domestic agencies. In the Moussaoui case the CIA and the Minneapolis branch of the Federal Aviation Administration were notified by the FBI but there was no sense of urgency or recommended action. And no one in the CIA connected the case of the young Muslim with known links to fundamentalists to the 'peak threat' that their agency knew existed during the summer of 2001. They were still focused on the wrong target – American interests abroad – and it was a fatal mistake.

In an incredible last-minute twist to the tale of Zacharias Moussaoui, on 7 September the Minneapolis FBI agents gave up their battle with their own lawyers to get a search warrant and prepared to ship their prisoner back to France. There they knew his computer *would* be searched and the results passed back to the FBI. But September 11 dawned before the deportation got under way and Moussaoui's computer was at last unlocked. It contained information about crop-dusting, wind currents and the aerial spread of pesticides. His phone records tied Moussaoui to Ramsi bin al-Shibh, the Hamburg cell and the flow of funds from Mustafa Ahmed, al-Qaeda's financial chief.

The tragedy is that obtaining this information just a few days earlier might have given investigators a chance to crack the membership of the Hamburg cell and identify Mohamed Atta and Marwan al-Shehhi before they boarded the planes on September 11.

16

The European Connection

'I have never met [Bin Laden], but if I had I would consider it a good thing, not something to be ashamed of. He is a good Muslim who responds to the cause of the nation of Islam.'

—Abu Qatada, November 2001

Zacharias Moussaoui's whole life story illustrates how al-Qaeda was able to run rings around many Western governments by establishing a deep-rooted network right across Europe. He was born in the sunny city of Narbonne in the South of France, the child of immigrants from Morocco. His mother, who worked for the local telephone company, had struggled to raise her two sons, Abd Samad and Zacharias, and her two daughters after she had divorced their father.

Aicha Moussaoui never wore the veil and brought up her children to consider themselves a modern French family rather than North Africans. 'Zacharias showed no especially religious feelings until a cousin of ours, Fusia, came from Morocco because her father was having problems with her fundamentalism,' Aicha told *Panorama*. 'She started telling the boys that real Muslim men should not help around the house and they should take several wives.'

Relations within the family became strained. Aicha felt her sons were becoming alienated from their former French

existence. The two brothers moved to Montpellier after their
mother told them it would be better if they left home.

'It is very important that you should know that I, as a
Muslim, unequivocally condemn the September 11 attacks,'
Abd Samad Moussaoui said after Friday prayers at the
Montpellier mosque. 'I am deeply wounded that people could
exploit our religion by daring to create so many innocent victims.' Abd Samad wanted to talk about his brother, Zacharias,
and how he had become enmeshed in the world of al-Qaeda.

'As a kid Zacharias loved playing rugby, laughing and fool-
ing around. He wanted to perfect his English. He said he'd be
"marketable" in the employment field,' Abd Samad explained.
'So he set off for England in 1992 with just a rucksack. He didn't
know anyone – he just landed up in London on his own.'

When Zacharias returned to France six months later, he
seemed a changed person – harder, disillusioned. He complained that British society was closed and class-ridden. 'He'd
been living in a hostel for the homeless, surrounded by promis-
cuity, which was difficult for him. It was full of drug addicts,
the mentally ill,' according to his brother.

Abd Samad could see that Zacharias had been deeply
affected by his experience. He had started going to a mosque
for the first time in his life, and had developed radical ideas
which shocked even his devout brother. Zacharias started quot-
ing what his brother considered to be 'pseudo-theologians' like
Sayyid Qutb, propounding the teachings of Mohamed ibn Abd
al-Wahhabi. Abd Samad considers the sect of Wahhabism to be
totally at odds with the Muslim tradition of tolerance, as practised in the majority of Islamic communities in Europe.

'Zacharias was espousing a racist ideology, an ideology of
exclusion and terror.' Abd Samad was clearly very upset at the
rift that had opened between the two brothers. 'I argued with
him that this was nothing to do with mainstream Islam. I tried
to cite examples from the Qur'an to draw him back, but he
would not listen.'

Zacharias Moussaoui returned to London, taking with him a

white French friend called Xavier Djaffo who, according to his family, converted to Islam under the influence of Moussaoui. It was now that the French intelligence officers involved in Operation Chrysanthemum, an investigation into bombings by Islamic extremists against French targets in Algeria, began to pick up rumours about a 'Zacharias' who lived in London. A French investigating judge, Roger Leloire, came to London to make inquiries but says he found the British security services unable to help.

By now Moussaoui was enrolled at the South Bank University, taking a degree in International Business Studies, a worldly and somewhat unlikely subject for a devout Islamic student. None of his teachers or fellow students had any idea of his extreme views or even felt he had any political convictions at all.

Yet in 1995, when Moussaoui returned again to Montpellier, Abd Samad found his brother's religious views even more radical, causing him to distance himself, he claims, from his troubled relative. 'Zacharias told me it is totally legitimate to commit mass murder and excommunicate a whole nation,' said Abd Samad. The most shocking aspect of all was his assertion that the actions of militants who killed women and children in Algeria were justified.

Abd Samad was convinced his brother had been radicalised by a militant North African Islamic sect while in London. He could identify the meeting place where they gathered only as 'somewhere near Baker Street'. He never found out more because Moussaoui cut all links with his family that year.

The views expressed by Moussaoui are those of extremist Algerian fundamentalists like the GIA, the Groupe Islamique Armé, who by now were carrying out horrifying massacres of Algerian families, slitting children's throats and beheading women – justified, they claimed, because their menfolk had committed 'sins' and were 'unbelievers'. Algeria was being dragged down into a vortex of blood, madness and chaos as the government struggled to maintain order. Osama bin Laden, however, was beginning to form links with the GIA and their splinter groups despite the fact that their excesses against their own people had caused even other hardcore terror groups to shun them.

Nineteen ninety-seven was a turning-point for Zacharias Moussaoui – it was the year he first went to Pakistan and Afghanistan for induction into the world of *jihad*. He reported his passport lost on his return, just like Mohamed Atta and Marwan al-Shehhi would do in 1999, in order to erase evidence of his journeys. He was to obtain three new passports in as many years, showing the extent of his movements in and out of global hotspots of Islamic militancy. The French authorities issued him with these passports although they were later to claim they suspected him of extremist links.

Moussaoui became obsessed with the *jihad* in the breakaway republic of Chechnya, travelling there with his French child-hood friend, Xavier Djaffo, who was killed in the fight against Russian troops. The death of Xavier in May 2000, Moussaoui's family believe, may have been the last straw which prompted him to sign up for a terror mission against the West.

By the spring of 1998 Zacharias Moussaoui was training at the Khaldan camp for foreign fighters. Mohamed Atta was there at the same time. From that moment Moussaoui became part of a small and secretive pool of recruits who would spread across Europe. Atta would later draw on this reserve after he formed the Hamburg cell. When Ramsi bin al-Shibh, with his suspect Yemeni background, failed to get a visa to join Atta, al-Shehhi and Jarrah on a flying course in America, Moussaoui, with his French passport and British residence, was the obvious choice to take his place as a pilot and ultimately, perhaps, as the twentieth hijacker.

Moussaoui and Atta travelled a similar road with their experiences in the West, but whereas Atta was shocked by the cultural shift he experienced in Hamburg, Moussaoui came to reject his adopted home in Britain more gradually. Both men, like so many hundreds of others, fell prey to the persuasive arguments of people on the look-out for converts to the cause of *jihad*. Just as Atta was recruited at the al-Quds mosque in Hamburg, so Moussaoui spent time in a religious community near Baker Street run by a militant Islamic teacher, and he is thought to have attended private tuition sessions at his tutor's home in Acton, west London.

I pulled my blue shawl closer over my forehead with a mixture of self-consciousness and annoyance as I approached the flaking front door of the semi-detached house. A few rusty cans, bottles and plastic carrier bags were scattered around the unkempt front garden. I had asked an Egyptian contact, a known sympathiser of Osama bin Laden and a suspected member of his organisation, whether I should be entirely covered for this meeting. 'It would be better,' came the response. My contact, Yasser al-Siri, had been arrested that morning, charged with involvement in the assassination of Ahmed Shah Masoud, the Afghan resistance leader, just days before the September 11 attacks – charges of which he was later cleared. I had seen the headlines on the *Evening Standard* hoarding by the tube station – 'Bin Laden's Man Seized' – and I hoped my meeting would still be on. Parliament was debating a new law in the wake of the hijackings to make it easier to detain militants who had for decades exploited British laws of freedom of expression. 'Londonistan', as French intelligence contemptuously called the community of militant exiles in the British capital, was getting jittery. The net was closing around the outspoken proponents of *jihad*, and the man I had come to meet had always been one of militant Islam's most fiery preachers.

Oman Mohamed Othman, better known as Abu Qatada, certainly cut a prominent figure as he opened the door and beckoned me to step inside with my crew and remove our shoes. Large and rotund, he was imposing in his long white robe. He had a luxuriant black beard and a definite presence despite his glowering look. Throughout the hours we spent at his house, somewhere above there were scuffles and whispers and a glimpse of black veil from Mrs Othman and her four young children.

We sat on the floor in a room lined with leather books, religious texts, as a large computer system whirred in the corner. A sixteen-year-old disciple of the cleric explained he was there to translate. He would give me only his first name, 'Amir' – because his parents disapproved of his connections with Abu Qatada's group, he said.

Abu Qatada understood all my questions perfectly and was capable of answering them in English, but preferred to watch me closely while Amir relayed his answers, explaining that his group believed in combat and preaching. Their creed was *Salafi*, based on the teachings of the first three generations of notables which followed the Prophet Mohamed, the proponents of the original, pure form of Islam.

'We are not modernist,' Amir explained softly, with a smile. That is an understatement. What Abu Qatada did not spell out was that his group has for many years been classed as an Algerian terrorist organisation by most European governments. The GSPC or 'Salafist Group for Call and Combat' has been banned in the UK since the Terrorism Act came into force in March 2001.

I had heard Abu Qatada's name muttered for some time by frustrated intelligence officers in the UK, France and the Middle East. In Israel and Jordan they were itching to get their hands on the cleric, who is wanted for involvement in terror attacks in the Christian, Jewish and Muslim Holy Land. I had been told everywhere that Abu Qatada issued the religious *fatwas* and rulings which provided cover for Bin Laden's murderous exploits. The word 'inspiration' was always used in connection with Qatada – his teaching and charismatic preaching had converted many young men to the cause of *jihad* and sent them on their way to the camps of Afghanistan. Abu Qatada is a bit of star in *jihadi* circles, with videos of his hate-filled sermons available under the counter of selected Islamic bookshops in Birmingham and London. Several of these videos were found in an apartment used by members of Mohamed Atta's Hamburg cell.

Abu Qatada's past is shrouded in mystery. He has used nine different aliases and three different dates of birth. He confirmed to me that he is Palestinian, was born on the West Bank and spent several years at university in Pakistan, where he studied Islamic law, during the years of *jihad* against the Soviets. Intelligence agencies say Abu Qatada met Bin Laden there, although the cleric denied this to me.

'I have never had an organisational role with Bin Laden. I respond to anyone who seeks my advice, be it Bin Laden or anyone else. I am an independent scholar,' he maintained. 'I have never met him, but if I had I would consider it a good thing, not something to be ashamed of. He is a good Muslim who responds to the cause of the nation of Islam.'

Abu Qatada was not shy in promoting his views about holy war to me, the views he taught in his classes. 'Only through *jihad* can our enemies be thwarted. We teach that only through *jihad* can Islam be proclaimed. It both protects the nation which Islam created and brings non-Muslim people to Islam.' It sounded as if this bringing of non-believers to Islam would not be entirely voluntary, more like the forced conversion of those vanquished in bloody battle. And who were the enemies of Islam? Could he be thinking of America?

'The reality we are witnessing is unequivocal proof that America is neither friendly nor impartial towards us. They are the enemy,' declared Abu Qatada emphatically. He enumerated America's familiar sins: its support of Israel, its military presence on the Arabian peninsula and its support – along with Britain – of sanctions against Iraq.

Despite his condemnation of Britain as America's lackey, London was the place where Abu Qatada chose to seek political asylum in 1994. He had been sentenced to life imprisonment for his part in terror attacks on cinemas and other targets in Amman, leading him to flee from Jordan. He was granted asylum with his family and began drawing on the largesse of the British welfare state. He received £322 a week in social security payments and £70 a week in 'disability' payments. Qatada, a hale and hearty-looking figure, claimed to be too ill to work while issuing blood-curdling *fatwas* which al-Qaeda interpreted as legitimising their murderous actions in East Africa and elsewhere.

The British view was that the evidence presented by Jordan was too vague to allow extradition to a country which practises the death penalty. Jordanian investigators gnashed their teeth, just like Egyptian investigators had over the protection Islamic Jihad suspects like Yasser al-Siri had enjoyed for years in London. But no one was more angry than the French, with their extensive knowledge of North African terror networks and their harsher approach which had driven many of the militants across the Channel to Britain.

Abu Qatada seemed safe in Britain to continue his preaching at The Four Feathers, a community centre not far from London's biggest mosque in Regent's Park, where he would give a sermon on Fridays after the main prayer at midday. A group of around one hundred young men would turn up and a few of them would be invited to his house afterwards, for more private discussions.

Throughout the 1990s Britain was a haven for fundamentalists. The emphasis on traditional liberties, the UK's generous welfare benefits and its legal system, with many built-in safeguards for defendants in which extradition hearings proceed at a snail's pace, all contributed to an atmosphere of tolerance bordering on indulgence. By February 2001, however, the warning signals about Islamic militancy in Europe were coming through loud and clear. Abu Qatada was picked up by the police in Operation Odin, the crackdown on militants in several countries suspected of planning the attack on the Christmas market in Strasbourg. The penniless cleric was found to have £180,000 in cash stuffed under his bed. British intelligence were well aware of his role as a religious authority in extremist circles. They knew too that there were recruiters who sent impressionable young men, fired up by Abu Qatada's rhetoric, on the well-worn routes to Afghanistan and Chechnya financed by Bin Laden. Yet the discovery of the money under the bed was still not enough to link him to specific offences. And so the cleric was released.

In their skirmishes with Islamic extremists, MI5, Britain's domestic security service, have had to rely on those who can infiltrate the tight-knit groups around them. One such agent was Reda Hussein, an Algerian who spent time undercover in mosques with a radical clientele and fiery preachers. He frequented the Finsbury Park mosque, an ugly red-brick building in north London where a one-armed imam with a sinister iron claw, Abu Hamza, regaled his congregation with anti-Western rhetoric. But when Reda tried to find out what Abu Qatada was up to, his experience put him off working as a spy for life.

Reda is an engaging man who sports a baseball cap pulled down low over his eyes, a legacy perhaps of his days undercover. He is passionate about the danger radical imams in London pose to the West and to moderate Arab regimes, and still shivers at the memory of the videos he has had to view in the course of his work. The Algerian terror groups, Qatada's GSPC and the GIA, relish appalling footage of massacres and their aftermath sprinkled with subtitles glorifying 'Soldiers for Allah'. The victims have suffered unspeakable atrocities in which the militants are seen to delight, dabbling in blood and showing off their handiwork.

In 1999 Reda Hussein would go twice a month to The Four Feathers to listen to Abu Qatada. 'He would stand on a box in front of the audience urging people to contribute to the Islamic holy war,' he told me. Some people would contribute up to £50. 'He said in his proclamations that it was legitimate for fighters engaged in *jihad* to kill women and children in countries like Algeria,' Reda went on. 'They were the families of security forces and they had a right to go to Paradise, according to Qatada.' Hussein was never invited back to the Acton house and his career as an undercover agent came to an abrupt end when one of Abu Qatada's bodyguards became suspicious of him and gave him a bad beating. 'The intelligence people, they do nothing about these dangerous extremists,' complained Hussein.

I had brought some pictures to my meeting with Abu Qatada. One was of Zacharias Moussaoui, whom investigators in America and Europe are convinced came to the cleric's private seminars in the same book-lined room in which we were now sitting. Other pictures were of individuals who had confessed to being part of Bin Laden's network in Europe and were known to have once been part of Abu Qatada's impromptu *jihad* circle.

Abu Qatada looked at the photos briefly, his face impassive. He said he didn't think he knew any of them, but added elliptically, 'I have no idea whether this man Moussaoui came here or not. Or these others. Many people come to my house and I solve their problems for them.'

'My house is open,' he declared. 'I simply talk about Islam, after which it is up to the individual to decide the correct way to implement what they have learned. I am very pleased that my videos circulate among Muslims and that they listen and benefit from them.'

In my conversation with Abu Qatada he complained long and loud about the activities of MI5, which he seemed to feel had behaved in an unsporting manner with him. He claimed they had threatened him when they arrested him the previous February. 'They said I should leave Britain, or they would tarnish my reputation,' he alleged. When I told a Whitehall contact that Abu Qatada was not happy with Her Majesty's Government's methods he silkily replied, 'Well, those chaps are bound to have made their message pretty clear.'

One militant who had thought himself safe in the UK had already had a rude awakening the morning I arrived at Abu Qatada's house. It was a message reinforced when a photographer from the Associated Press banged on the door demanding a picture of the occupant. In the confusion over the many Muslim names, addresses and aliases floating around in those fraught days after September 11, he had come to the wrong place looking for the arrested man. It was an omen and I could see that Abu Qatada was nervous, well aware that his would be the first name on the list of those to be detained when the new law came into effect a few days later. That law would authorise internment for people suspected of terrorist links but against whom nothing concrete could be proved.

The cleric was being called 'Bin Laden's European ambassador in London' by the authorities in Madrid, and a Spanish judge wanted to question him about his links with al-Qaeda agents in at least six different countries. 'I have to accept that I am a big target,' Qatada said resignedly as he showed me to the door, which was now fastened on its security chain. The man who had lived so cosily in west London under the noses of the security services was about to experience a change in his fortunes.

Just before Christmas 2001, Abu Qatada's sessions at the Fatima Centre in Shepherd's Bush, the venue which succeeded The Four Feathers when things got too hot in Baker Street, were abruptly cancelled. The bulky and unmistakable figure of Abu Qatada, frequently seen driving a large Ford Transit van through the streets of Acton, somehow gave his minders the slip. Leaving his family, including a new baby, to the mercy of the British social services system – which had done them so proud – Abu Qatada disappeared. For nine months he eluded capture while the press speculated that he was actually an MI5 agent. But then he was seized at dawn in a terraced house just a stone's throw from the Houses of Parliament. Abu Qatada now resides at Her Majesty's pleasure in Belmarsh Prison, where he faces an indeterminate stay under the new anti-terrorism laws.

In the wake of the September attacks Britain's intelligence services and their masters in Whitehall were forced to confront some real home truths, just as the CIA, FBI and other American government agencies had to face the implications of the massive failure of their intelligence-gathering.

Two days after the Twin Towers attacks an air of panic pervaded Whitehall as Moussaoui's London connections were revealed and a new detainee's name hit the papers. Lofti Raissi, an Algerian pilot, had been arrested on suspicion of helping train some of the hijackers. He lived right under the Heathrow flight path in west London. More and more names with a British connection would be revealed with each passing week, just at a time when MI5 and MI6 were stretched to breaking-point in heading off new attacks by Bin Laden.

In a central London bar a nervous Whitehall official looked exhausted. 'We never thought they would shit on their own doorstep,' he said, a reference to the unspoken pact that had governed the stand-off which had existed for years between the pursuers – the police and intelligence agencies – and the pursued, the Islamic militants. Britain's asylum laws were part of the reason for that stand-off, a traditional regard for human rights reflected in the country's legal framework. But there was also an unspoken policy in keeping with the *Realpolitik* practised over many decades with such skill by the Foreign and the Home Offices. The policy had been to keep things low-key, not pursue suspects with the more hard-line policies and more flexible attitude to the law that French security services and politicians had adopted.

Instead the extremists would be watched, and some pumped for information on attacks being executed elsewhere. A steady drip-feed of intelligence would flow, enabling the British to stay in the know and to foil other plots in the making. It may have been cynical and it intensely annoyed the intelligence services of many other countries, who were vocal in their complaints, but it had its successes.

In the days leading up to the September attacks another major al-Qaeda plot was in the process of being uncovered before it could be brought to its murderous conclusion. The

British security services played a large part in this, in concert with French, Belgian and other agencies. The plan had been to blow up the US Embassy in Paris on 13 September. At least six of those involved had lived in Britain at some point while the conspiracy was being hatched.

The plot was revealed by the 35-year-old French–Algerian, Djame Beghal, who had been arrested in July while travelling through Dubai with a fake passport. He had confessed his part in the plot in prison in the Emirates, apparently under pressure from Muslim clerics. Once extradited to France he changed his mind about what he had said, alleging torture. But it was too late. Beghal's confession had revealed a network of dozens of individuals who were rounded up in the UK, Spain, the Netherlands and France.

However, after the seismic collapse of the Twin Towers the public and press were not very interested in a foiled plot. The attack that had succeeded dominated everything else. And the big and uncomfortable political question was, why did no one do anything about the hardcore of individuals who inspired, recruited for and actively assisted al-Qaeda in Britain? Beghal himself had operated out of Leicester and London and was believed to have been a key organiser of the network. He had been another of the attendees at Abu Qatada's sessions.

The French have long been critical of the way Britain became a sanctuary for extremists, believing that the IRA held the attention of the British intelligence services to the detriment of other global threats. They claimed that their warnings about Islamic extremists, particularly from North Africa, and the many requests they sent to London to monitor certain individuals, were often ignored.

The famed anti-terrorist investigating judge Jean-Louis Brugière has been among the most insistent critics of the *entente cordiale*, if only in a discreet way. I had visited him several years ago in his fortress-like eyrie at the top of the Palais de Justice on the Ile St-Louis in Paris. He was protected by a phalanx of metal detectors and a succession of gendarmes sitting on hard wooden chairs. I was there to discuss Carlos the Jackal, one of his most celebrated cases in the days when Middle Eastern terrorists were Marxists and their rationale was somewhat different. The judge had shown me the gun he kept in his desk drawer, obviously revelling in his on-the-edge existence. The British were letting the side down then, in his view – and nothing seemed to have changed.

After September 11 Judge Brugière was again in the thick of it, responsible for the case against Djame Beghal, the biggest catch so far in Europe. The judge was smarting over the criticism that he had jeopardised the operation to catch the Paris embassy plotters identified by Beghal, because the French had held up the raids in order to build a legally bullet-proof dossier.

Judge Brugière was pointed in his remarks about the British security services and in particular the case of Zacharias Moussaoui, the would-be twentieth hijacker who had so nearly achieved his aim. He insisted that the British had been warned about Moussaoui's links with Islamic extremists.

'The danger is within, the threat is at home. Mr Moussaoui was known to British intelligence. He lived a long time in the UK,' he smoothly pointed out. 'You have to have operational information, a database on someone like him, and we had that kind of profile on Moussaoui.' He added that the Americans too had been advised by the French to keep a close eye on Moussaoui, presumably only after they had arrested the aspiring jet pilot. But Brugière conveniently ignored the fact that the French had issued three new passports in quick succession to a man of whom they were very suspicious – passports which enabled him to erase the evidence of his forays into Afghanistan.

The judge put the problems in the UK down to a lack of co-ordination. 'In the UK you have the intelligence services, MI5 and MI6. Then you have Scotland Yard which also has its intelligence arm. There is no bridge, no connection between the intelligence service and the police.'

While sniping across the Channel is a time-honoured tradition, there is no doubt that there has been poor co-ordination in recent years in Britain and not only between the intelligence agencies and the police, a problem often exacerbated by legal restraints. There have also been organisational problems between MI5, the domestic security service, and MI6, the Secret Intelligence Service, whose remit is global.

Until ten years ago there was a joint section, G7, which straddled the two services to co-ordinate counter-terrorism. Seven officers from each service and a back-up staff ran the unit. People who spoke the relevant languages and had the expertise worked closely together with successful results. 'Out of a clear blue sky,' I was told, came the order to disband, a result of the many and confusing turf-wars fought in Whitehall. MI5 felt they should have their own operation – they were not getting the right 'product' from MI6, 'The Friends' in Whitehall parlance, who were more preoccupied with the nuances of the Middle Eastern political scene than the nitty-gritty of which extremists posed a threat at home.

There was a breakdown in communication and an uneasy relationship replaced the camaraderie. Intelligence suffered in those crucial years just as al-Qaeda was expanding its operations. It is only in the past few years that there has been a determined attempt to build a strong working relationship again. It is now bearing fruit, according to insiders. But lead-times inside the intelligence community are long and the cogs turn slowly. Osama bin Laden, once again, found it easy to exploit the weaknesses he found in another Western bureaucracy.

17

The Muscle Arrives

'He had character, he had discipline, he was dedicated. He seemed timid but I could see he was competitive. I was teaching him to do what we all have to do, to blend into our society.'

—Bert Rodriguez, Ziad Jarrah's martial-arts teacher

Throughout the summer of 2001 Mohamed Atta moved up and down the coast of Florida, taking advantage of the shifting cultural kaleidoscope of the Sunshine State to lose himself among the holiday-makers and different ethnic communities there. He rented a series of short-stay apartments – sometimes with Marwan al-Shehhi, sometimes on his own. Number 122 Tara Gardens, Coral Springs, was a typical choice, pastel-coloured blocks set among palm trees and peaceful lawns. The manager of this apartment noticed nothing untoward about the well-dressed, polite but reserved Arab men who lived there.

Atta then moved on to Hollywood in Florida, less than two miles from where Ziad Jarrah had rented an apartment. Al-Shehhi took a smart flat at the Hamlet Country Club in Delray Beach. On his application form in the box marked 'residence' he wrote, 'None, I'm wandering.'

In May and early June a dozen other members of al-Qaeda arrived in various parts of Florida. These were the final members of the hijacking team. They came in ones and twos, via

Dubai and different parts of Europe, to avoid attracting attention. They were all Saudi Arabians with valid tourist visas
issued in their home country. Most importantly, they were
'clean skins' with no record of links to Islamic extremism. Five
listed addresses in Delray or Boynton Beach, two in
Lauderdale-by-Sea, two in the Bimini Hotel in Hollywood and
one in Pensacola. 'Nice kids', 'clean-cut', 'lots of hellos and
thank yous' were some of the remarks made about them by
their landlords. They spent time around the pool but would get
out and leave if other residents, especially young women, came
to swim.

Mohamed Atta moved between the new arrivals in a red
second-hand Pontiac he had bought. He was co-ordinating
their arrangements and ensuring they kept a low profile. Bin
Laden himself would later confirm that full details of the
mission were kept secret from most of the members of the
group.

It is clear there were three tiers of hijackers. First were the
'untainted' pilots from Hamburg, unknown to the CIA – al-
Shehhi, Jarrah and Atta himself, the overall commander, the
only man who knew the full details of the plot. The second tier
– the two San Diego-based al-Qaeda 'veterans', Khalid al-
Midhar and Nawaf al-Hazmi – were also a vital part of the
planning. Hani Hanjour, the Saudi, and Zacharias Moussaoui,
also unknown to the intelligence services, were both gearing up
during 2001 to become the fourth pilot and probably had limited knowledge of what would happen on September 11.

The third tier, which investigators quickly dubbed 'the
muscle', was comprised of the new arrivals from Saudi Arabia,
Bin Laden's homeland. They had been hand-picked by
Mohamed Atef, the head of al-Qaeda's military committee,
through a rigorous selection procedure. Each man had to have
a clean record and a high level of commitment followed by the
requisite training.

The twelve Saudis who joined the plot in its last few months
of planning all trained in Bin Laden's camps at various periods

in 1999 and early 2000. The CIA believes that Khalid al-Midhar, the Saudi operative running the California cell, may have played a pivotal role in gathering the 'muscle' together. He left America for just over a year, travelling to Saudi Arabia, the Yemen and Afghanistan and returning on 4 July, just after the last of the new group reached the States.

The Asir mountains in Saudi Arabia divide the coastal plain along the Red Sea from the vast desert of the interior of the Arabian peninsula. To the south lie the tribal lands of the Yemen, the birthplace of the Bin Laden patriarch and stronghold of his clan. To the north of Asir province lies the city of Jeddah, which became the home of Osama's family and the base of the construction company on which its wealth was founded.

Asir, a province of great natural beauty but lacking the oil riches that lie beneath the barren sands in the interior of the country, was the place which would foster the greatest number of the September 11 hijackers. Conservative and religious, in the Wahhabi mould, it was fertile recruiting ground for al-Qaeda, with its disaffected youth, many of them caught in the kingdom's recent economic downturn. There were fewer opportunities for them in the tougher job market of the late 1990s. And its universities, like others in Saudi Arabia, turned out many graduates who were poorly qualified for anything but religious studies of the most austere Islamic kind.

Many of the Saudi hijackers were part of an interconnecting web of young men, linked through family, mosque and college. They had all expressed a willingness to fight in the current *jihad*, the war in Chechnya; all were angry at the situation of their fellow Arabs, the Palestinians; all were ultimately open to Bin Laden's call to man the hijacked planes.

In Asir, in the town of Khamis Mushayt, a wealthy Peugeot dealer, Mohamed al-Shehri, had lost contact with his sons, both studying to be teachers. The oldest, Wail, had a mental illness and had gone to seek the guidance of a religious scholar in Medina. His youngest brother Waleed went with him.

Intelligence agencies would later discover that Wail had trained in Bin Laden's al-Farooq camp, a favoured destination for young Saudis who wanted to join the *jihad*. Wail followed a 1998 alumnus of that camp, Nawaf al-Hazmi, who would form part of the al-Qaeda vanguard at the flight school in San Diego. Nawaf's younger brother, 21-year-old Salem, who would board Flight 77 with him, had made his way to al-Farooq at the same time as Wail al-Shehri.

The face of Wail would later stare out from an FBI poster, a troubled young man in his early twenties with a sparse beard. Waleed, beside him, looks more solid. Both men wear the che- quered red and white *keffiyeh*, the Arab head-dress. Both men would board American Airlines Flight 11 with Mohamed Atta, the plane that ploughed into the North Tower of the World Trade Center. A few minutes behind them, on United Airlines Flight 175, would be another al-Shehri, possibly a relative, 28- year-old Mohand.

With the three men based in California – al-Midhar, al- Hazmi and Hanjour – the total number of Saudis involved in the terror attacks would be fifteen. Later, in the video found in Afghanistan in which Bin Laden discusses the September 11 hijackers, he pointedly boasts of the participation of various Saudi tribes from the south-west. It was a message to the ruling family and the Saudi elite, who have always looked down on the south-west's tribal culture, that he had strong support in these populous lands.

Mohamed al-Zulfa, a member of the Saudi ruling council who comes from the province of Asir, told the Saudi news- paper *al-Watan*: 'It looks as if he [Bin Laden] very carefully chose from the leading tribes as if to say, "This is not only me against the House of Saud and the US, it is also the new gen- eration of these tribes of Saudi Arabia that have joined this fight."'

'You can come up with theories about who these young men

were,' countered Adel al-Jubeir, a senior adviser on foreign affairs for the palace, 'but in the end they are fifteen individuals out of sixteen million Saudis. They do not represent a trend in Saudi Arabia, any more than David Koresh represented a trend in Christianity or Timothy McVeigh represented a movement in America.'

While Wail al-Shehri was training at al-Farooq, another Saudi youth, Abdulaziz al-Omari, was the imam at the camp who led the five daily prayer sessions. He would board AA Flight 11 alongside Atta and sit close to Wail al-Shehri in the cabin. Al-Omari came from al-Makwah, a town just north of Asir, and had studied at Mohamed bin Saud University. Another student from that university, Majed Moqed, would join the group. And there were other students, too: Satam al-Suqami, who studied at a university in Abhar, the capital of Asir; and Ahmed al-Nami, a graduate from the King Khaled Islamic Law School in the city.

Three other local youths, Ahmed al-Haznawi and Ahmed and Hamza al-Ghamdi, disappeared from Khamis Mushayt at the same time as the al-Shehri brothers. There were reports they were part of the same circle at the al-Seqly mosque. They would later turn up in Florida along with another al-Ghamdi, Saïd, who would board Flight 93.

Ahmed al-Haznawi prepared a 'martyrs' video in an al-Qaeda training camp in Afghanistan in March 2001. Wearing combat fatigues and a black and white *keffiyeh*, the young man with haunting eyes declaims, 'It is time to kill the Americans on their own ground, among their families and soldiers.' Waving his finger al-Haznawi emphasises again, 'The time of humiliation and enslavement is over, and the time has come to kill the Americans on their own turf.' A year later an image of the burning Trade Towers would be electronically added and the tape sent to al-Jazeera, the Arabic station chosen to distribute al-Qaeda's video propaganda.

At the end of June, the nineteenth and last hijacker to join the group emerged from his home in the United Arab Emirates at the same time as Bin Laden's mysterious money man, the Saudi-born Mustafa Ahmed al-Hawsawi, flew back to Dubai for the second time. Little is known about Fayez Benihamed, but US court papers reveal that on 25 June, just before Fayez left for the States, both he and Mustafa Ahmed opened checking accounts at the Standard Chartered Bank in Dubai. They were preparing a conduit for unused funds to flow back later into al-Qaeda coffers. Three weeks later Fayez Benihamed signed a document giving Mustafa Ahmed power of attorney over his account. With this the Saudi financier was able to collect a number of Visa cards in Benihamed's name and ship them to Florida on 1 August. These new credit cards would be used to purchase airline tickets in America.

The September 11 plotters lived either singly or in pairs, never appearing in public as a large group of foreigners. They used Mail Boxes Etc, an anonymous mailbox company, to collect their post. They frequented Kinko's, a chain of photocopy and stationery shops, to send their e-mails, or they visited local libraries and used the public computer facilities there. They brought no laptops or personal computers to the States which might contain valuable information if they were arrested. Mohamed Atta used the Internet anonymously to establish a communications channel back to Bin al-Shibh in Hamburg. He pretended to be a woman called Jenny using a chat room to talk in German, not Arabic, to a friend in Europe. He was using a code to co-ordinate the movements of others in the plot.

Senator Bob Graham acknowledges that the hijackers 'were able to plan to a level of sophistication that reduced to a minimum their need to communicate. Then our inability to intercept those few communications there were shows how out of sync our current intelligence capability is with the challenges we're facing.'

'They were very Internet-savvy, they could look for rental agencies out of the way, get apartment guides.' Bob Blitzer

believes that the mainstay of the American way of life, the
Information Superhighway, had helped them plan. 'There are a
lot of tools out there if you know where to look. The lead
people were sophisticated, they'd lived in the West in Germany
and travelled widely in Europe.'

Mohamed Atta was, however, taking risks travelling in his
red Pontiac all over Florida. On 26 April he was picked up by a
highway patrol car for speeding. He had no Florida driving
licence, so instead of just paying a fine he was booked by the
Broward County Sheriff's Office to appear in court. Five weeks
later the court date came and went. Atta had ignored the sum-
mons. A warrant was issued for his arrest but it was a mere
formality. Among the vast backlog of cases no one picked him
out, or came looking for him. The al-Qaeda manual stresses
the need to have all the right documents to hand to back up
operatives' cover story, and Atta quickly learned his lesson.
Within five days he had obtained a Florida driving licence; so
too had Ziad Jarrah, who was living less than two miles away.
Within the next few weeks six other hijackers would get their
Florida driving licences too.

Atta promptly sold his conspicuous red Pontiac, which was
now known to the police, and hired a succession of different
cars for the longer journeys he was starting to make. Just as he
had chosen Huffman Aviation, a flying school which asked few
questions as long as its students could pay, so Atta chose a
rental company which was not anxious to know what its clients
were doing.

The peeling blue sign outside on the sidewalk in Pompano
Beach announces 'Warrick Rent-A-Car, We Rent Cheaper!'.
Brad Warrick, the owner, is matter-of-fact about the secret of his
business success. 'I know a lot of criminals come here because
we're a little guy, out of the way and a lot less conspicuous
than going to a big place,' he stated. 'We don't have software in
our computer system that checks the background of drivers
like the major companies do.'

Atta had seemed the perfect customer – well-dressed, carrying a briefcase. Accompanied by his 'cousin' Marwan al-Shehhi he had rented three cars from Warrick in the space of a month. All his documents – his new Florida driving licence, his insurance and his credit cards – matched, according to Warrick.

'He didn't rent the best car we had, he rented the cheapest, a white Escort, then a blue Chevvy Corsair, then back to the Escort,' said Warrick. 'I noticed he put a lot of miles on the clock, 1,900 on one occasion just driving round Florida. Another time he told me he was going up to New York State.'

Warrick found that Atta left his hire cars scrupulously clean. The only item he ever discovered left behind was a scrap of paper with an Arab name and an address in Delray Beach scribbled on it. It was stuck to an ATM withdrawal slip from the SunTrust Bank in Florida. After September 11 both vehicles were sold to a dealer as 'notoriety cars', with one entrepreneur reportedly wanting to buy them so he could charge people to hit them with sledgehammers.

The 'muscle', the rest of the hijackers, had little to do except get themselves fit for their coming mission. They joined various health clubs in Boynton and Delray Beach, taking out short-term memberships for July and August only at $60 apiece. Ziad Jarrah, however, chose the US One Fitness Center in Dania, a busy professional gym frequented by law-enforcement and prison officers whose work demands strength and fitness.

'We call it "close-quarter aggressive and defensive tactics", and it's for people who have to be in control in difficult situations. This is what Ziad wanted to learn,' explained Bert Rodriguez, panting from his exertions with the gym's punch-bag. 'It entails everything from grappling to choking, to striking, to guns.' Shaven-headed, with a gold earring and thick cords of muscle running down his neck, Rodriguez is a formidably fit figure with a penchant for martial arts.

Ziad Jarrah's photograph and membership details were still in the computer when we visited the gym – Ziad smiling as usual, wearing his stylish glasses, clean-shaven with a towel slung round his neck. The explanation he gave was plausible. 'Ziad said he was a businessman and travelled a great deal and might get into awkward situations where he would need some self-defence tactics,' said Rodriguez.

Jarrah signed up for twenty classes, one-on-one, with Bert Rodriguez as his instructor. Of all the dozens of Americans who fleetingly came into contact with the hijackers Rodriguez was the only one who spent many hours of intense physical and psychological activity with one of the al-Qaeda members. Yet no chink appeared in Jarrah's armour. Bert Rodriguez was totally taken in by the polite Lebanese student who spoke with a heavy German accent and who admitted to a fear of heights which he said he had conquered by learning to fly.

Ziad Jarrah listened intently as Rodriguez explained that martial arts were not about power and strength, but about knowing the moves. Jarrah, fit, well co-ordinated and totally focused, practised diligently at home. He said he was teaching his new-found skills to some of his friends as well. 'He wanted to learn how, if someone attacked him, to stop them quickly – using as little effort as possible,' said Rodriguez. 'Although he was mild-mannered, putting on an air of timidity, I could see he was clearly very competitive, very disciplined.' Rodriguez now realises that he had unwittingly been teaching Jarrah to blend into someone's thoughts, to anticipate their physical moves; he had contributed to the Lebanese man's special skill in blending, chameleon-like, into the society around him.

As our interview ended Bert turned back to the floor of the gym. Stealthily and deliberately he demonstrated how he could disarm a colleague who was holding an ugly, long-bladed knife. I thought of Ziad Jarrah on Flight 93 on September 11, as a terrified passenger whispered into his mobile phone that hijackers, wielding knives, their heads bound in red bandannas, had seized control of the plane.

A curious incident which happened during the hijackers' time in Florida still puzzles investigators and raises worrying questions about the research Atta and others in the team were conducting into crop-spraying. In June, Ziad Jarrah and Ahmed al-Haznawi, the young Saudi who had already prepared his 'martyr' video, turned up at the emergency centre of the Holy Cross Hospital in Fort Lauderdale. Al-Haznawi was seeking treatment for an ugly lesion he had developed on his leg. He told Dr Chris Tsonas that he was a pilot and had bumped into a suitcase. Tsonas cleaned the wound, which was an inch wide with a black scab, and prescribed an antibiotic. The men left and the doctor thought nothing more about the incident.

After the September 11 attacks the United States became gripped with a new fear following the deaths of several people who had received letters laced with anthrax spores. FBI agents visited the Holy Cross Hospital and interviewed Tsonas, showing him pictures of the two hijackers, whom he identified as the individuals who had come to his clinic. Reading his own medical notes from the time Tsonas realised what the wound probably indicated. 'Oh my God – my written description is consistent with cutaneous anthrax,' he later told the *New York Times*. The FBI, however, who scoured all the locations and belongings associated with the hijackers after September 11, could find no trace of anthrax anywhere. Despite the doctor's testimony the authorities leaned towards the theory that the letters containing such a deadly biological agent were the work of a deranged scientist in the US, rather than al-Qaeda.

In March 2002, however, the revelation of the contents of a memo prepared by experts at the Johns Hopkins Center for Civilian Biodefense Strategies re-opened the debate. The memo, which drew on the Center's own interview with Dr Tsonas, concluded that the diagnosis of cutaneous anthrax, which causes skin lesions, was 'the most probable and coherent interpretation of data available'. It went on to say: 'Such a conclusion of course raises the possibility that the hijackers were . . . the perpetrators of the anthrax letter attacks.' Dr Tsonas believed the hijackers

did manage to get hold of anthrax: 'What were they doing looking at crop-dusters? There are too many coincidences,' he told
the *Times*.

The al-Qaeda manual outlines three stages of any operation:
research, planning and execution. The group were now about
to enter the final phase of their mission. The manual states: 'In
order to discover any unexpected element detrimental to the
operation, it is necessary to rehearse it in a place similar to that
of the real operation.'

And so the leaders of the teams took test flights in May, June,
July and a final one at the beginning of August, on various
routes across America from east to west. Exercising caution,
they did not take the actual flights they would hijack on
September 11. Al-Shehhi flew from JFK in New York to San
Francisco, Jarrah from Baltimore to Los Angeles, Atta from
Boston to San Francisco and Hani Hanjour from Dulles near
Washington DC to Los Angeles. On his trip, Mohamed Atta
tried to request access to the cockpit to test the airline's security
measures. He was politely but firmly turned down. The trips
enabled the men to determine that a Tuesday morning was the
least busiest time to fly, with fewer passengers to subdue and a
better chance the planes would keep to schedule. They also
worked out how long it would take to reach cruising altitude
and which seats in the first-class cabin would provide the eas-
iest access to the cockpit.

On 1 August the Hollywood actor James Woods was doing
what he normally did on the long flight home to Los Angeles
from Boston. He was watching people, trying to imagine who
they might be. Four men travelling together caught his eye
because of their strange behaviour. 'When the flight attendant,
who was a woman, came up to them, they literally ignored
her – like she didn't exist,' Woods later told Fox Television. The
men did not drink alcohol and seemed oddly detached. 'It was
as if you were at a nightclub and everyone is focused on the
singer,' said Woods, 'except four people in the room who are

doing something else, connecting only to each other . . . like guys who are undercover or on a mission.' Woods was so concerned he told the aircraft's first officer that he feared the men were going to hijack the plane. Both the first officer and a flight attendant later filed a report with the Federal Aviation Administration, but nothing further was done. After September 11 Woods contacted the FBI and learned that two of the men he had seen that day were members of the al-Qaeda hijack teams, one on Flight 175 and one on Flight 77.

Each of the return flights for the hijackers had layovers in Las Vegas, and the exact purpose of these stops still puzzles the FBI. Ziad Jarrah flew in ahead, on 25 June, to scout out the city. Atta arrived four days later with al-Shehhi and stayed for three nights at the EconoLodge, a run-down motel on the seedy end of Las Vegas Boulevard. Atta and Jarrah used a local Cyberzone Internet café to send urgent e-mails. Hani Hanjour, the Saudi flying student from the west coast, was there with Nawaf al-Hazmi. Their accomplice, Khalid al-Midhar, flew back at the beginning of July from the Middle East, suggesting further instructions were being relayed to the team in Las Vegas. A flurry of activity now ensued. The cell was entering the final countdown to the terror attacks.

The various meetings in Las Vegas would most likely have been to co-ordinate the attacks on the chosen targets or to decide who would be the pilot of the fourth plane. Moussaoui was running into trouble with his lessons in Oklahoma and Hani Hanjour's flying skills were poor. Investigators also believe the Las Vegas summit may have been called by Atta to allow all the team leaders to meet, well away from Florida and San Diego. They could discuss the layout of the planes and decide which seats to book to give them the best lines of sight of each other and the cockpits.

Atta, according to US court documents, then set off to Madrid, via Zurich, on 7 July. He spent four hours at Zurich airport where he bought what might have seemed, to the casual observer, typical Swiss souvenirs – chocolates and two Swiss

Army knives. It is believed he was trying to see if the knives would be detected by the airline's security system.

Once in Spain he travelled extensively, clocking up more than a thousand miles on his rental car in just a few days. He was seen meeting three Arabs in the resort town of Salou. Hotel records confirm Atta's presence there and it is known that his old flatmate from Hamburg, Ramsi bin al-Shibh, also travelled to Salou at this time.

This late trip of Atta's to Spain, where al-Qaeda maintained an extensive network, is still a mystery. Its timing, so close to the attacks, would suggest that last-minute instructions from Afghanistan were handed over by Ramsi bin al-Shibh. It must have been important as Atta's new, six-month, visa issued in January after his grilling by the immigration service had by now run out, and he was running a big risk in going back into Miami on 18 July. However, this time he was unchallenged by the INS.

Ziad Jarrah flew back to Germany for a week to see his girl-friend Aysel Senguen. It was to be the last time they saw each other, but he gave no hint of it. The couple were due to attend another family wedding back in Beirut on 22 September and Ziad phoned his uncle in the Lebanon for a chat. 'Ziad was his usual sociable self,' Jamal Jarrah confirmed. 'He said he had bought a new suit for the occasion, in the States. We were joking about giving the car we were saving for his and Aysel's wedding to his cousin instead.' There would be no Ziad at the family get-together in September, and no wedding for Aysel and her Lebanese boyfriend.

In the Emirates, Marwan al-Shehhi's family had grown concerned at his estrangement from them. Seven months had passed since he had last been home and they had no idea he had been to the United States, let alone learned to fly. On his last visit, Marwan had given in to their wishes and married a local girl. But he had refused to live with her, and after a few weeks vanished again. The family contacted the government, which had sponsored his studies in Germany. They began to make discreet inquiries. 'By contacting his friends in Germany we did know that he had some close relations with people linked to radical Islamic groups,' Sheikh Abdullah told me, 'but we did not know then that it was Bin Laden or anyone linked with Bin Laden.' The al-Shehhi family would still be looking for their son on September 11.

18

Countdown to Zero Hour

'I don't think anyone could have predicted that these people ... would try to use an airplane as a missile, a hijacked plane as a missile.'

—Condoleezza Rice, May 2002

On 6 August 2001 George W. Bush was on vacation on his ranch in Crawford, Texas. A photo shows him in a Stetson hat and open-necked shirt, leaning on a fence. The President is smiling, relaxed, while an aide, sweating in a suit beside him, shuffles awkwardly. But the holder of the most powerful office in the world is never truly on holiday and that day was no exception. Bush had just finished going through his PDP, the Presidential Daily Briefing. It made for worrying reading with its headline, 'Bin Laden determined to strike in US', and its analysis that al-Qaeda hoped to 'bring the fight to America'.

The briefing memo was the result of Bush's request in July to Condoleezza Rice, the head of the National Security Council, for a summary of possible attacks by al-Qaeda within the United States. Most of the 'chatter' in the intelligence system that summer had revolved around threats to US interests abroad, but it prompted the President to look at the risks at home as well. He would have been shaken by information received from Italian intelligence that al-Qaeda had been thinking of targeting him and other world leaders, using missiles, at a recent G8 summit in Rome. The President's aides were beginning to work on a strategy for dealing with al-Qaeda.

The Bush administration was conscious that it had taken its eye off the ball since assuming office seven months previously. Clinton's outgoing NSC Director, Sandy Berger, had warned Rice she would be spending most of her time on al-Qaeda, but under a new Republican Attorney General the FBI had focused more on violent crime and drugs than terrorism. Over at the Pentagon, the Defense Secretary had decided not to relaunch a surveillance plane that had been tracking Bin Laden in Afghanistan. A request to plough $800 million more into counter-terrorism had been vetoed and the money diverted into the new pet project, missile defence. Nothing had yet been done about tackling al-Qaeda despite the FBI's belief that they had clear evidence linking the organisation to the bombing of the USS *Cole*.

Rice later said that the page-and-a-half presidential briefing was 'not a warning' but more 'analytic' and 'historic' and only focused on 'hijacking in the traditional sense'. It contained information, which had first originated from British intelligence in 1998, that al-Qaeda members had discussed a hijacking to force the release of the blind Sheikh. Omar Abdel Rahman was still languishing in an American jail for his part in the plot to blow up New York City landmarks. 'I don't think anybody could have predicted that these people . . . would try to use an airplane as a missile, a hijacked plane as a missile,' Rice later claimed.

Moussaoui would be arrested ten days later but the information on his case was never forwarded to the NSC or Rice, who was ultimately the President's chief adviser on the threat posed by terror. And, as we have seen, the FBI Phoenix memo, already in existence, had been filed under 'routine' rather than 'urgent'. Neither was there mention in the briefing of the Philippines report on the suicidal pilot, Murad, nor the planned airborne attack on the Eiffel Tower by Algerian militants. The President was left with only a 'vague' impression, Rice conceded, of terror threats at home. No one was connecting the dots and no one issued a warning to airlines or the American public.

While the President was on his ranch the three Saudis who had been living in San Diego, Hanjour, al-Midhar and al-Hazmi, drove across America in their blue Toyota Corolla to Maryland on the east coast. They were joined there by two of the recent Saudi arrivals, Majed Moqed and Salem al-Hazmi. Room 343 of the Valencia Motel in Laurel became the staging-post for those who would hijack American Airlines Flight 77 on its departure from nearby Dulles airport and fly it into the Pentagon.

Gail North, the motel's housekeeper, said the five men would only open the door a crack to pass out dirty towels and receive clean ones. They were living cheaply, paying a weekly rate of $280 plus tax for one bedroom, a kitchenette and a tiny living area. Still, she noticed they always appeared in well-pressed khaki trousers and button-down shirts, different from the other, more seedy residents of the motel. By now they were being extra careful, paying their bills in cash distributed to them by Atta, who was using money orders drawn on a store in Punta Gorda called The Shipping Post and ferrying it from Florida to Maryland.

Despite their caution, there were setbacks in the final weeks before the attacks: yet more clues as to their existence. Each time they overcame them. Hani Hanjour got a ticket for speeding on 1 August in Arlington, Virginia, close to his target, the Pentagon, which no doubt he was busy sizing up, as the al-Qaeda manual recommends be done, exhaustively, with every target.

Conscious of the brush with the law that Atta had already had, the group in Laurel decided to get their own identification documents. Again they had tested the US system and found its weak spot, right there in Virginia. A loophole in the local law allowed non-Virginia residents to obtain licences on production of a form notarised by a third party.

There were always a few shady characters hanging around

the Department of Motor Vehicles, who, for the appropriate fee, would provide a signature to confirm that the applicant lived in Virginia. One such man signed forms for Hani Hanjour, Salem al-Hazmi and Majed Moqed, who would strike the Pentagon, and later Ahmed al-Ghamdi and Abdulaziz al-Omari, hijackers aboard the planes which hit the World Trade Center.

By now, another staging-post had been established, near Newark airport in New Jersey, from where UA Flight 93 would leave on September 11.

Patterson, NJ is the archetypal American melting-pot, the home to 170,000 people from over fifty different countries. As you wander down the streets, Middle Eastern spices, Chinese laundry steam and snatches of unfamiliar, plaintive music assail you on all sides. The hijackers blended in here seamlessly, their lack of English hardly noticeable. After the attacks their landlord, a Syrian–American, could remember little about them apart from their pleasant manner and their fondness for doughnuts and Chinese food. At least six of the hijackers lived in the apartment at some point. Mohamed Atta made his last trip up from Florida, using a rental car from Warrick's, to check on his Patterson crew.

There was now less than a month to go to the day of the attacks. For Atta in particular, the only man aware of the timing and probable outcome of the plan, the arrest of Zacharias Moussaoui on 16 August would have been an enormous blow.

Despite the links to the September 11 plot, highlighted in the US Justice Department indictment of Moussaoui, there is still no absolute certainty that he was to have been the twentieth hijacker. His financial and communication links to the Hamburg cell, in the wake of Ramsi bin al-Shibh's failure to get a US visa, plus the involvement of Mustafa Ahmed in the money chain, make that a strong likelihood. Moreover, the first three planes would take off with five al-Qaeda men on board, suggesting that the fourth plane, with only four, was destined to have one more person. However, Moussaoui may have been part of a second wave of attacks, designed to follow September 11, perhaps involving the crop-dusting scenario he was so avidly researching.

Moussaoui's luggage yielded up some interesting articles: binoculars and flight manuals, a notebook with Bin al-Shibh's telephone number, and a hand-held aviation radio. There were fighting gloves and shin guards in his car, and two knives. And yet with these alone the FBI could not convince their lawyers to allow them to break into the detainee's computer. If they had, they would have uncovered a flight simulator program, software explaining Boeing 747 procedures and a computer disk containing information about the aerial application of pesticides.

Despite the arrest of Moussaoui and the danger of discovery, Mohamed Atta kept his cool, displaying the usual meticulous attention to detail. All nineteen men still had to buy their plane tickets without arousing suspicion. The targets had been chosen, the flights to get there had now been settled on.

On 22 August Ziad Jarrah walked into a store in Florida and purchased antennae and equipment for a GPS, a handheld Global Positioning System. And according to US court documents he bought 'the schematics for a 757 cockpit instrument diagram'.

Following Jarrah's footsteps led to Tropic Aero, in Fort Lauderdale, the town in Florida where Ziad Jarrah lived during the last weeks before the attacks. Jerry Carbone, the helpful owner of the store, admitted he had a 'couple of hits' with the names the FBI gave him to run through his database. He was enthusiastic about one of his top-selling items, the handheld GPS.

'With a GPS you can pre-programme it before you get on the plane,' Carbone explained, 'then once on board you switch it on, let it lock on to the satellite system above the earth and tell it, "I want to go to a certain spot." And it will tell you the bearing, distance, time and how to get from your present position to anywhere else in the world.' It was perhaps ironic that of all the pilots, Ziad Jarrah, the model flying student with the martial-arts training and disarming manner, who had equipped himself with the state-of-the-art GPS, would be the one who failed to achieve his mission on September 11. Flight 93 crashed before reaching its intended target.

On the same day Jarrah bought his GPS, Fayez Benihamed used his Visa card in Florida to obtain nearly $5,000 in cash. It had been deposited in his account in Dubai the day before by the indefatigable Mustafa Ahmed. Over the next seven days the hijackers would buy their tickets, singly and in pairs, by cash, credit card and over the Internet. Investigators would later discover that the co-ordination was so thorough that each of the four hijacking teams had its own bank account and each team's cash card used a single PIN number.

On 25 August Mohamed Atta, using his own name, opened a frequent-flier account on the American Airlines website, perhaps to allay any suspicions which might be aroused when three days later he bought one-way tickets for himself and Abdulaziz al-Omari. It seems incredible now that so many young men could buy one-way tickets on the same four flights, just days before, without any checks being carried out. Some of the tickets were paid for in cash and several were bought on the same credit card, but still no alarms were raised.

'One of the deficiencies is we had two levels of security – a very heightened level for international travel and a much lower level for domestic travel,' David Stempler, President of the Air Travellers' Association, later admitted. 'By paying cash for one-way international travel it sets off all kinds of alarm bells, but in domestic transportation it just doesn't.'

It seems hard to believe, given the warning bells that sounded within the US aviation industry prior to the September 11 attacks, that there could be such complacency. In the spring and summer of 2001, as a 'major spike' in threats from al-Qaeda was noted in the American intelligence community, there were a number of warnings issued to US airlines flying foreign and domestic routes. The Federal Aviation Administration (FAA) received fifteen notifications of threats to American airlines from terrorists between June and September 2001, at least one of them specifically mentioning hijacking, and passed them on to the airlines. In July one of the alerts, known as ICs, or Information Circulars, focused on domestic airports when Ahmed Ressam, the man foiled in his attempt to bomb Los Angeles airport by a vigilant customs officer on the Canadian border, appeared in court. 'An airport is sensitive politically and economically,' Ressam stated. There was a further warning to the FAA, from the FBI this time, in mid-August after the arrest of Zacharias Moussaoui. The alert centred on his interest in learning to fly a Boeing 747 but the FAA did not pass it on to the airlines because they felt they did not have enough information to warrant issuing an advisory notice. Yet again in the puzzling Moussaoui case, no one 'joined up the dots', as an FBI agent put it.

Once the tickets had been bought the teams moved into their final positions in the last few days before September 11. Atta and al-Shehhi's groups made their way to hotels in Boston. Jarrah's team took rooms at the Marriott Hotel at Newark airport and Hani Hanjour and his team remained in Maryland, close to Dulles airport. Hanjour was now confirmed as the fourth pilot, perhaps by the removal of Moussaoui from the scene. Hanjour was known to be the weakest link in the chain. He was the only one to risk last-minute flying lessons, at a local airfield close to Washington. This would have enabled him to make a final aerial reconnaissance of his target, the Pentagon. His instructor later remarked on his poor flying skills but paid no more attention to the clearly nervous but friendly young Saudi.

Back in Europe, in Hamburg, the birds had flown the coop. Ramsi bin al-Shibh left on 5 September using money sent to him from Dubai. He flew to Madrid again and on to Pakistan, and then disappeared over the Afghan border, back to the al-Qaeda leadership which had sent him to Germany three years before. Saïd Bahaji, the computer expert, who ran the prayer room at the Harburg Technical University with Atta and signed the lease on 54 Marienstrasse, had flown out three days earlier, bound for Karachi and a Bin Laden guesthouse. His wife and young son were abandoned in Hamburg.

The last man to leave his base was Mohamed Atta. As the cell commander he had the responsibility to obey the good housekeeping rules of al-Qaeda, the return of unspent funds to be used in future operations. A number of last-minute wire transfers were arranged in his own name and the names of two other hijackers, and then, spreading the risk yet again, Atta packed up a last bundle of cash in an envelope and went down to Kinko's store. On 4 September he sent the package, by Federal Express courier, to 'Almohtaram', the 'respected one', in Dubai.

I picked up the trail of Mustafa Ahmed again, in the Emirates, this time in the sprawling, dusty and traffic-choked centre of Sharjah. It was no accident that Bin Laden's money man chose Sharjah to risk a personal appearance on the morning of September 11 local time – still the dark hours, before dawn, in America, where the hijackers were completing their final preparations.

Although it is just twenty minutes' drive from Dubai's designer shopping malls, Sharjah is one of the most conservative of the seven Emirates, where the puritan Wahhabi sect of Islam dominates. Alcohol is forbidden, strict dress codes are enforced and the only shopping mall here is a vast Islamic supermarket designed like a mosque, a kind of cross between a mausoleum and a railway station.

Outside the al-Ansari money exchange, off the al-Arouba thoroughfare, one out of twenty-eight branches in the UAE and the one which Mustafa Ahmed chose, a crowd of expatriate workers milled around on the day I visited. It was Friday, the weekend, and Pakistani labourers and Filipino housemaids had come to wire money home, through the money exchange, via Western Union. Inside the exchange branch manager Abdul

Jaleel wearily told me that about two dozen international money transfers were processed there each day. 'It just takes seconds and we only require ID that proves this is the person who is to collect the money. How can we trace it?' Jaleel demanded.

'Just look at the timing,' Sheikh Abdullah, the UAE Information Minister, told me. We were sitting in the sumptuous hotel suite in Dubai in early November, as the Emirates authorities and FBI investigators were unravelling Mustafa Ahmed's last known movements. 'He collects the cash, around $5,000 from each of three hijackers. Within hours he's on a plane for Pakistan, just as the terror attacks are beginning to unfold.' The Sheikh was clearly much taken with his role as amateur sleuth. 'I would hardly call it a coincidence,' he concluded.

It was no coincidence either that, on that same day, Mustafa Ahmed, using his power of attorney, collected the last remaining $8,055 in the account of the young Emirates hijacker, Fayez Benihamed. Gathering together all the cash from the hijackers in America, the bagman transferred it to the Visa card connected to his own Standard Chartered Bank account before closing it.

And so the industrious Mustafa Ahmed flew out of Dubai, with no loose ends behind him, all al-Qaeda's funds gathered safely in. Instead of the $40,781 cash in his briefcase, which would have drawn attention to him had he been stopped, he had only a small square of plastic in the pocket of his robe.

19

The Last Night

'When the hour of reality approaches, the zero hour, whole-heartedly welcome death, for the sake of God. Say a prayer before you hit the targets.'

—Document found in Mohamed Atta's luggage,
11 September 2001

On the morning of Sunday 9 September Jan Shineman, checking in for Flight 11 to Los Angeles at Logan, Boston's international airport, noticed a man behaving oddly. He was staring at her and seemed out of place among the soberly dressed Boston crowd. 'He was wearing summery, holiday-type clothes, like you would see in Florida, and he had no baggage, just a folder with a notebook,' recollected Shineman, a smartly dressed businesswoman with a blonde bob.

She described the man as 'aloof, an intense expression on his face, with very penetrating eyes': an echo of the way a woman flying student at Huffman had described a fellow pupil. Then Shineman saw the man again, at the gate for Flight 11. 'He was taking notes, watching the pilots in the cockpit through the window by the gate. They were running through their pre-flight checks,' she said. On arrival in California she told two friends about her experience and how strange the man had been. 'I told them that if he had got on my flight I would have told the captain about him, he was so odd.' But he did not board Jan

Shineman's flight, at least not that day. Two days later, watching
television as the first pictures of the hijackers were shown,
Shineman realised it was Mohamed Atta she had seen.

No one else at Boston airport seems to have noticed Atta's
activities at the gate. Until September 11 anyone, not just passengers, was allowed to wander down to the very entrance to
the plane in US airports. Massachusetts Port Authority had
long been criticised for lax security at Logan. It had the fifth
highest number of security violations recorded by the FAA, the
Federal Aviation Administration, between 1991 and 2000.

A phone message from Ziad Jarrah would later be recovered from Atta's mobile. It was received that day, 9 September,
and referred to the Egyptian as 'the boss'. The next day Atta
was in New York. Investigators would later determine he had
used his credit card in Manhattan that day and one agent told
the *New York Daily News* that he believed Atta had visited the
public observation deck at the top of the World Trade Center to
get a 'fix' on his target. Atta is thought to have had a Garmin
GPS 111, a global positioning satellite device similar to the one
Jarrah had just bought. It seems likely that, having plugged in
the start-point co-ordinates at the gate in Boston airport, where
Shineman saw him, Atta then travelled to his ultimate destination to enter the final waypoint into the machine to allow him
to pre-plan the jet's final approach.

Later that day Atta, accompanied by Abdulaziz al-Omari,
drove their rented blue Nissan north to Portland, Maine. No
one knows why they separated from the main group of hijackers
waiting in Boston. It may have been to reduce the numbers of
Arabs checking in at Logan airport at the same time. They were
probably obeying the al-Qaeda manual's instruction to always
'board at secondary stations' to avoid attracting attention.

The two men checked into the Comfort Inn, but there was to
be little comfort for them that final night. CCTV cameras
caught images of them aimlessly wandering the local strip of
twenty-four-hour convenience stores and petrol stations.

At 8:41 P.M. the camera on a bank machine caught al-Omari's

face in a series of four stills. First in serious mode, punching in
the code, Mohamed Atta watchful and grim-faced behind him;
then wryly grimacing at his leader and finally smiling broadly
as he turned away. Later, pundits would cite this final picture
as proof that Abdulaziz al-Omari had no knowledge of his
impending death.

At 9:15 P.M. Atta, in a distinctive polo shirt, two-thirds black,
one-third white, filled the car with petrol. And finally, seven
minutes later, a camera in the ceiling of a Wal-Mart store
showed him strolling the aisles, buying batteries. Atta and al-
Omari then returned to the Comfort Inn to spend their last
night on earth preparing for their mission.

A five-page, handwritten document in Arabic would later be
discovered in a bag belonging to Mohamed Atta. Other copies
were found in a car belonging to the hijackers at Dulles airport
and in the wreckage of Flight 93.

It is clearly written for the group taking part in the September
11 attacks, but the document is not a detailed guide as to how to
carry out the hijacks; indeed, it makes a vague attempt at obfus-
cation. This must have been done in case the document was
discovered before the planes took off. No mention is made of the
targets and letters substitute for names and places; 'M' is used
for *matar*, or airport, and 'T' for *ta'irah*, or plane.

It is likely, but not certain, that the pages were written by
Atta, as the commander of the group. It divides the operation
into three phases and it reads like a medieval devotional
manual. It quotes the experiences of the 'forefathers', the first
generations after the Prophet. The hijackers are reminded of the
great battles of Islam in the past and assured of an even more
glorious afterlife awaiting them.

Some Islamic commentators have interpreted the writing as
confirming the group's adherence to the extremist *takfiri* sect,
with its fervent prayers to God to give 'victory over the infidels'. There are passages on the evils of Western culture and
admonitions to slaughter the 'unbelievers' as if they were animals, as an offering to God.

The object of the work is to stiffen the resolve of the hijackers, to make sure they act as a committed, tightly-knit group, with no last-minute qualms about their own impending deaths, or the deaths of their victims. The tone is one of exhortation reaching levels of religious ecstasy in places. The hijacking mission to destroy the World Trade Center and the Pentagon is likened to the ten-year period of state-building between 622 and 632, by the Prophet Mohamed himself: 'Remember the battle of the Prophet . . . against the infidels, he went on building the Islamic state . . . consider that this is a raid on a path. As the Prophet said, "A raid . . . on the path of God is better than this World and what is in it."'

The first part of the document is headed 'The Last Night', which is to be spent in prayer and undergoing various rituals. There should be 'a mutual pledge to die and a renewal of intentions' to carry out the mission. Ritual washing should take place, the shaving of excess hair, and the application of perfume to the body. There is a final list of practical requirements. The men are reminded to check their bag, passport and knives and, specifically, to sharpen their blades. There are stern instructions to 'forget that thing which is called the World. The time for amusement is over and the time of truth is upon us.'

Near Dulles and Newark airports on the night of 10 September the other teams of hijackers would have been reading the same document, praying and following the prescribed rituals to screw their courage to the sticking point. It is likely the remaining group in Boston with Marwan al-Shehhi also had a copy.

In Dubai, where al-Shehhi came from, I talked about the suicide mission with HRH Sheikh Abdullah bin Zayed, the Information Minister, and member of the ruling family. He was utterly bewildered. 'I can't believe that nineteen people were aware they were going to die and that none of them disappeared in the last days before the attack or at least gave some hint of what was to happen.' He preferred, like many Muslims, to believe that some of the young terrorists were lured unwittingly to their deaths by Bin Laden.

However, Osama bin Laden himself, in the video discovered after the attacks, made it clear that all of the men knew they were on a 'martyrdom mission'; it was the targets, the exact details of the plan, that not all of them knew about. Bin Laden went on to tell the unidentified Sheikh, 'They were trained, but we did not reveal the operation to them until they [were] there . . . just before they boarded the planes.' In the light of this it would seem the document entitled 'The Last Night' played an important part in revealing the mission in full to the whole team, and exhorting them to face their own deaths without wavering.

Previous suicide bombers – Bin Laden's own teams and the Palestinian foot soldiers of Hamas and Islamic Jihad – have performed their missions singly or in pairs. Suicide squads are high-maintenance. They need to be kept close to their targets, physically and psychologically, to avoid a last-minute change of heart. It is rare for them to be more than a short bus or taxi ride away before the mission. Often they are encouraged to make a video to leave behind to explain their actions to their families. So far only a tape made by Ahmed al-Haznawi has emerged, not intended for his grieving family when he died but held back for seven months after the attacks to be released as part of an al-Qaeda propaganda exercise. To this day all of the hijackers' families cannot comprehend what happened to their sons and many of them continue to deny their children were involved. Isolating the Saudi 'muscle' in a hotel room with committed leaders, the pilots and one or two others in each group, plus an inspirational religious text, may have been the way al-Qaeda ensured there were no last-minute changes of heart.

It seems to have been Mohamed Atta whose fanaticism and undoubted strength of character managed to conquer not only his own fear but to keep eighteen other people on the path to the very end, even in the last days when they were hundreds of miles apart. Some of them – Atta himself, al-Shehhi and Jarrah, al-Midhar and al-Hazmi – had lived with the knowledge they would die for at least eighteen months. But the document would have been most valuable in steadying the nerves of the 'muscle', the more recent Saudi recruits.

That night Ziad Jarrah, alone among the hijackers, wrote a note to a loved one, his girlfriend Aysel Senguen back in Germany. 'I am what you wish me to be but unfortunately you have to wait a bit longer until we can be together again,' he wrote, even now being evasive about the truth of his situation. 'I did not escape from you but I have done what I had to do. You should be proud of me, for this is an honour.' To the end, Jarrah displayed the smiling mask, hiding the killer. 'Keep your chin up, stay strong and do what you always wanted to do.' He could not even be honest with the girl he had callously left behind to pick up the pieces of her shattered life.

The 'second step' of the operation was described in the 'Last Night' document as beginning when the hijackers made their journey to the various airports to board the planes. Atta and al-Omari made that journey by catching a connecting flight from Portland to Boston at 5:45 A.M. on Tuesday, 11 September. A camera caught them passing through the security machine, smartly dressed, relaxed, unhurried. They were obeying the document's injunction 'do not seem confused or show signs of nervous tension; be happy, optimistic, calm'. A year later the Director of the FBI would tell Congress that Atta had run the perfect terror operation. 'There were no slip-ups. Discipline never broke down,' Robert Mueller ruefully admitted. 'They gave no hint to those around them what they were about. They came lawfully, they lived lawfully. They trained lawfully. They boarded the aircraft lawfully. They simply relied upon everything from the vastness of the Internet to the openness of our society to do what they wanted to do without detection.'

Mohamed Atta's religious exhortation had promised the religious warriors that 'all their equipment and gates and technology will not prevent, nor harm, except by God's will'. The security machine failed to pick up the craft knives, or 'box-cutters', that the men were carrying. And if it had done, it is unlikely they would have been stopped; any knife with a blade under four inches long was allowed on board American planes before September 11.

Atta and al-Omari made it to Boston's Logan airport with only minutes to spare to board AA Flight 11. Not all their luggage arrived in time. Atta's case containing the 'Last Night' document, the will he had drawn up at the al-Quds mosque and a copy of the Qur'an, would be discovered later that day. There were also jet simulator manuals and videotapes of Boeing layouts inside the bag.

All five hijackers sat in First or Business Class, with Atta in seat 8D. There were eighty-one passengers and eleven crew members aboard AA Flight 11. Behind, on another plane on the tarmac, was the faithful Marwan al-Shehhi, shadowing Atta to the end. There were sixty-five passengers and crew aboard United Airlines Flight 175 to Los Angeles, including the five hijackers. Both jets were Boeing 767s loaded to capacity with fuel for their cross-country flights; time-bombs in the hands of al-Qaeda.

The last words between the two friends who had travelled together so far, from Germany to Afghanistan and America, were spoken on their mobile phones, minutes before Atta's plane took off shortly after 8:00 A.M. Authorities say the call was to confirm that the mission was going ahead. In a few minutes American Airlines Flight 77, a Boeing 757 travelling from Dulles to Los Angeles, would also take off. Delayed on the ground for forty minutes, the fourth plane would finally depart at 8:42. It was another Boeing 757, United Airlines Flight 93 from Newark to San Francisco.

The 'third phase' outlined in the document of exhortation had begun: 'Pray for yourself and your brothers that they may be victorious and hit their targets.' There are instructions to clench the teeth before battle, as the early generations did, and to 'strike like champions who do not wish to return to the world'. This section of the document leaves no room for doubt

that those for whom it was written knew they were on a suicide mission. Its whole content revolves around the glories of
martyrdom, its rationale is to keep the reader focused on the
imminent moment of death, which he has chosen. The lure of
Paradise is lyrically described in terms of the many virgins,
the sexual pleasures, that will be their reward. 'Know that the
gardens of paradise are waiting for you in all their beauty and
the women of Paradise are waiting, calling, "Come hither,
friend of God." They have dressed in their most beautiful
clothing.'

Many Islamic scholars have reacted with horror to this document, with its justification of martyrdom for those who kill
civilians. 'The idea that martyrdom is a pure act of worship,
pleasing to God's specific command, is a terrifying new kind of
nihilism,' Hassan Mneihmeh and Kanan Makiya pointed out in
the *New York Review of Books*. For Western intelligence and law-
enforcement agencies the 'nihilism' of the mass suicide mission
signals a new phase in terror tactics which makes the war they
are waging ultimately unwinnable. For what sanction can there
be against people prepared to give up their lives and to engineer such ingenious, diabolical ways to do so?

Mohamed Atta's father, in Egypt, reacted angrily when
asked what could have made his son become the leader of a
suicide squad. He was still in denial about the role Atta played
in the massacre, still ranting about Israel and America's responsibility for the growth of terror. Nevertheless, he acknowledged
the tremendous strength of his own child's willpower and in a
sudden outburst he came closest to defining the real story of his
troubled son's life.

'Without oppression, terrorism cannot exist. How then are
terror groups formed?' he demanded. 'One person convinces
another, who convinces another, and another, of a valid reason
to destroy himself, even though life is the most precious possession a person has. It means this person dies because of his
deep-rooted conviction; he does not care about his own life.'
Atta senior was unwilling to complete the thought; in not

caring for his own life the terrorist foot-soldier is just the vehicle for his master's plan – the taking of so many innocent lives.

Fifteen minutes after take-off the hijackers on Flight 11 struck, wielding their knives. No one knows how many crew or passengers they killed but Atta was able to seize the controls of the plane and turn it south, towards Manhattan. The final words of his document, couched in that most poetic of languages, Arabic, echo in the memory. Those words reveal the extent of Mohamed Atta's fanaticism, his frustration and his madness. They will stand for ever as a testament to Osama bin Laden's perversion of his religion, his evil and his cowardice in setting nineteen young men on a path to acts of self-destruction which would kill over 3,000 people and destroy the lives of countless thousands more.

'When the hour of reality approaches, the zero hour, wholeheartedly welcome death for the sake of God. Either end your life while praying, seconds before the target, or make your last words, "There is no God but God, Mohamed is his messenger." Afterwards we shall all meet in highest heaven, God willing.'

At 8:45 A.M. American Airlines Flight 11 crashed into the North Tower of the World Trade Center in New York City.

At 9:03 United Airlines Flight 175 flew into the South Tower.

At 9:43 AA Flight 77 smashed into the south-west face of the Pentagon, in Washington.

At 10:03 UA Flight 93 crashed in an open field in west Pennsylvania.

Part III

WAR ON TERROR

20

Draining the Swamp

'There's a poster I remember way out west; it says, "Wanted, Dead or Alive".'

—President George W. Bush, September 2001

New York, October 2001

Ground Zero in the autumn of 2001 was a place full of purpose. American zeal and efficiency were fast obliterating the physical evidence of the attacks, but the nation's mental trauma was harder to erase. I watched from the gantry running round the southern edge of the jagged hole left in the heart of Lower Manhattan. Beside me a woman cried silently for a dead relative as the cranes swung to the rhythm of the procession of slow-moving trucks passing beneath us. Twenty-four hours a day they transported the debris to a site in New Jersey, where it was minutely sifted for human remains and clues to the mechanics of the attacks. The ceaseless activity in the blasted acres below – the pinpricks of yellow helmets, the tiny earth-movers – highlighted the vast scale of what nineteen fanatics armed only with knives had accomplished. Amid the forest of buildings a whole block of New York, a big slice of the city's financial district, had been levelled; it was as if it had been targeted by the most sophisticated of 'smart weapons' – a thermobaric bomb at least, or even a small nuclear device. It was no longer possible to imagine how high the Towers had once stood. Occasionally the site would fall silent as a small coffin draped in the Stars and Stripes made its way back along the line, handed from shoulder to shoulder.

The real heart of Ground Zero was not the place where the Twin Towers once stood but the black, marble-walled corner just outside the hoardings put up around the site. The memorial to New York's firemen, established long before September 11, should have filled gradually over the years, a name or two added at a time, after tragedies of more normal proportions. Now there were hundreds of names and numbers: police and fire station precincts, groups of lost colleagues listed on handmade posters, many of them Italian and Irish names. There were ribbons and teddy bears and tributes inscribed on photographs. Most poignant of all were the helmets and the badges, battered and twisted, once worn by men who trudged up hundreds of stairs inside the Towers that day; a dogged procession moving against the tide of office workers flowing down and away from the stricken buildings. 'Thank You Dad,' wrote Tom Farino. 'You died in a very honorable way and the world thinks so and it is thankful that you saved people and you are a Hero.'

In the corner of the memorial wall stood an easel which read: 'John P. O'Neill, Special Agent, retired after 31 years'. A photograph showed a darkly handsome, square-jawed man, the epitome of a 'Fed'. John O'Neill, the former FBI head of counterterrorism, had started a new job as Head of Security at the World Trade Center less than three weeks before September 11. O'Neill made it down to the street from his office on the thirty-fourth floor and called to tell his girlfriend he was safe. 'Exited safely but went back in to assist others,' read the citation. John O'Neill was still inside the South Tower when it collapsed.

O'Neill's career through the ranks of the FBI paralleled the rise of al-Qaeda; he was one of the few who never underestimated the threat the terror group posed to his country. He had

been the FBI point-man on many of the al-Qaeda investigations since arriving in the New York office in 1995, on the very
day that Ramsi Yousef, the first Trade Center bomber, was
apprehended in Pakistan. John O'Neill had accompanied the
FBI's chief, Louis Freeh, to Saudi Arabia, where he had been
frustrated by the regime's attempts to block the Riyadh and
Khobar Towers investigations. O'Neill had despatched a 500-
strong team of agents to East Africa after the US Embassy
bombings and established a new, aggressive, blueprint for FBI
operations abroad in poorly policed countries where US citizens had been killed. It was O'Neill who had investigated one
of Ahmed Ressam's accomplices in the abortive Millennium
Plot to target Los Angeles airport; the FBI man warned his
superiors then that all roads in the case led back to the United
States, where he feared al-Qaeda was busy organising terror
cells. O'Neill had aggressively tried to pursue al-Qaeda in the
Yemen after the bombing of the USS *Cole*, as well, but his stand-
off with the authorities and his own ambassador had resulted
in his recall to America.

Ironically, it was September 11 which forced the Yemenis to
save their own government from America's wrath by allowing
the FBI to again begin the hunt for al-Qaeda figures behind the
Cole attack. It was then discovered that some of those involved
in the bombing of the warship had links to the September 11
attacks. If US pressure had been exerted earlier, when O'Neill
was alive and chafing with impatience in his hotel room in
Aden, al-Qaeda terrorists with knowledge of the plot against
America might have been caught and interrogated.

O'Neill spent his career fighting official bureaucracy, inertia
and the kid-gloves American approach to Arab governments
which he believed was sapping the ability of people like him to
go after al-Qaeda. A friend joked with O'Neill, when he heard
about his new job at the Twin Towers, that at least al-Qaeda
would not bomb the same place again. 'They'll probably try to
finish the job,' O'Neill replied sardonically. The supreme irony
would be that it took his own death and the deaths of

thousands of others in New York and Washington to bring home to America's politicians and public that Bin Laden had declared war against the United States, and that the war would have to be won.

Washington, September 2001

'The Pearl Harbor of the twentieth century took place today . . . We think it's Osama bin Laden.' These were the words George W. Bush dictated for his diary on the night of September 11, as he told the *Washington Post*. All day the President had been shuttled around the continent of North America in Air Force One, from secure air base to underground bunker; the Secret Service even had to assess the credibility of a threatened attack on the presidential plane itself. Finally Bush had returned to Andrews USAF base near Washington in the late afternoon; his helicopter took him back to the White House over the smouldering wreck of the Pentagon. 'We think there are other targets in the United States, but I have urged the country to go back to normal,' Bush's diary entry continued. 'We cannot allow a terrorist thug to hold us hostage. My hope is that this will provide an opportunity to rally the world against terrorism.'

Thousands of innocent Americans and people from seventy-two different countries had perished on September 11. The apocalyptic vision of Ground Zero in the heart of New York was beamed live on television to the furthest corners of the world. To most people it was an atrocity of unimaginable proportions but some in the Islamic world saw it as a humiliating defeat for America, the toppling of its symbols of economic and military might. 'The mighty aura of the United States has been seen to collapse in the eyes of the Muslim world,' Dr Sa'ad al-Fagih, the Saudi dissident, told me that day.

The United States government itself had indeed come close to disintegrating as the Senate and House of Representatives were evacuated, the leaders of the Congress spirited away to secure underground bunkers. For more than three hours there was a vacuum of power as the nation waited for its leaders to reassure them that the United States had survived its worst blow for more than fifty years. A group of Islamic extremists in the mountains of Afghanistan, using a terror cell of nineteen people inside America, had brought the strongest and richest country on earth to its knees. After those initial, halting hours, however, it was soon clear that America had found a new strength and purpose.

George Tenet, the CIA Director, quickly informed the President that three known al-Qaeda operatives had been listed on the flight manifest of the Pentagon plane, American Airlines Flight 77. Intelligence monitoring had picked up conversations between known Bin Laden associates congratulating each other after the strikes. 'Get your ears up,' said Bush to Tenet. 'The primary mission of this administration is to find them and catch them.'

The CIA Director told the President that the Taliban had effectively merged with al-Qaeda, seduced by Bin Laden's millions. 'Tell the Taliban we're finished with them,' Tenet urged. Donald Rumsfeld, the hawkish Defense Secretary, was already taking the line that it was the countries supporting terrorism which were the real problem. 'We have to force countries to choose,' said Bush grimly. That night he told the nation: 'We will make no distinction between the terrorists who committed these acts and those who harbour them.' It was the beginning of the so-called Bush Doctrine, to commit the United States, with or without allies, to a broad-based, long-term war against terrorism that would take the fight to the heart of enemy territory.

The Clinton doctrine for dealing with al-Qaeda had been to do nothing that would have put the lives of American soldiers and innocent civilians at risk or upset the delicate diplomatic web in the Middle East. Finally, when provoked by the 1998 embassy bombings, military action had been at arm's length and ineffective. The failure to do real damage to the terrorist

network had only emboldened al-Qaeda and added to Bin
Laden's prestige. But it would be Bin Laden's fatal mistake, a
mark of his physical isolation and his lack of understanding of
Western democracies, that he chose to deal his ultimate blow
against a very different American administration. Dick Cheney,
a former Secretary of Defense; Colin Powell, the Chairman of
the Joint Chiefs of Staff and architect of the Gulf War strategy
during George Bush senior's term; and Donald Rumsfeld, a
Secretary of Defense in Gerald Ford's government were just
the front ranks – behind them were many other individuals
inclined by both nature and experience to take a tough stand.

President Bush knew he needed to push the risk-averse generals in the Pentagon to think differently about the war he had
in mind; they would resist committing forces to a mission
which had not yet been defined. 'They had yet to be challenged
to think on how to fight a guerrilla war using conventional
means,' Bush later told the *Washington Post*. Rumsfeld and Bush
had already discussed, before September 11, how US military
policy must change from what Rumsfeld dismissively called
the Clinton pattern of 'reflexive pullback'. Rumsfeld now
reminded the President of the embarrassment caused by the
1998 attacks on Bin Laden. 'Tell the Afghans to round up al-
Qaeda. Let's see them or we'll hit them hard,' said Bush.

By the morning of 12 September, the CIA had presented the
President with more evidence of al-Qaeda's guilt and the
danger it still posed. There were intercepts in which associates
of the group spoke of the attacks as 'the beginning of the wrath'
and others which identified Congress as having been the target
of Flight 93. Shortly after the Pentagon was hit al-Qaeda members in Afghanistan had spoken of following through with 'the
doctor's programme', a clear reference to Ayman al-Zawahiri,
the Egyptian second-in-command. And intelligence reports
showed that Abu Zubaydah, the recruiter and chief field commander of the mission, had referred to 'Zero Hour' – the same
phrase used by Mohamed Atta in his last exhortation to the
hijackers.

The CIA seized the initiative with a series of proposals on how to go after Bin Laden, al-Qaeda and the Taliban regime. George Tenet had been a hangover from the Clinton administration but had forged a strong relationship with Bush in the early days of his presidency. George Bush senior, an ever-present shadow at his son's side, had spent a year himself as CIA Director and had schooled George W. in the importance of the daily intelligence briefing, which he received in person from Tenet each day. Clinton had wanted only a written submission.

In the first traumatic days after the attacks open criticism of America's greatest intelligence failure since Pearl Harbor, a failure which gave birth to the CIA, was still muted. Tenet and the new Director of Counter-Terrorism, Cofer Black, seized their opportunity, giving a persuasive performance in front of Bush and his War Cabinet. They proposed bringing together covert action teams inside Afghanistan with expanded intelligence-gathering and sophisticated technology to fight a war against terror using local opposition forces. CIA paramilitary teams had been authorised to operate inside Afghanistan since the attack on the USS *Cole* a year earlier. They would now be expanded and tasked with organising the various commanders of the Northern Alliance, a motley collection of Afghan warlords and their 20,000 fighters, to form a new spearhead. Along with Special Forces teams from the US military they would provide the 'ears and eyes' on the ground for further military action. The Northern Alliance would be invigorated by a substantial injection of US cash and sophisticated American weapons technology to give them the edge over the Taliban and al-Qaeda fighters.

It was Donald Rumsfeld who voiced the key question in the War Cabinet: 'Do we focus on Bin Laden and al-Qaeda, or terrorism more broadly?'

'Start with Bin Laden, which [is what] Americans expect,' was the President's response. 'Then if we succeed we've struck a huge blow and can move forward.' Killing or capturing Bin Laden and destroying his network was the main objective, from the start, of the 'war on terror' that the President announced. It would be achieved, in Rumsfeld's words, by 'draining the swamp' of Taliban-ruled Afghanistan.

The new political determination and the shift in military and intelligence strategy to deal with al-Qaeda was paralleled by a re-think on other ways to pursue and neutralise the more broadly based network of terror. The first priority, even above the war against terror, was to secure the country against further attack. Tom Ridge was appointed Director of Homeland Security but it was the Justice Department, responsible for the FBI and the courts, which became the key to preventive action.

John Ashcroft, a former Senator and State Governor, was the new Attorney General. A commanding figure, he had been widely attacked for his conservative, Christian views; Ashcroft had only narrowly survived a bitter confirmation battle in the Senate. He would now preside over a fundamental shift in priorities, both in the law-enforcement community and in the courts. Prevention would now be the watchword, not prosecution. The FBI would focus on taking out the threat and not, as in the past, on protecting information while prosecutors painstakingly built a case against individual terrorists. The public needed no persuading that Bin Laden and al-Qaeda were guilty and dangerous, and that sentiment effectively untied the hands of the Justice Department. 'It was made very clear to me that we had to do everything in our power and find a way to do those things which we otherwise might not think about,' John Ashcroft told *Panorama*. 'Our highest priority has to be preventing this kind of terrorism. We've got to think outside the box.'

The emphasis was now on capturing all al-Qaeda and Taliban suspects, wherever they were, and interrogating them to glean information about other attacks in the pipeline. The administration moved quickly to establish military tribunals to short cut the legal process and right of appeal. Across America Muslim men were rounded up and taken into custody, some 1,300 in the first few weeks alone. The FBI aggressively pursued the case against Lotfi Raissi, the Algerian pilot arrested in Britain, until a lack of evidence forced them to drop extradition proceedings seven months later. The sweep of detentions across the States signalled a shift in legal tradition which strained the sinews of a system where liberty and the rights of the individual had always been held sacred. Hardly a word was uttered in protest, not even in the liberal media; it was part of a new climate where Arab men were encountering hostility and sometimes violence on the streets of a nation once known for its tolerance and multiculturalism.

In the first few days after the attacks Americans had agonised over the hatred felt for their country, their government's policies, their way of life; it was a hatred they could not fathom. Then the 'weakness' which Bin Laden had detected in his enemy, the vacillation caused in the past by a lack of political will and the lack of a public mandate, was transformed as America hardened its heart against world opinion. 'If you are not with us, you are against us,' became the administration's slogan – one that was whole-heartedly endorsed by the people.

In diplomatic circles Colin Powell was stitching together a coalition of nations to pursue the war on terror in Afghanistan and further afield. Pakistan was the key to its success and General Pervez Musharraf, the Pakistani President, was given an ultimatum – reject the Taliban, seal your borders and call your renegade security service to heel, or else. The ISI, the 'kingdom within a state' which had done so much to foster al-Qaeda and the Taliban, would now be asked to destroy its own creation. Musharraf, a 'dead man walking' as an American White House aide described him to me, had no alternative but to acquiesce. The widespread support for Bin Laden in the north-west tribal areas of Pakistan and other parts of the country would, if unchecked, sound his own death-knell. The Saudis, however, proved a tougher nut to crack.

'I felt as if the Twin Towers had fallen on my head,' Prince Bandar bin Sultan, the Saudi Ambassador to Washington, described the moment George Tenet called him to say the CIA believed that as many as fifteen of the hijackers had come from Saudi Arabia. The ebullient cigar-smoking prince, a legendary operator in the corridors of power, had been the acceptable face of the Saudi regime for years: he now realised his hardest ever task was at hand. Several members of the Bin Laden clan who had been happily ensconced in pleasant apartments around Boston, where the family had generously endowed a Harvard chair, were whisked out of the country. Bandar provided the plane. 'The message was, get them out,' according to a source close to the family. 'An Arab had had his head-dress pulled off in public, Muslims were being attacked in the street and the Bin Laden name stank.' Matters weren't helped when another Saudi prince, the billionaire Alwaleed bin Talal, visited Ground Zero and graciously handed over a cheque for $10 million to the New York Mayor, Rudy Giuliani. The prince, after standing on the rubble surrounded by rescue workers still digging away, then rather tactlessly reminded Americans that it was their policy towards Israel which had inflamed opinion in the Middle East against them. Thomas Friedman, the influential *New York Times* columnist, spoke for millions when he addressed the Saudis in an open letter: 'Whatever you do, stop lying to us and yourselves. Because we're sick of it and we're not alone.'

American public opinion was incensed at the Saudi royal family's refusal to allow bases in the country to be used for the planned attacks on Afghanistan. A classified US report of a Saudi Arabian intelligence survey of educated Saudis between the ages of twenty-five and forty-one found that 95 per cent supported Bin Laden's cause. The Saudis let it be known that it would not be a tragedy if the US were to withdraw its forces from their land. Many American Senators agreed; they could not wait to see the back of a nation many of them regarded as duplicitous and which had not only funded extremist Islamic movements and spawned Bin Laden himself but also fifteen of the nineteen hijackers. Relations between the two governments sank to their lowest ever point as the *Washington Post* opined in its influential leader column that 'the [US] administration must now recognise that Saudi political policies have become not just an unpleasant sideshow but a genuine menace to the United States'. It was, however, reluctantly recognised by both sides that bringing US troops home, Bin Laden's central demand, would cede victory to al-Qaeda at the worst possible time.

The firing of Prince Turki al-Faisal as head of the Saudi intelligence service did not appease Washington. 'Oh God save us from Satan! . . . You are a rotten seed of Noah,' Prince Turki railed against Bin Laden in a Saudi newspaper. Many in the West wondered why it had taken so long for Prince Turki to publicly renounce his erstwhile friend. Behind the scenes the royal family was badly shaken: despite their initial protestations that the hijackers had stolen the identities of innocent Saudis, it soon became impossible to deny the unpalatable truth. Bin Laden had sent an unambiguous message to the regime he hated and wanted to bring down; his power and influence over young, disaffected Saudis was greater than theirs.

Afghanistan, October 2001

On the night of 7 October, three US cruisers and a destroyer in the Arabian Sea let fire a salvo of fifty missiles. A wave of aircraft swept across Afghanistan; twenty-five F-18 strike aircraft from the USS *Missouri* and fifteen B-1 and B-52 bombers sent from the base at Diego Garcia. American and British submarines launched Cruise missiles as General Richard Myers announced at the Pentagon that the US was only 'in the early stages of on-going combat operations' against thirty-one al-Qaeda training camps and Taliban targets. The Taliban regime knew they would pay for allowing Bin Laden to hijack Afghanistan, but they were incapable of imagining how heavy the price would be – the ten-year-old son of Mullah Omar was reported killed in the first night of bombing, the first of many hundreds of Afghan civilian casualties. A single missile was fired on the village of Sansegar, destroying the mosque where Omar started his movement in 1995. By 19 October the first of around three hundred US Special Forces were deployed on the ground, co-ordinating and bolstering the Northern Alliance as it began to rapidly roll back the Taliban's forces.

The Bin Laden propaganda machine was ready and primed to counter the US offensive. A videotape, clearly recorded before the attacks, was delivered by a messenger to the offices of al-Jazeera Television in Kabul on the day the first bombs hit Afghanistan. 'God has blessed a vanguard group of Muslims, the forefront of Islam, to destroy America,' declared Bin Laden, clad in camouflage jacket, his back to a wall of rock. 'May God bless them and allot them a supreme place in heaven,' he continued. With him was al-Zawahiri, underscoring the fact that the September 11 terrorists had been led by an Egyptian militant. The message from al-Qaeda was that 'every Muslim should rush to defend his religion' in a world now divided into 'faith' and 'infidelity'. It was a call for an Islamic uprising of the whole Muslim *umma*, or nation, in the face of the threat posed to Afghanistan by America and the international coalition. Bin Laden had long dreamed of such an uprising and it seems certain that al-Qaeda knew the September attacks would bring a massive retaliation and had calculated that this would enable them at last to spark a wider Islamic conflict with America and the hated regimes of the Middle East. But Osama bin Laden was to be disappointed.

The Bush administration brought pressure to bear on the ruler of Qatar not to allow his television station, al-Jazeera, to broadcast any more tapes delivered by al-Qaeda. Much was made of the danger that the video could contain coded messages, designed to trigger more terror attacks from the underground network in America and Europe. The point was not too subtly underlined when al-Jazeera staff in Kabul received a warning to evacuate their office; minutes later one of the surgical strikes carried out by US smart bombs hit the house full square. The first bomb fell, unexploded, through the mezzanine floor and ended up in the back garden. The second bomb detonated in a massive explosion. Wisely, al-Jazeera decided to close down its operations in Kabul and not to broadcast another tape they had received from al-Qaeda.

As well as bombs the US dropped food, medicine and supplies into Afghanistan. 'The United States of America is a friend to the Afghan people and at the same time is a friend to more than half a billion Muslims world wide,' Bush insisted. On the ground the tactics of using American cash, weapons and training to beef up the Northern Alliance seemed to be working; opposition forces advanced as the Taliban crumbled under the onslaught from the air. Frank Anderson, former chief of the CIA's Near East Division, a man with long and bitter experience of Afghan politics, remarked on the powerful effect US bribes had in winning warlords in the south away from the battered Taliban: 'The wonderful thing about Afghanistan is the role which treachery plays,' he observed.

Treachery would later play a significant role in the hunt for the real prize in the war against terror – Osama bin Laden himself. In the first month of the campaign Bin Laden taunted his pursuers with tantalising glimpses of his movements. On 6 November, Hamid Mir, a journalist from the Pakistani paper *Dawn*, was brought blind-folded to a secret location near Kabul, 'to a place where it was extremely cold and I could hear the sound of anti-aircraft guns firing away', according to Mir. Bin Laden, accompanied by the faithful al-Zawahiri and a dozen bodyguards, had a new warning for America: 'I wish to declare that if America uses chemical or nuclear weapons against us, then we may retort with chemical and nuclear weapons as a deterrent,' he said, employing his usual twisted logic.

The US-led coalition was gathering pace as relentless US bombing and the Northern Alliance's ground offensive rapidly pushed the Taliban from the northern half of the country. The strategic town of Mazar-i-Sharif fell on 9 November. The Northern Alliance pressed on south, towards Kabul. Taliqan, where Taliban fighters changed sides with hardly a shot being fired, and Herat in the west, also fell to the Alliance. Then they surged south through the Shamali valley to the mountain pass guarding the entrance to Kabul. On 12 November ecstatic crowds welcomed the Western press, which continued on into the city while the Northern Alliance forces halted grudgingly on the outskirts, in deference to their American masters' wishes. The anger felt by many Afghans towards the hated foreigners, the 'Arabs' of al-Qaeda, who had enjoyed special status under the Taliban, was given free rein; mutilated bodies were found in a small park in the town while the citizens of Kabul were celebrating their liberation by shaving off their beards and tuning their radios to music again.

Three days after the fall of Kabul one of al-Qaeda's top three leaders, Mohamed Atef, was killed when a US air strike was launched against a house near Kandahar where al-Qaeda members were meeting. It was a serious blow to al-Qaeda: the Egyptian ex-policeman had been with Bin Laden since the defeat of the Soviets in the late 1980s. He was the man who had been behind al-Qaeda's military strategy since the early days in East Africa, and he had set up the training regime in the terror camps of Afghanistan. It now seemed that Bin Laden's boast, that he would teach the Americans the same bitter lesson as the Soviets had learned in Afghanistan, was a hollow threat. Al-Qaeda's commanders and foot soldiers fled as Afghans scavenged in the wreckage of Atef's bombed house and other abandoned al-Qaeda buildings and training camps. One of the looters would find a treasure-trove of information which weeks later would yield valuable clues to al-Qaeda's network in Europe and reveal new plots to spread terror and fear in the West.

21

The Road to Tora Bora

'The Americans can bomb all they want, they'll never catch Osama.'

—Maulvi Younis Khan, November 2001

They call it the most dangerous road in the world; ninety kilometres of spine-jarring roller-coaster track, frequented by bandits, obliterated by dust clouds kicked up by groaning lorries or obscured by downpours of rain which fill the vast craters with deep, cloying mud. For six hours our convoy of three jeeps negotiated the deep gullies in the road, climbed peaks and crept along precipices on the route from Kabul to Jalalabad. This was the same road along which Bin Laden and his al-Qaeda fighters had fled eastwards as the Northern Alliance moved in on the capital in November. The fugitives were making for their leader's old stamping-ground, the natural mountain fortress of Tora Bora, where he had fought off the Soviets fourteen years earlier.

We drove through stunning gorges cut by the turbulent river through granite rocks the colour of ginger and black shining slate. Children and old men were engaged in the Sisyphean task of shovelling sand into the pot-holes that held the road together. We threw them *afgani* notes and two tiny girls, clad in emerald and turquoise rags, caught the money expertly as we lurched by. In the distance a mountain shot through with iron ore glowed purple in the sun as we breasted the pass at the half-way mark and coasted down towards Serobi; a mean, ragged little town with a reputation as a smuggling centre. It was here, in the main street just in front of the metal bridge spanning the river, that four journalists, an Italian, a Spaniard, an Australian and an Afghan, died in a hail of bullets in November when gunmen held up their taxi. We needed fuel and the drivers stopped just short of the fateful spot. Our armed guards jumped out and stood protectively around us. The ancient pump took an eternity to dole out the petrol; we were relieved to move on and shake the dust of Serobi from our wheels.

Jalalabad, an ancient trading centre on the old Silk Road between the Khyber Pass and the Central Asian states to the north, has always been a traditional meeting place for Pashtun tribesmen from the area bordering on Pakistan. Beyond the tall palm trees, unique to this eastern Afghan town, rise the peaks of the Spin Ghar, the White Mountains. In the vast bowl of white crags, one peak, Tora Bora, stands highest of all. Two days before the fall of Kabul on 12 November a local builder's merchant, Ahmad Sdiq, told me he had seen a large convoy of vehicles, as many as three hundred cars, four-wheel-drives and trucks, gathered in Jalalabad. 'The convoy was full of Arabs,' he said. 'I asked them where they were going and I was told they were on their way to their base at Tora Bora.' Sdiq described seeing three different types of al-Qaeda fighters – tall, thin Saudis with long faces; others with more muscular physiques, who told him they were from Egypt; and a third group of well-built men with black skin, probably Sudanese. Sdiq was told that Osama bin Laden was sitting in the third vehicle in the convoy but his face and those of the six others around him was covered.

Others in Jalalabad claim to have heard the al-Qaeda leader rally local tribesmen at an Islamic centre in the city – the Pashtun areas had spawned the Taliban and there had been much support historically for al-Qaeda in these parts. 'The Americans had a plan to invade but if we are united and believe in Allah, we'll teach them a lesson, the same one we taught to the Russians,' Bin Laden announced, according to tribal leaders who were there. The al-Qaeda leader was dressed in grey robes, his Arab fighters around him clad in green fatigues with brand new Kalashnikovs; they shared a communal feast of lamb kebabs and rice. Then he made a last appeal to the Afghans: 'God is with us and we will win the war. Your Arab brothers will lead the way. We have the weapons and technology. What we need most is your moral support.' To encourage their support the clan leaders received thick envelopes of a more practical commodity than moral certainty – Pakistani rupees. Then Bin Laden and his escort swept out of town towards the mountains. The Afghan residents of Jalalabad wished him good riddance. 'The Arabs thought they owned this country, but people here hated them,' Sdiq said. 'We told them, why don't you go to Palestine and fight the Israelis instead of your fellow Muslims?'

It was in a Jalalabad house in mid-November, as al-Qaeda fled the city, that the videotape was found which showed a relaxed Bin Laden sitting with a Saudi Sheikh, smiling about the September 11 attacks, saying how he had surprised even his closest confidants with his daring plot: 'They were overjoyed when the first plane hit the building,' said Bin Laden, 'but I said to them – be patient . . . We stayed until four in the morning listening to the news. Everyone was most joyous.'

I followed in Osama bin Laden's wake towards Tora Bora across a plain strewn with large boulders, the detritus of glaciers swept down from the mountains. In the foothills of the mountains near the village of Choprikor we found a group of three large, square, walled compounds. These were Bin Laden's houses where one of his four families had sometimes stayed and where many of his fighters had been stationed. The largest building, nearest the road, had been torn apart – a large sign painted in red with a cross proclaimed that the site was still to be checked for mines and unexploded ordnance. Turrets at each corner were pierced with slits – for machine-guns, according to the neighbours gathering to tell us about the house, which had been comprehensively ransacked. A local boy confirmed that Arabs had lived here and that there had been much coming and going late at night. 'Everyone knew he lived here sometimes with his family,' said another man when I asked him about Bin Laden. The villagers pointed to the permanent concrete guard posts outside, and the piped water and mains electricity, a luxury no locals enjoyed. Inside the compound I was shown eight small dormitories where Chechen fighters had lived. I found crumpled leaflets in the rubble; they had been dropped from American planes and bore the image of a smiling, clean-shaven American, wearing a *pakhul*, the traditional felt hat, holding out the hand of friendship to bearded Afghan men.

It was ironic, I thought, to find these leaflets dropped in Bin Laden's house, with their idealised vision of Americans and Afghans hand-in-hand against the evil of al-Qaeda. For what happened at Tora Bora taught the US a salutary lesson: beware of the duplicity and treachery of local warlords and do not expect to deal successfully with the threat of al-Qaeda at arm's length only. 'Close up and dirty is the only way to do it,' was the succinct opinion expressed by someone who had experience of the undercover operations in Afghanistan.

Bin Laden disappeared, once he reached the village of Milawa, into the network of caves excavated by the *mujahideen* in the war against the Soviets. American B-52 bombers began to pound the hillsides in the last week of November. The USAF was confident they could blast al-Qaeda's positions apart; there was much talk in the press of 'daisy-cutters', 'bunker-busters' and bombs which could suck air out of both the caves and the lungs of anyone inside them. On the ground, members of the US Special Forces, Delta Force and Navy SEALs, were tasked with guiding the bombs to their targets by 'painting' the mouths of caves with laser devices.

It was two months into the war which President Bush had declared on al-Qaeda, but General Tommy Franks, the overall US commander, was effectively running the military campaign from Central Command headquarters in Florida. There was no US commander in Afghanistan above the rank of lieutenant colonel. Franks had decided it was too risky to put US soldiers on the ground at Tora Bora, and, following the pattern established with the Northern Alliance since the war began, the Americans now started enlisting local warlords to do the front-line fighting. Franks told subordinates it was vital that at Tora Bora, the first battle to include allies from Afghanistan's Pashtun majority, America take a supporting role rather than just pushing the locals to one side.

The American contribution on the ground consisted largely of covert groups, Special Forces liaison troops and CIA paramilitary units from the Special Activities Division, many of them veterans re-hired after September 11 for their experience in Afghanistan. Flush with a billion dollars' worth of extra funding sanctioned by the President, the CIA's job was to identify local groups who had the will and ability to fight the Taliban and al-Qaeda and provide them with the cash and the weapons to do it. 'Today I have more spies stealing secrets than at any time in the CIA,' James Pavitt, the Agency's Director of Operations told an academic conference in America. 'We are training ten times as many case officers as five or six years ago,' he continued, confirming that the battered Agency was re-establishing itself 'on the souls of 3,000 innocent men, women and children from September 11'.

The first warlord to establish his credentials with the Americans after al-Qaeda fled Jalalabad was Hazret Ali, one of Masoud's former commanders from the north. I met Hazret Ali in the echoing marble lobby of the mournful Spingar Hotel in Jalalabad; a place almost devoid of guests owing to the gun battles that erupted nightly beyond the unkempt rose garden in the grounds. A small, wiry and hard-eyed man, Ali had forsaken more traditional Afghan dress for a natty Quiksilver jogging suit, several sizes too big. 'I don't really know exactly who the Americans were who came to me in November,' he said. 'They were a special group and when the battle started all our work was in co-ordination with them and with the Air

Force. The group was with us everywhere we went and they are still with me today.'

Hazret Ali was not the only one to benefit from the expertise of US Special Forces and the money liberally handed out by the CIA. At least two other warlords played a part in the American plan, each with their own liaison teams: Haji Qadeer, an expatriate Afghan who had returned from America, and Haji Zaman Gamsharik, lured back from Dijon in France by the US as a Pashtun counter-balance to Ali. Gamsharik had British as well as US Special Forces attached to his command. There were a plethora of lesser commanders under these three warlords and a number of local powerbrokers involved themselves as well, including Maulvi Younis Khan, a Jalalabad religious leader who was in favour of allowing the Arabs to leave instead of attacking them. 'America can bomb all they want, they'll never catch Bin Laden,' Khan said confidently. With local rivalries, in-fighting and hidden agendas the warlord scene at Tora Bora was a recipe for confusion and disaster.

Ali and Gamsharik calculated that Tora Bora held between 1,500 and 1,600 of al-Qaeda's strongest Arab and Chechen fighters. 'We will fight until we are martyred,' was the message sent back through the emissaries. Bin Laden was expected to direct the battle himself with his knowledge of the terrain and the cave complexes. 'I think he was equipped to go to ground there,' Dick Cheney told ABC's *Primetime Live*. 'It's an area he is familiar with.'

Bin Laden was seen on 26 November, after the bombing started, by a group of his Yemeni fighters. He was nursing a glass of green tea and mumbling about the 'holy war'. Hazret Ali was certain the leader of al-Qaeda was in the caves and told me that documents found there later, as well as prisoners, confirmed it.

Bin Laden's own Saudi cook, Mohamed Akram, emerged later to relate how he was making dinner for his master when a huge bomb exploded at the entrance to the cave, blowing him back some thirty feet. On 30 November, Akram claimed that he and other fighters were given Iranian currency and told to escape from Tora Bora. According to Akram, Bin Laden left on foot with just a few followers. That account was backed up by another Saudi al-Qaeda man, financier Abu Jaffar, whose foot was blown off by a cluster bomb as he fled. He told reporters in the village of Upper Pachir in early December that Bin Laden had already headed for Parachinar, just over the border in Pakistan.

While these accounts from al-Qaeda insiders may well be deliberately misleading, American and British intelligence also believe that sometime during the first few days of December the world's most wanted man escaped the world's most powerful military machine, making his way through the mountains and into the border area of Pakistan. Bin Laden's ghostly voice was heard on a radio directing his troops around 5 December.

The exodus of the top leadership was followed by a rush from al-Qaeda's ranks, aided by local people and even some of the warlords who were supposed to be the spearhead of American efforts to crush the terror network. Maulvi Younis Khan, the al-Qaeda sympathiser, was busy behind the scenes; his own envoy, ensconced in the caves, radioed back to Hazret Ali and Haji Zaman Gamsharik that al-Qaeda was seeking a surrender agreement. 'This was just a tactic, but the battle eased for a day or two and this enabled many of them to escape,' admitted Hazret Ali, who accused Gamsharik of falling for this ploy.

Bin Laden's fighters were undoubtedly helped in their escape by local Pashtun villagers whose leaders had wisely been paid off before the battle commenced. 'All the *mujahideen* in the Tora Bora area were friends with Osama; he gave them weapons and money. All the villages in the mountains were in co-operation with Osama,' Ali told me ruefully. The warlords were less keen to describe the duplicitous role they played. Not only did they fail to block the exodus of al-Qaeda fighters, some of their commanders also accepted money for allowing the Arabs to melt away across the porous, 100-mile stretch of border with Pakistan.

'There were some technical problems because we were not very well organised and we were in a bit of a hurry. All sorts of groups joined us,' said Ali when I asked him whether his commanders had accepted Bin Laden's money. He was squirming visibly as he continued. 'Someone may well have helped him to escape. I can't point to any one person but I agree there was some kind of dishonesty here.' The warlords profited from both sides in the battle: 'Whatever was necessary, we received,' Ali confirmed when I asked him if he had been given money and weapons by his American minders.

When a final surrender was negotiated and the last cave breached on 16 December the al-Qaeda body count, according to the warlords, was between two and three hundred. Only around fifty bedraggled prisoners were taken out and paraded in front of the press. 'Those left inside for us were the stupid ones, the foolish and the weak,' complained another young commander, Haji Zaher. If original calculations of around 1,500 al-Qaeda members were accurate, that meant that well over a thousand hardened fighters had escaped either to Pakistan or southwards towards the equally mountainous Paktia province of Afghanistan, another Pashtun stronghold of Bin Laden's.

The Pentagon had left it to President Musharraf's Pakistani forces to try and seal the 100-mile stretch of rugged, lawless countryside that marked the border between the two countries. There was no effective siege of Tora Bora because the back door had been left wide open. 'The border with Pakistan was the key, but the Americans paid no attention to it,' said Pir Baksh Bardiwal, the intelligence chief for eastern Afghanistan. 'Al-Qaeda escaped right out from under their noses.' Donald Rumsfeld sounded unsure when Pentagon reporters asked him how effective Pakistan's forces could be in blocking the border: 'It's a long border,' he conceded, 'a very complicated area to try to seal, and there's simply no way you can put a perfect cork in the bottle.' Musharraf's forces succeeded in intercepting around two hundred of the fleeing al-Qaeda forces but many hundreds more got away. President Musharraf told *Panorama* that his troops had done their best to seal a porous border but conceded that they had failed. 'There are only small penny packets of al-Qaeda which made their way into our country and our cities,' he assured us. Subsequent events would prove the hollowness of his claim.

The big question raised by the abortive siege at Tora Bora is why the American high command did not place more US troops along the border to choke off the escape points. There were a thousand American Marines already in the country, at a base near Kandahar supporting Special Forces operations, and military experts have estimated that between one and three thousand well-armed, determined soldiers would have been sufficient to seal the stretch of border closest to Tora Bora. Washington was fearful of the impact significant numbers of troop deaths might have on US public opinion, so early in the war on terror. There were fears too of an anti-American back-lash if too many US troops entered Afghanistan, and Pakistan was reluctant to allow its territory to be used as a staging-post to ferry in foreign soldiers. And so many of al-Qaeda's finest fighters and its leadership were able to escape.

President Bush confided to the *Washington Post* in December that since September 11 he had kept a 'scorecard' of al-Qaeda leaders, drawing a cross through the faces of those his intelligence agencies thought were dead. But in the months following the failed siege of Tora Bora the President's rhetoric about taking Bin Laden 'dead or alive' became noticeably muted. No longer was the Saudi dissident branded Public Enemy Number One; instead, the American military command began to refer to 'HVTs' – High Value Targets. The Defense Secretary sounded irritable when asked how the hunt for the main quarry was going. 'As I get up at five A.M. and take a shower before heading for the office my wife says, "Don, where is he?"' Rumsfeld said. 'I tell her that if I want to bring up Osama bin Laden, I'll wake her up and bring it up myself,' he added pointedly.

The best chance of capturing Bin Laden had indeed been wasted at Tora Bora and Donald Rumsfeld was frustrated with General Franks and the whole climate of caution which still enveloped the top military establishment. And there was rancour further down the chain over a secret mission in the Spin Ghar mountains. Since September the covert war waged by the US in Afghanistan had been paralleled by another undercover operation carried out by the British, America's strongest ally in the coalition. Small teams made up of intelligence officers from MI6 and troops from the SBS, the Special Boat Service, had been working to prevent al-Qaeda and Taliban extremists destabilising the interim government of Hamid Karzai. Then in December, at Tora Bora, a bigger operation involving covert British forces began to unfold. Acting on information procured by British intelligence, two squadrons of the SBS, around sixty men, were sent into the area in what was described as a 'parallel' mission while the publicly-acknowledged siege of the Tora Bora caves was in progress. That mission involved killing known al-Qaeda targets, or 'slotting' them in the terminology favoured by British Special Forces. Having achieved what they set out to do, the undercover troops were stealthily leaving when they stumbled across information that Osama bin Laden himself was in the valley. They believed they could trap or kill him if they were allowed to sweep it thoroughly. The SBS, however, were under overall US command and members of Delta Force, their American colleagues – and rivals – were also in the area. The American generals wanted their own men to take the prize and the SBS were pulled off the job. But then valuable time was lost to indecision while the top brass debated what the risk of US casualties would be, whether local Afghan fighters should move in first and how low attack aircraft should fly. The delay allowed Bin Laden to get away and left the SBS feeling understandably cheated.

Five months later, in May 2002, the SBS would return to the valley to lead Canadian coalition troops investigating what had happened to Bin Laden and his bodyguards after Tora Bora. Intelligence had later been received that Bin Laden had been wounded during the bombing and there were hopes that, despite the failure to seize him at the time, he might have died not far away. Captain Philip Nicholson, the Canadian officer in charge, admitted their quarry had been there in mid-December during the battle for Tora Bora: 'He [Bin Laden] was located in the area at approximately that time,' Nicholson confirmed. The Canadians disinterred twenty-three bodies discovered at a shrine near the village of Ali Khel, where villagers revealed that the Taliban had told them to bury Arabs killed in the US bombing and to give the dead due respect. A thousand people from Afghanistan and nearby Pakistan had attended a ceremony on 30 December and the well-maintained graves were decorated with the white flag of the Taliban and illuminated by coloured lights. The villagers told the Canadians of 'a very big man who was buried in a special ceremony with his body booby-trapped', but the troops found no corpse which matched Bin Laden's 6'5" frame. DNA samples were taken from the bodies in an attempt to identify the dead, some of whom were dressed in military uniforms. Lieutenant Colonel Pat Stagran, another Canadian officer, said ruefully, 'We were hoping the big guy was there and I am still hopeful – but it doesn't look particularly likely.'

An outcast from his own country, Bin Laden had identified the Sudan as a weak state ripe for exploitation in the early 1990s. Then the failing, war-torn country of Afghanistan became a magnet for al-Qaeda during the second half of the decade. Now, fleeing for their lives from Tora Bora, Bin Laden's fighters began to congregate just across the border in the north-west provinces of Pakistan, another lawless stronghold of Islamic extremism. 'The Base has lost its base – the training camps in Afghanistan,' was the confident message coming from intelligence officers in the West. But Pakistan, a large Islamic nation with a history of unstable governments and military coups and an ambitious nuclear programme, now threatened to succeed Afghanistan as the new base for al-Qaeda. Bin Laden had calculated that America would strike directly at al-Qaeda following the devastating attacks on New York and Washington. He already had a plan to ensure the survival of 'the base' without its physical bedrock in Afghanistan, and that plan now swung into action. Immediately after the siege at Tora Bora there was confirmation that the terror network which carried out the September 11 attacks was far from being neutralised, let alone destroyed.

22

The Tentacles of Terror

'Don't touch me – I'm wired!'

—Richard Reid, the 'shoe bomber', on Flight 63,
December 2001

Miami, December 2001

In late December American bombers were still pounding
al-Qaeda positions in the mountains of Afghanistan. On television, retired generals were dusted off and engaged as
'consultants' to the networks; the extent of the fiasco at Tora
Bora was not yet known and the experts confidently predicted
that the remaining extremists could never have survived the
withering onslaught of the US Air Force. But just as holiday-
makers began to venture abroad again, to warmer climes for
the Christmas holidays, the terror network struck again.

On 22 December, TV stations in Europe and America inter-
rupted their coverage of the war with a dramatic announcement: a young Briton called Richard Reid had been discovered
in the act of trying to detonate explosives on a plane from Paris
to Miami. The so-called 'shoe bomber' had hidden PETN, a
plastic explosive, in the soles of his training shoes. The figure
driven away from the plane by armed police looked like a

misfit, his face scowling and swollen, half hidden by the hood of a scruffy sweatshirt. Other photographs showed a wild-looking man of mixed race, his hair in a long, greasy ponytail. Reid seemed a loser, the exact opposite of the disciplined, professional-looking Mohamed Atta, with his inscrutable stare and clean-shaven, well-dressed appearance. It would emerge, however, that far from being just 'a lone nut with a grudge', as rattled officials in Whitehall first thought, Reid was part of the al-Qaeda network. Richard Reid's story is one of alienation and loss and shows how Bin Laden's recruiters have begun to target vulnerable figures from more unlikely ethnic backgrounds. African, Afro-Caribbean and white men have become valuable assets for the network as suspicion of Arabs has increased in the West.

Richard Reid was born in south London in 1973. He was the second generation of his family to come from a mixed marriage. His father, Robin Reid, was the son of a Jamaican immigrant and a white girl; all his life Robin endured taunts of 'Go home, nigger'. He too married a white woman. In many ways it was an unlikely match for Lesley Hughes, the daughter of a magistrate. On the day of Richard's birth his feckless father was in jail, where he would spend eighteen years, on and off, for various offences. 'Car theft, breaking and entering, doing warehouses, you name it – I tried it,' Robin Reid, a grizzled but chirpy man with a Cockney accent, told *Panorama*. 'I was not much of an example to my son,' he admitted. A photograph shows an unlikely couple – Reid, tall and dishevelled, his arm around a prim-looking, bespectacled Lesley. Three-year-old Richard struggles to escape his father's arms, scowling with his lower lip thrust out: a child on the verge of tears.

A year later, Richard Reid's parents divorced. His mother remarried and moved to the country. Richard did not get on with his stepfather and left school at sixteen to drift back to London. Neither black nor white, he felt rejected, inhabiting a twilight world. At seventeen he followed in his father's footsteps when he was sent to prison for a mugging offence. Then, in 1995, Reid had a chance encounter with his father at the Elephant & Castle shopping centre in south London. The two men had a talk which was to change Richard Reid's life. 'I told Richard I had converted to Islam in prison,' said Robin. 'I asked him, why don't you become a Muslim? They treat you fair, like a human being and not like dirt.' Back in jail at Feltham, the institution for young offenders, Richard Reid attended the prison imam's prayer meetings and became a member of the fastest-growing religion in Britain. He took a new name: 'Richard is dead,' he told his father. 'I am now Abdul.'

Some clerics associated with proselytising Islamic groups are known to have targeted young black inmates of British prisons. 'Islam is a sort of natural religion for underdogs,' says Ziauddin Sardar, a British scholar of Islam, 'and that is why Afro-Caribbean people have found its message very attractive.' For years British prison authorities have allowed literature into jails without screening it, another example of a Western government's willingness to bend over backwards to accommodate Muslim sensibilities. Some of that literature was hate-filled, extremist material calling for *jihad*.

On his release from jail in 1996, Reid showed up at the Brixton mosque in south London, a place which had a reputation as an informal rehabilitation centre for wayward youths. 'When he came to us he was an amenable and affable young man, but impressionable,' said Abdul Haqq Baker, the head of the mosque. Zacharias Moussaoui, the French–Moroccan plotter arrested before September 11, also attended the Brixton mosque during his years in London before embarking on the path to al-Qaeda's training camps and the flying school in Oklahoma. His militant views put Moussaoui at odds with Abdul Haqq Baker and he was thrown out as a troublemaker. But Moussaoui had already made contact with Reid, and soon the gawky young man had fallen under the spell of Abu

Qatada, the religious 'authority' in Acton whose *fatwas* were tailor-made for al-Qaeda's aims. Intelligence agencies would later establish that phone calls were made between Moussaoui and Reid; a relative of Reid's confirmed that Moussaoui had visited him at her house. Richard Reid was also seen in the company of other young extremists at London's Finsbury Park mosque; men who would later turn out to be part of al-Qaeda's European network in Brussels and Amsterdam. In 1998 Reid disappeared from the Brixton mosque. 'Towards the end I saw a change in him, from wearing the beard and garments towards wearing army jackets,' recalled Baker. Reid followed in Moussaoui's footsteps, first to the *madrassas*, the religious schools in Pakistan, where he seems to have been immersed in extremist Islamic doctrine. His mother came looking for him at the Brixton mosque, concerned that she had heard nothing from him for months. But her son was now in Afghanistan. Like Moussaoui and Mohamed Atta before him, he had gone to Khaldan, where he received training in the use of explosives.

The next time Reid surfaced was in Amsterdam, in June 2001, just after Moussaoui returned to Britain before travelling to America for his flying lessons. A suspicious official from El Al, the Israeli airline, questioned Reid when he arrived to catch a flight from Amsterdam to Tel Aviv on 7 July. El Al's stringent security checks included examining passengers' footwear. Reid was allowed to proceed to Israel; there was nothing suspect in his luggage or his shoes and there was no reason to detain him or to undertake surveillance once he arrived. He spent seven days in Israel and left via the Gaza Strip, Palestinian territory. Later investigators would wonder if he had linked up with Palestinian extremists, members of Hamas, who specialise in building bombs from plastic explosives.

Richard Reid then returned to Europe and his base in Amsterdam, where he was faced with a problem familiar to al-Qaeda members – how to get rid of incriminating stamps in his passport, which showed he had been to Pakistan, the gateway to the Afghan camps. He told the British consulate in Brussels that his passport had gone through the wash with his clothes; a new one was issued. In December Reid was back in Amsterdam where he bought a pair of black trainers. A hundred grams of explosive was packed in the sole of each one by an unknown expert whose palmprint was later found on one of the shoes. The explosive, PETN, mixed with TATP, a volatile primer, is a favourite of Palestinian suicide bombers, who call it 'the Mother of Satan' because of its force and instability. A cord filled with gunpowder was then worked into each shoe as a fuse, designed to snake up past the ankles. Then Reid bought his ticket in Paris and hung around in the city; French intelligence suspect he was holed up in an al-Qaeda 'safe house' near the Gare du Nord. During this time he made much use of an Internet café, The Happy Call, sending e-mails to contacts in various mosques saying he would become a 'martyr of the Islamic cause'. He also sent an e-mail to his mother on 20 December calling it his 'will', writing: 'The reason for me sending you this is so you can see I didn't do this act out of ignorance nor did I do it just because I want to die, but rather because I see it as a duty upon me to help remove the oppressive American forces from the Muslim land and this is the only way for us to do so, as we do not have other means to fight them.'

Richard Reid's arrival at the American Airlines check-in on 21 December sounded alarm bells. He had a business-class ticket to Antigua via Miami but no luggage apart from a knapsack containing a copy of the Qur'an and a Walkman with religious tapes. He was taken aside for questioning and the interrogation took so long he missed the flight and had to spend the night in a hotel, paid for by the airline. In Afghanistan the bombs were falling on al-Qaeda's hideouts but the terror network's controllers were still functioning somewhere in the region. French intelligence sources say Reid e-mailed his contact in the terror group to ask what he should do. 'You have to go back, you have to do it, this is your mission,' came the stern reply.

Reid successfully passed through the security checks the next day and boarded American Airlines Flight 63 with 195 other people. It is extraordinary that the airline, which had lost two jets to terrorists just three months before, still allowed on board a man with a one-way ticket and no luggage; someone passengers later described as 'weird-looking' and 'a druggie' who stared blankly at the people around him. Once the plane reached cruising altitude Reid, seated over the wing near the fuel tanks, put his suicide plan into action. When the woman next to him got up to visit the toilet he bent down surreptitiously to fiddle with his shoes. An alert flight attendant, Christina Jones, decided to investigate the sulphurous odour she could smell, unusual on a non-smoking flight, and discovered Reid trying to light the fuse on his trainers with a match. She screamed for help as Reid shouted, 'Don't touch me – I'm wired!' Passengers nearby immediately overpowered the terrorist and a doctor injected him with a sedative from the plane's medical kit.

Flight 63 was then escorted by fighter jets to Boston airport, where Reid's shoes were examined and the explosive discovered. Just as the September 11 attacks had been foreshadowed by Ramsi Yousef's 1993 attempt to destroy the World Trade Center, so Richard Reid's abortive attempt to blow an airliner out of the sky bore an uncanny resemblance to Yousef's other foiled plan.

Security sources in Israel who have dealt with many PETN devices told me that if Reid had placed his foot in the right spot the shoe bombs would have had sufficient force to blow a hole in the fuselage of the plane, sucking out passengers nearby and causing the depressurised airliner to tumble out of the sky in an uncontrolled dive. What saved American Airlines Flight 63 was the rain in Paris that morning; Reid's shoes were damp and the fuse had failed to light.

For weeks after his arrest Richard Reid's connection with al-Qaeda was shrouded in mystery; he denied all links to Bin Laden and claimed he had bought the explosive himself to make the bombs. The British security services were shaken – first Moussaoui and now Reid had emerged from 'Londonistan' with no known links to the extremist network. 'Pretty cack-handed' was their verdict on the shoe bomber. But Richard Reid was more than just a lone, bungling incompetent; his links with al-Qaeda were finally confirmed when a thief made a quick buck in a market in Kabul.

A journalist from the *Wall Street Journal*, Alan Cullison, bought a used computer from an Afghan who told him it came from an office abandoned by al-Qaeda in November as Kabul fell to the Northern Alliance. It took weeks to crack the computer files, which were protected by passwords. 'Many of the text documents were couched in elliptical, coded language,' according to Cullison. 'The Taliban regime is referred to as Omar & Brothers Company, and al-Qaeda as the Abdullah Contracting Company.' It harked back to Bin Laden's early days as 'The Contractor' in the war against the Soviets, when he had often used his *nom de guerre*, 'Abu Abdullah', the father of Abdullah.

Another memo, written in the summer of 2001 under an alias used by Ayman al-Zawahiri, concerns an unnamed 'project' which would bring an end to internal lethargy and squabbling. 'It may well be a way out of this bottleneck and transfer our activities to the stage of multinationals and bring joint profit,' suggests the writer. The business language first used by al-Qaeda's top command in the Sudan years was now being applied to the impending September 11 attacks; at the time the memo was written, the plot was in its final planning stage.

The code which locked one file took five days to break; the document proved to be the travel itinerary and debriefing record of a peripatetic operative called 'brother Abdul Ra'uff'. It details how Ra'uff had concealed his puritanical faith by dumping empty alcohol bottles and cigarette ends in his hotel wastepaper bin in Amsterdam. It relays the information that he easily obtained a replacement British passport after putting his old one in the washing machine and removing a visa sticker for Pakistan. It describes an uncomfortable trip Ra'uff had made to

Israel where security staff had 'searched his shoes' and then put him in a seat at the back of the plane where they could keep an eye on him. Ra'uff was frustrated at being unable to report back on the security precautions El Al operated around its cockpits. The al-Qaeda operative then listed the places he had visited in Israel: Bethlehem, Haifa and Jerusalem, where he checked out security at the Wailing Wall and found it 'minimal'. The diligent tourist then cased railway and bus stations and a kibbutz in Tiberias.

The identity of the al-Qaeda operative was finally confirmed when the commander of the Khaldan camp was captured in Afghanistan and told his interrogators that Richard Reid was also known as 'Abdul Ra'uff' and that he had been enrolled on training for a 'solo suicide mission'. In the summary of the reconnaissance trip the writer makes it clear why a British drop-out was so valuable to the network, despite his shortcomings and his suspicious appearance: 'It appears that brothers with European passports are able to move about in Israel with greater freedom and can be treated as Israelis,' states the report. From the range and content of the documents on the computer American intelligence has concluded it belonged to Mohamed Atef, the head of al-Qaeda's military committee and one of the individuals behind the September 11 attacks. Eventually Richard Reid would plead guilty in an American court to attempting to blow up a passenger plane because he was an avowed enemy of the American people and a follower of Bin Laden. 'Basically I got on the plane with a bomb. Basically I tried to ignite it. Basically I intended to damage the plane,' Reid said to the judge with a smirk. However, Richard Reid refused to reveal who his co-conspirators in Europe had been, leaving security services in Britain, France and Holland unsure whether cells of expert bomb-makers and other al-Qaeda 'sleepers' remained hidden there.

The passengers of Flight 63 were lucky. There was to be no mass slaughter, thanks in large part to the quick reactions of the flight attendant. But unravelling the story of Richard Reid was

ultimately to have tragic consequences for one citizen of the
United States and his family. Ironically, the tragedy was indi-
rectly the result of the *Wall Street Journal*'s scoop in getting hold
of Reid's computerised itinerary.

Karachi, Pakistan, January 2002

Daniel Pearl, the South Asia bureau chief for the *Wall Street
Journal*, was working on a follow-up story investigating
Richard Reid's connections to militants in Pakistan. Pearl was
Jewish and had spent much of his life in Israel; he was married
and his wife, Mariane, was expecting their first child. On 23
January the reporter set off for a restaurant in Karachi where he
thought he was meeting an Islamic cleric whose followers
included Reid. Instead, Pakistani investigators believe, Pearl
was lured into an elaborate trap by another British member of
al-Qaeda; unlike the misfit Richard Reid, this man was a cunning and ruthless charmer whose persuasive skills had already
led at least four unsuspecting Westerners into his clutches.

Three years earlier I had tried to persuade the Indian authorities to allow me to interview a British Asian locked up in a
Delhi jail. Ahmed Omar Saïd Sheikh was a member of the
Kashmir group then called Harkut al-Ansar, one of the half-
dozen extremist Islamic organisations known to shelter under
the umbrella of al-Qaeda. The Indian authorities called him
'the poster boy for the Islamic *jihad*', and I was intrigued by
Omar Sheikh's background, so unlike that of the militants
around Bin Laden at the time. He was born in Essex, the son of
well-to-do parents. His father was a cloth merchant who sent
his son to a minor public school in Snaresbrook and then to the
prestigious London School of Economics, where fellow students and lecturers told me how bright and charming Omar
was. He became interested in the plight of fellow Muslims in
Bosnia, a war in which Bin Laden's money and al-Qaeda's military training were already secretly playing a part. In 1993 the

LSE student went on a mercy mission, delivering aid to belea-
guered communities in the Balkans; during that trip he became
drawn into a wider *jihad*, seduced by the arguments of
Pakistani militants he met there who were committed to ending
Indian control over the disputed region of Kashmir.

The following year Omar Saïd Sheikh kidnapped four
Western tourists in Indian Kashmir, luring one of them, a
British backpacker he met at Delhi bus station, with the promise of a free holiday on board his houseboat. The hostages were
released following a shoot-out with Indian authorities and the
British militant was imprisoned. It was during 1998 that I tried
to talk to Omar Sheikh in his Indian prison cell, where he had
written a diary; I was interested to speak directly, in English, to
an Islamic extremist connected to al-Qaeda to find out what lay
behind his hatred of the West. But Indian bureaucracy moves
slowly, and my application was still being processed in 1999
when hijackers seized an Indian Airlines jet. They demanded to
fly to Kandahar in Afghanistan, the power-base of the ruling
Taliban, and the pilot was not surprised to see the hijackers
greeted as comrades by the Taliban guards when the plane
landed. The release of Omar Saïd Sheikh and other Kashmiri
militants was demanded by the hijackers in return for letting
the passengers go. The Indians complied and the Briton was
brought to Kandahar and set free. Indian intelligence main-
tains that Omar Sheikh then began to work directly for
al-Qaeda as the link-man in Pakistan operating through a new
and virulently anti-Western militant organisation, Jaish-i-
Mohamed.

Four days after Daniel Pearl disappeared in January 2002,
threatening e-mails were received saying that Pearl would be
killed if the kidnappers' demands were not met. These
demands included the release of Pakistani prisoners taken since
the war began in October, the return to Pakistan of the Taliban's
former ambassador, and access to Pakistani citizens jailed in the
US following the September 11 attacks. The FBI's cyber-crime
unit traced the e-mails to two young men who were arrested in

Karachi. They confessed that Omar Sheikh had given them the text of the messages to send and that the object was 'to kidnap a person who is a Jew and who is working against Muslims'. A third man was arrested who turned out to have connections to the Pakistani intelligence services, raising suspicions that Pearl had uncovered information which linked Richard Reid and Islamic extremists once again to the all-powerful ISI.

For weeks the Pakistani police scoured the graveyards of Karachi while Pearl's wife, Mariane, waited in her hotel room, pleading with the kidnappers through the newspapers to release 'an innocent man, with an innocent wife and an unborn son'. On 21 February Mariane Pearl received the grim confirmation of her husband's death: a videotape had been received by the US Embassy showing the barbaric act itself, the cutting of Daniel Pearl's throat in front of the camera, followed by footage of his body in convulsions on the ground as a voice intoned the group's demands in Urdu. Omar Saïd Sheikh had already given himself up to the ISI to save his relatives from an uncertain fate in police custody. The murky details of the part the British militant played in Pearl's murder will probably never emerge; a master of deception and intrigue, Omar Sheikh ran rings around the police, changing his story about whether his followers killed Pearl before or after his own arrest.

The revelations about Omar Sheikh gave British intelligence another uncomfortable jolt. But the embarrassment ultimately added impetus to the lobbying inside Whitehall. For years 'Londonistan' had been perceived by some as the weakest link in Europe. Now that changed as new legislation was passed which enabled non-British residents who were suspected of belonging to terror organisations to be detained indefinitely.

'We got everything we wanted,' a quietly satisfied Whitehall source told me, relaying the information that certain 'troublesome' individuals who had needed to be monitored for years at great expense had recently decided to go abroad, mostly to Pakistan. They were taking open-ended holidays there, realising they would be arrested if they set foot again in Britain. The

fiery rhetoric of some extremist mullahs, who had been preaching anti-Semitic and anti-Western diatribes for years, was
suddenly muted in the face of new strictures against those who
preached race hate. The Blair government was at one with the
Bush administration and a climate of steely determination pervaded both Downing Street and the White House.

Not even the embarrassing pictures of shackled Taliban and
al-Qaeda prisoners at Camp X-Ray in the hot and steamy
swamp of Guantanamo Bay in Cuba could undermine American public support for the war on terror. A few liberal
newspapers tried their best to stir a sense of outrage but only in
Britain were tough questions asked about civil liberties and the
Geneva Convention. Most of the detainees at Camp X-Ray
turned out to be insignificant individuals, not hardcore members of the terror network, and it was unlikely there would be
enough evidence against them to warrant their appearance
before military tribunals. The seven British men at Guantanamo Bay were almost all from the Pakistani community in
Tipton, a small town in the Midlands, who had made their way
to Afghanistan in the days following September 11. They were
seen as lost souls by the intelligence officers who interviewed
them, youngsters who had volunteered for a new *jihad* but who
had become cannon-fodder, thrust into the front line by al-
Qaeda and the Taliban when the bombing of Afghanistan
began.

Faisalabad, Pakistan, March 2002

Al-Qaeda's Pakistan connection yielded up its biggest prize at
2:00 A.M. on 28 March. American FBI agents and Pakistani
police from the elite Special Services Group raided Shahbaz
Cottage, a two-storey house in a middle-class suburb of
Faisalabad, an industrial city deep in the heart of the Punjab,
200 miles south of the Afghan border. A roof-top gun battle
resulted in the capture of twenty-eight Yemenis, Saudis,

Pakistanis and Palestinians, one of whom was shot three times, once in the groin, as he tried to escape.

'He's singing in a higher pitch,' said an unnamed American official gleefully after agents walked among the captured and the wounded, comparing them with photographs in an intelligence dossier. They were looking for a handsome thirty-year-old who wore glasses and a neat beard. The injured man was now clean-shaven but there was no mistaking his likeness to the photograph. It was Abu Zubaydah, his full name now revealed as Zayn al-Abidin Mohamed Husayn, the mysterious and powerful individual responsible for screening recruits to al-Qaeda's camps since 1995. Once they graduated, he would assign them to front-line fighting in Afghanistan or direct them to various sleeper cells around the world. Zubaydah speaks at least three languages fluently, including English, and balances his scholarly side with an expertise in weaponry, including mortars and truck bombs. The most senior member of the second generation of al-Qaeda leaders, Abu Zubaydah was known to have had an operational role in the African embassy bombings and to have been the field commander of the USS *Cole* attack. He was one of only a handful of people privy to the details of the September 11 atrocities. When Mohamed Atef was killed by an American bombing raid in November 2001, Zubaydah effectively replaced him as al-Qaeda's number three, charged by Bin Laden with reconstituting and regenerating the terror network outside Afghanistan.

'Al-Qaeda has many tentacles but one of them has been cut off,' said the White House spokesman. American investigators looked forward to questioning Abu Zubaydah about his encyclopaedic knowledge of the global network. 'There is no question but that having an opportunity to visit with him is helpful,' said Donald Rumsfeld. 'Sometimes I understate for emphasis,' he added drily.

The celebrations at Abu Zubaydah's arrest were tempered by the sobering confirmation that the terror network was still active and still using the tried and tested formula which had been so successful in the past. A Pakistani man with fake business cards and a plausible story had found the house in Faisalabad. He paid a generous deposit and the first month's rent up-front in exchange for a year's lease, much as Mohamed Atta had done in Hamburg. 'It's a peaceful area and it's just my luck that I had to rent it out to al-Qaeda,' said Shaheen Kauser, the travel agent who owned the house. Her words had a familiar ring; Thorsten Albrecht, the German estate agent who rented 54 Marienstrasse to Atta and his friends, had said much the same. Zubaydah's group had slipped up, however, when they used a satellite phone and sent an e-mail which triggered electronic monitoring systems run by American intelligence.

Abu Zubaydah was the biggest fish the coalition had caught to date; other al-Qaeda captives had confirmed he was responsible for planning attacks even post-September 11. The abortive plot to blow up the US Embassy in Paris, for example, had been directed by Abu Zubaydah. His satellite phone number was also discovered in the memory of another telephone belonging to a man accused of plotting to destroy the US Embassy in Sarajevo. Zubaydah was 'an ideal candidate' for the military tribunals introduced after September 11 to try senior al-Qaeda people; tribunals which could impose the death penalty. Donald Rumsfeld rejected the idea of using truth drugs on him or sending him to a third country where torture might be employed, but assured the American public that 'we intend to get every single thing out of him to try to prevent terrorist acts in the future'.

Raids on other houses in Faisalabad and Lahore netted fifty more extremist suspects, evidence that Pakistan's militant Islamic fringe was providing key assistance to al-Qaeda in its efforts to regroup. The suicide bombing of a Protestant church within Islamabad's diplomatic enclave, earlier in March, had killed an American embassy employee and her seventeen-year-old daughter. It had been the most serious challenge yet to the embattled President Musharraf as he walked a precarious tightrope between satisfying American demands to root out terrorism and keeping control of his own nation of 135 million Muslims. He had rounded up 2,000 militants in January and banned five Pakistani groups which sympathised with al-Qaeda, but most of those detained had quietly been released or were only under house arrest. But in the aftermath of the discovery of Abu Zubaydah and large numbers of al-Qaeda's terror network within his country, Musharraf found himself in a corner. He – and, more significantly, his intelligence service, the ISI – could no longer claim their limited co-operation with their American counterparts was sufficient. A shaken President Musharraf gave in to pressure to expand clandestine US Special Forces operations in the border areas to become a joint military operation to flush out al-Qaeda fighters.

The capture of Abu Zubaydah held out the biggest hope yet of cracking the network's future plans. A terror alert was put out to over 7,000 US banks and financial institutions, the result of information Abu Zubaydah provided, but intelligence officers in Europe were sceptical. 'Will anything he tells us be the truth?' one wondered. 'It's more likely to be disinformation.' As spring arrived the jigsaw of the terror network was being pieced together from an avalanche of leads, many of them probably false ones, provided by numerous captives. The White House had compared al-Qaeda to an octopus, boasting that in capturing Abu Zubaydah the US had severed one of its tentacles. But the coming months would prove that al-Qaeda not only had many more legs than an octopus, it was also capable of quickly growing back any limb of the organisation lost to the Americans. Abu Zubaydah had replaced Mohamed Atef, who had been killed by US bombs. And no sooner was Zubaydah in custody than his place was taken by another veteran operative, Khalid Sheikh Mohamed, the architect of the September 11 attacks. And while the terror network was secretly re-grouping outside Afghanistan, the day of reckoning on the battlefield between al-Qaeda's remaining fighters and the coalition approached.

23

Operation Anaconda

'Do not underestimate your enemy. If he is a mouse, prepare to fight a lion.'

—Afghan proverb

Afghanistan, April 2002

The RAF Hercules was plunged into darkness as the loadmaster extinguished the lights. The plane banked sharply and dropped swiftly towards the few scattered lights of Kabul below, the two Land Rovers and mounted gun in the belly of the aircraft groaning as their chains tightened. It was 2:00 A.M. and I climbed stiffly off the canvas roof of the jeep, where I had been sleeping, and buckled myself into a webbing seat. Silently guns and flak jackets were passed out among the crew. The pilots' faces, clad in 'night-owls', glowed an eerie green; the night-vision goggles locked on to infra-red signals set on the runway to guide the plane down. As we trundled along the runway towards the bombed-out buildings where the RAF had made their base, the hulks of wrecked Soviet planes, testament to the country's war-torn history, loomed in the shadows beyond. In the darkened streets of Kabul, notwithstanding the curfew, the nightly round of gunfights and rocket attacks was proceeding as usual.

I had arrived in Afghanistan in the final stages of Operation Anaconda, America's bloody spring offensive against al-Qaeda, which had so far claimed the lives of eight Americans and perhaps as many as eight hundred of Bin Laden's fighters. No one knew the true figure. 'Success for us will be to deny al-Qaeda and the Taliban a sanctuary in Afghanistan and hand the country back to the Afghan people,' Major General Frank 'Buster' Hagenbeck, the US commander in Afghanistan, had said. One of his officers offered a pithier definition of what lay in store: 'We're coming up on their campaign season here in Afghanistan,' he said. 'It's not baseball, it's war in the springtime.'

The base for the American and coalition forces engaged in the fight against al-Qaeda lies at Bagram in the Shamali valley, more than an hour's drive north of the capital. Kabul was humming with activity by the time we drove out of the city through the market area; row upon row of shops, each squeezed into a metal shipping container lying on its side. Tin Alley with bright kettles and giant pressure cookers gave way to a visceral meat market via a jumble of wheelbarrows heaped with spring onions and tomatoes. Finally Kabul petered out along a street which seemed to be the garden centre, crammed with pots of geraniums and roses. On the surface, life seemed to be returning to normal – but this was the capital, hundreds of miles from the troubled eastern and southern Pashtun provinces.

The Shamali valley offers a graphic and shocking impression of what twenty-three years of war has done to this country. Once the breadbasket of Afghanistan with its orchards and vines, the valley lies between towering peaks stretching out on all sides. The mountains, purple or gold depending on the light, with long streaks of snow reaching down from their peaks, are untouched and timeless. But the valley bears the scars of the many battles that have ebbed and flowed along it. Soviet, Northern Alliance and Taliban bombardments have left row upon row of twisted and blackened vines, stumps of trees and termite-like heaps of mud, the ruins of villages. Fresh craters punctuate the road where the latest ordnance, American this time, has added another layer of destruction. Most deadly of all is the unseen horror, the landmines lurking under the inviting carpet of wild pink tulips. Rows of stones line each side of the road, the majority painted red to warn that areas beyond have not been cleared. The odd white stone indicates where a mine has been removed. Children dice with death to gather flowers in the minefields and sell them for a few coins to passing truck drivers.

At the gates of Bagram base, where the Soviets lived for a decade in their fruitless attempt to subdue the *mujahideen*, US military police now frisk the beards and turbans of Afghans waiting patiently in long lines for manual work inside the razor-wire perimeter. Once through the sandbags the long dusty road through the centre of the camp is filled with American soldiers jogging to keep up their fitness levels on this high altitude plain. Explosions shake the ground as wrecked buildings are cleared of unexploded ordnance. Rusty piles of tanks and skeletons of trucks remain in heaps but between them neat rows of green tents have been erected and a Stars and Stripes flag flutters against the backdrop of the snow-covered mountains. The old Soviet MiGs still rust in the minefields scattered throughout the base but beside them a sparkling blue mountain of bottled mineral water has sprung up. Australian troops in shorts and T-shirts ride dirt bikes around the tents of a Spanish field hospital; Bulgarian mine-clearers work alongside Danish medics. The international coalition assembled at Bagram has many different uniforms and languages.

There is a purposeful, efficient air at Bagram; Chinook and Black Hawk helicopters drone incessantly along the flight line, ferrying troops and equipment in and out. A vast and derelict hangar holds the inner sanctum, the Tactical Operations Center or TOC, the nerve centre of the war, where intelligence is collated and strikes against al-Qaeda planned and directed. Burly men in jeans and polo shirts, sporting pistols in leather holsters, pass in silence between the command centre and the Special Forces tents, off-limits to the press. These are the so-called 'squirrels', the CIA men and military intelligence officers whose war this has been from the start. Inside the TOC the intelligence services of other nations, most notably Britain, have their representatives too, exchanging information on an hourly basis.

Night after night our tent on the edge of the runway reverberates to the sound of Special Forces Chinooks taking off. Fast pick-up trucks driven by 'squirrels', their headlights blacked out, deliver weapons and equipment in unmarked crates to the choppers to take to undercover units in the field. The secret war is still in full swing but now it is integrated within a more conventional military framework.

The Americans learned a salutary lesson at Tora Bora in December 2001, when it was brought home to them that a combination of US air power and Afghan allies could not defeat al-Qaeda. By February 2002 three infantry battalions from the 10th Mountain Division and the 101st Airborne Division were preparing for a big offensive under a two-star American general. Major General Hagenbeck had been brought in to command the military campaign on the ground in Afghanistan after the débâcle at Tora Bora. 'The lesson we learned is that the enemy knows the terrain well and will take advantage of it, and they will exploit any weakness they can detect on the part of coalition forces,' Hagenbeck told me in his office, hung with sports pennants of the baseball teams the former PT instructor supports. A slight, fit man with sandy hair and an unassuming air, Hagenbeck is not the archetypal American general. 'Tora Bora taught us there is no silver bullet for defeating al-Qaeda,' he went on, 'but we clearly need more than just Special Forces or air power alone. We need all our assets, both high tech and low tech – boots on the ground.'

American high-tech assets were telling Central Command that al-Qaeda fighters were regrouping in the eastern province of Paktia as the harsh Afghan winter began to abate at the end of February. Satellites and signals intelligence showed them collecting in a valley south of the town of Gardez, again in a mountainous area close to the Pakistan border. 'After Tora Bora we were looking for concentrations of al-Qaeda and our human intelligence sources indicated they were gathering in the Shah-i-Kot valley,' Lieutenant Colonel Jasey Briley, the chief military intelligence officer at Bagram told me. 'Locals were being bought out or forced out by the Arabs.'

To add to the signals intelligence and human assets on the ground the Americans had a powerful eye in the sky, a drone or unmanned aerial reconnaissance vehicle called the Predator. Operated remotely by CIA officers on the ground at Bagram, the twenty-six-foot long drone can fly at up to 26,000 feet photographing activity below at distances up to twenty miles away. Armed with Hellfire missiles it can deliver a devastating blow without endangering the lives of airmen. Predator is an important step towards the 'automated battlefield' that the American defence establishment dreams of.

I saw some of the top-secret pictures that Predator had taken of the build-up of al-Qaeda forces in Shah-i-Kot. The colour resolution and the detail were extraordinary; on a sheer slope of boulders and rocky scree covered with snow, two fighters had somehow pitched a fragile tent, glowing blue in the wintry light. They were crouched in the entrance. The camera had moved in for a closer look at the mountaintop position; this time an al-Qaeda soldier had his back towards me; tall and slightly stooping, he was hunched against the cold in his traditional *shalwar kameez*. The man was guarding a machine-gun position, the weapon carefully protected from the elements by an oiled tarpaulin. 'You can see from his clothes, his posture, his height; he is clearly an Arab,' I was told.

The Predator pictures backed up the spies' information on the ground – al-Qaeda and the remnants of the Taliban were gathering for another fight. 'We estimated there were between 150 and 250 men in Shah-i-Kot,' Briley told me. They were believed to be the hard-line fighters, fanatical Chechens, tough Uigurs from China, and experienced Saudis, the backbone of

Bin Laden's forces. Former Taliban commanders, Ibrahim Haqqani and Saifur Rahman Mansoor, were also suspected of being in the command chain. There were whispers that HVTs, High Value Targets, were holed up in the mountains and that their purpose was not only to strike at the American forces but to attack the interim Afghan government of Hamid Karzai.

On 2 March Operation Anaconda was launched with the intention of encircling al-Qaeda like a snake and squeezing the life out of it for ever. The first phase of the battle called for 400 local Afghan forces under the command of a young general, Ahmad Zia, with US Special Forces alongside, to form the vanguard of the attack. Zia's men would advance southwards from the town of Gardez, swinging left to enter the Shah-i-Kot valley from the west, sweeping al-Qaeda before them. Unlike at Tora Bora, this time troops from the 101st Airborne would be stationed along the mountain ridges to the north, east and south of the valley, to block al-Qaeda's escape. The Americans expected them to try to flee through the channels which ran, like the spokes of a wheel, from the valley through the mountains to the Pakistan border. The coil of the snake would form a vast ring encompassing seventy-two square miles at an altitude of up to 12,000 feet. Seventeen hundred US and Canadian forces would then turn their firepower on al-Qaeda, trapped in the middle.

'Unfortunately, the enemy had a vote,' the Deputy Chief of Staff Walter Piatt ruefully observed as he showed me the map of the battlefield. 'Instead of fleeing, this time they were prepared to stand and fight.' Local people in Gardez were mindful of the old Afghan proverb: 'Do not underestimate your enemy. If he is a mouse, then prepare to fight a lion.'

When Zia's forces arrived al-Qaeda troops were already waiting for them with a mortar ambush, killing a US Special Forces soldier, Chief Warrant Officer Stanley Harriman, and three of Zia's men. It was dark and wet and Zia and his Afghans quickly withdrew under fire, bogged down by the mud. Once again, as at Tora Bora, Afghan forces had not proved capable of spearheading the assault. As American Chinooks poured troops into the various landing sites in the mountains around the valley they were met by a barrage of small-arms fire, mortars and rocket-propelled grenade attacks from well-entrenched al-Qaeda fighters. 'We hit the dirt as the mortars came in from behind us,' Captain Tom Murphy, a fire support officer with the 101st, told me. 'It sunk in pretty quickly that things weren't going the way we'd planned.'

The resistance was fiercest at the spot in the south named Blocking Position Ginger where troops of the 10th Mountain Division were pinned down for more than forty-eight hours. The intelligence picture had been wrong: far from there being a couple of hundred al-Qaeda fighters, there were at least five times that number. 'There were many others along the eastern ridge line in fighting positions and trenches and sophisticated infill positions,' admitted intelligence officer Briley. 'We found we had landed on top of them instead of landing outside of where they were, and that stirred up the hornet's nest.'

On the ridges American officers called in close air support from F-15, F-16 and B-52 bombers while Apache gunship helicopters laid down a wall of steel on al-Qaeda positions around Ginger. So far the Americans had suffered only the one initial fatality; the troops pinned down at Ginger had suffered casualties but no one else had been killed. 'The Apaches couldn't clear the area because every time they went near it they were taking [fire from] RPG and small arms as well as some 50-calibre weapons,' said Chief Warrant Officer Jeff Simon, a Chinook pilot who had taken the first wave of troops in, the men now under intense fire. 'We couldn't understand why the commanders would not authorise us to return immediately with back-up forces, as our guys were in so much trouble on the ground.'

The decision was made by Hagenbeck to attempt to insert two special-ops surveillance teams to identify al-Qaeda positions at Ginger. It ended in the US military's single largest loss of life since the battle for Mogadishu in 1993.

At 3:00 A.M. on 4 March, two days into the battle, a Chinook codenamed 'Razor 3' carrying US Navy SEALs approached the Takhur Ghar mountain where the Ginger landing zone was located. As the chopper came in to land, RPG fire severed the chopper's hydraulic line and the pilot jerked the craft up and away without putting down the SEAL team. The second helicopter was unharmed but pulled out to shadow its damaged twin. It was only when the crippled helicopter put down some miles away that a head count was taken and it was realised that Neil Roberts, a Petty Officer 1st Class, had fallen out of the Chinook during the aborted landing. A Predator was launched to scan the area and beamed back pictures of Roberts being captured and taken away by al-Qaeda fighters.

In the command centre Walter Piatt was among those who saw the pictures. 'We were not going to leave a fellow soldier on the field, we were going to go in after him,' he said. 'Nobody hesitated, nobody questioned it.' It was also a cold-blooded calculation made to stop a valuable source of intelligence falling into enemy hands, especially the hands of Chechens, infamous for their use of torture. 'Operationally and strategically it was vital to get him out because we knew what al-Qaeda would do if they got a US soldier in their hands,' said Piatt. 'They pay money to anyone that can deliver one, dead or alive.'

Major General Hagenbeck ordered two more Chinooks, 'Razor 1' and 'Razor 2', to launch a quick-reaction force into the area to search for Roberts. His fellow SEALs had immediately requested this. 'They all but told me, we're going to turn this chopper back once it's re-armed and fuelled and get him, and I supported that decision,' Hagenbeck told me. 'It was an incredibly brave thing for those soldiers to do – to search for their buddy,' said Piatt, watching events unfold on screen in the command centre.

Just after the helicopters took off from Bagram the officers in the bunker saw pictures from the Predator which they had been dreading. Before them, the real-time images showed Neil

Roberts being executed by his captors. 'Revenge was what flashed through your mind,' admitted Walter Piatt. 'I knew then that these people would never surrender, so great was their hatred of us.' As foreigners the Arabs and Chechens were unwelcome in Afghanistan, unwanted back home. They knew they had nowhere to go but to die on the hillsides of Shah-i-Kot.

As the sun rose over Ginger, the enemy greeted the two Special Forces Chinooks with heavy machine-gun fire and RPGs. The glass cockpit bubble of Razor 1 was shattered, the pilot hit in the thigh; Razor 2 was immediately called out of the zone. The first Chinook plummeted to the ground and the soldiers ran out of the back ramp into a hail of bullets. Three dropped dead immediately and despite returning fire from the chopper one of the two American gunners was also picked off. Inside the cargo bay of the downed Chinook two medics worked to save the lives of their wounded colleagues, even after the forward compartment of the helicopter caught fire. All the while the Predator was beaming back pictures of the crash site and the al-Qaeda fighters swarming around it.

Four hours into the firefight one of the medics, Senior Airman Jason Cunningham, a 26-year-old on his first combat mission, crossed the enemy line of fire seven times to drag his wounded colleagues out of the Chinook on a sled to a safer position. He moved them a second and a third time until he was hit in the abdomen, suffering severe internal injuries. Eight hours later he died in the snow. 'Our motto is "That others may live",' one of Cunningham's colleagues in the Air Force Combat Search and Rescue corps told me. 'He is deserving of the highest military honour we can give him.' Six Americans died on Ginger but, thanks to Cunningham's medical skill and heroism, ten wounded soldiers survived.

In the skies above Ginger, Matt, an A-10 Thunderbolt pilot, was acting as the airborne traffic cop as fire, missiles and bombs from dozens of aircraft began to turn the tide against al-Qaeda on the ground. 'I could not believe it – six months before

I had seen the World Trade Center collapse and now here I was in my plane looking down at the ground and seeing gunfire raging,' Matt told me. The risk of 'friendly fire' was now a serious one with US soldiers on the ground calling down laser-guided bombs within a hair's breadth of their own positions. 'It was very chaotic, planes everywhere in a very small piece of sky,' according to Matt. 'There were guys on the ground who knew their own position but didn't know specifically which aircraft they were talking to.' Miraculously there were no own-goals that day.

It took ten days of fierce fighting for the Americans to gradually gain the upper hand. US military sources estimated that as many as 800 al-Qaeda and Taliban forces had been killed. On the coalition side eleven had died, eight of them American, and there were eighty-eight casualties. In the Pentagon there was a growing feeling that the battle marked the climax of the war in Afghanistan.

In the tents and Mess halls at Bagram soldiers of all ranks expressed grudging admiration for al-Qaeda. 'I had respect for the enemy before and even more so now,' Hagenbeck said. 'There was not a single occasion of any of them attempting to surrender even when they knew death was imminent, eyeball to eyeball.' Infantrymen remarked on the coolness of al-Qaeda, who could be seen almost strolling to their positions to pick off Americans, one by one. 'Their tactics were clever,' said Captain Murphy. 'They were smaller in numbers but they chose their moments to harass us, waiting for the right chance to strike and inflict casualties.' Military intelligence officers were surprised at what the bodies and the field camps yielded. 'They were well supplied, well equipped, well trained,' Briley told me. 'They had solar panels, Gore-Tex clothing, some of the best waterproof equipment in the world.'

The biggest puzzle of all was why the enemy had fought so tenaciously instead of melting away in the earlier stages when they had the Americans on the defensive. Could they have been protecting some top leader in a bunker or a cave, maybe

Bin Laden himself? 'No doubt there was some kind of leadership there,' Briley concluded. 'They had command and control but we cannot say who was there for sure.' For Walter Piatt, Operation Anaconda had rectified the tactical mistake made at Tora Bora. American infantry had borne the brunt of the battle, engaging the enemy themselves, not relying on their Afghan proxies. 'Al-Qaeda chose to stay and fight this time and that was a terrible mistake,' Piatt said. 'They lost people it took them years to train, the mid-level management of the group. It was a success for us.'

Following the operation American troops swept the caves and camps of al-Qaeda around Shah-i-Kot. They discovered documents, currency and computer records to add to the intelligence picture on the terror network. There were personal diaries kept by some of the fighters detailing ways of countering US high-tech equipment and disabling helicopters. But there were no high-ranking commanders among the dead and reporters wondered why so few al-Qaeda and Taliban bodies had been discovered when US military sources were briefing, less than a week into the battle, that eight hundred had been killed. Some may have been buried or carried away but even General Hagenbeck was reluctant to put a definite figure on the enemy death toll. 'The numbers are in the hundreds but I don't think we will ever know for sure because of the types of killing that went on – with laser-guided bombs, for example.'

When the eight flag-draped coffins of the American dead arrived home, the public backlash against the war, which the military feared, did not materialise. The unspoken 'V' word – Vietnam – had shaped America's outlook on warfare for decades. General Franks, the Commander of Operation Enduring Freedom, receiving the coffins of the Anaconda dead back home, made a significant slip in his speech. 'Our thoughts and prayers go out to the families and friends of those who lost their lives in our ongoing operations in Vietnam,' Franks said. 'Certainly that sacrifice was appreciated by this nation.' It was a revealing moment which underscored how the loss of thousands of American lives in a protracted guerrilla war abroad still haunted the older generation of US generals.

It took Operation Anaconda, a full-scale military confrontation with al-Qaeda, to lay to rest a more recent humiliation, the ghost of Mogadishu, created in part by the hidden hand of Osama bin Laden. The spectre of Somalia had hung over military and foreign policy for nearly a decade but now Bush and Rumsfeld had taken the decision to exorcise the ghost of the dead Rangers – and the nation and younger military officers stood behind him. 'We see it as a fight against terrorism,' said Jasey Briley. 'That's what motivates each and every one of us to go after the al-Qaeda network, whatever it costs.' His view was echoed by Walter Piatt when he told me: 'We knew what our country wanted us to do as a military force. It was clear the American people understood there were going to be casualties. It was vital to defend our way of life.'

'The hunt continues' was the mantra repeated every day at 9:00 A.M. at the Bagram base when Major Bryan Hilferty, Hagenbeck's spokesman, held his daily meeting with the press. Each morning, before relaying the latest details of the war – the incursions, the deaths and injuries on both sides – Hilferty prefaced his remarks with a portrait of one of the American victims of September 11. We heard in turn about the baseball player, the father of two, the jazz musician, the immigrant who worked in the Twin Towers. There was no doubt that for every American soldier at Bagram, the fight was deeply personal. On one of my flights over Afghanistan with the military, I flew on a C-130 transporter belonging to the Minnesota National Guard. Down the fuselage of the plane, behind the soldiers' backs, hung eight large, brand-new Stars and Stripes banners. 'We can say these flags have flown over Afghanistan and have played a part in our war on terror,' one of the airmen explained. 'We take them home to hang from public buildings in Minnesota to remind the American people of what we are doing.'

As weary US troops returned to Bagram from Shah-i-Kot, the military consensus was that Anaconda had been a success for the coalition forces despite the uncertain enemy death toll and the unknown quantity of fighters left in the mountains. US Central Command had learned their lesson at Tora Bora but they knew that al-Qaeda too would be wiser, after Shah-i-Kot. 'We expect them to disperse, be harder to deal with, become more of a guerrilla-style operation,' said Lieutenant Colonel Briley. For Matt the pilot, who had stared at the enemy down the barrel of an A-10's lethal Gatling gun, the chances of finding large groups of al-Qaeda fighters again were slim. 'It's not going to be large group formations any more, it will be small pockets of resistance,' he predicted. 'That negates our power, the large weapons we would want to bring against them, and it forces us to get down on the ground and mix it with them in person.'

'This is not the last battle of this war, but as long as al-Qaeda want to send them here, we will kill them,' Major General Hagenbeck warned. 'And if they want to go somewhere else, we will kill them there.'

Gardez, Afghanistan, April 2002

The road climbed suddenly to 10,000 feet as our convoy zig-zagged up the mountain. Behind us the plain lay shrouded in mist, the scattered tents of the Kuchi nomad tribes were mere dots, their herds of sheep and camels smudges in the distance. We were in the snowline now, descending sharply into Gardez, the town north of the Shah-i-Kot valley in the province of Paktia. This was warlord territory, where al-Qaeda had chosen to make its stand and profit from the divisions which still bedevilled Afghan society.

Gardez has a frontier feel with its dusty streets and battered buildings; men with spectacular beards and turbans patrol with ancient guns and bandoleers of bright bullets slung around them. The Mujahideen Photo Studio now sported dubious pictures of women with lush hair and smiling lips but there was hardly a *burkha* to be seen in the streets. Any American or European, let alone a woman, was in danger of provoking strong emotions in this troubled area: a grenade had recently been lobbed through the window of a car carrying a Canadian journalist, who was seriously wounded. *Shabnama* or 'night letters', the handiwork of al-Qaeda, were circulating in the town offering a bounty of $100,000 for any Western soldier or journalist delivered alive; $50,000 for a body. I shrank down in my seat and pulled my chequered scarf, the standard male head covering, round my face. We rattled on towards the large whitewashed fortress on a rocky hill which dominates the town of Gardez.

I had come to the wild Pashtun province of Paktia, on the border with Pakistan, where the Taliban and al-Qaeda had historically enjoyed the support of many tribes, to escape the sanitised bubble of the Bagram military base and get a reality check on what was really happening on the ground. At Bagram the daily press briefings assured us that 'mopping-up' operations were all that was needed in Paktia in the wake of the success of Operation Anaconda and the reported deaths of some eight hundred al-Qaeda guerrillas. Inside the medieval Gardez fortress General Zia Huddin, commander of the local forces, received me in a room strewn with cushions and lined with bodyguards nursing Kalashnikovs. 'I believe that only a hundred, at most, were killed,' Huddin said, offering me green tea and almonds. 'The problem was that the Americans did not know the area well, they were inexperienced and they did not have proper information about the situation on the ground.' The general and his troops had been called upon to provide reinforcements later in the battle, after the young Afghan protégé of the US Special Forces, General Ahmad Zia, and his men had pulled back as al-Qaeda threatened to overwhelm the coalition.

In the compound of the Governor's house in Gardez, they were gearing up for trouble; men stacked large quantities of ammunition and rockets into the back of ancient vehicles.

Inside the house two secretaries sat cross-legged signing documents in a corner as an imposing figure with a large white beard argued loudly with various tribesmen. This was Taj Mohamed Wardak, lately returned from Los Angeles to take over the most unenviable job on earth – Governor of Paktia Province. He was charged with keeping the peace in Paktia and preventing local warlords from tearing each other apart while the election of representatives to the *Loya Jirga*, the council to shape the future government of Afghanistan, proceeded.

'The end of al-Qaeda does not depend on Bin Laden or anyone else,' Wardak explained, 'it depends on the co-operation of the people and only real democracy here can kill this disease.' The Governor explained that al-Qaeda was up to its old tricks, exploiting local rivalries to foment acts of terror against US and Afghan government forces. Unknown gunmen had just attacked a convoy of coalition forces patrolling in the area; one soldier had been killed and seven injured and the attack had provoked a firefight with American soldiers. 'If it had gone on much longer it would have been disastrous,' Wardak said. 'Gardez would have been bombed by the Americans and there would have been many casualties.' Hundreds, perhaps more than a thousand Afghan civilians had already been killed by American bombs, many of them the victims of complex local rivalries. In the first three months of the war the US had been too trusting of its Afghan allies, too willing to bomb what they were told were concentrations of al-Qaeda and Taliban sympathisers but which turned out to be innocent people, including women and children.

Wardak claimed that al-Qaeda had joined forces with a commander working for a local warlord, Pacha Khan. Khan was sulking in a small patch of territory near Shah-i-Kot; ousted from Gardez by the Karzai government and replaced by Wardak, Khan still believed he was the rightful ruler. 'Al-Qaeda is not small in numbers; we know there are opposition groups in Afghanistan supporting them and that has effectively

swelled their ranks,' Wardak sighed. 'They will work together
to change the tactics of this war because al-Qaeda know they
cannot continue a face-to-face confrontation with the Americans.'

I headed out of Gardez towards the valley of Shah-i-Kot; in
front of me a band of guards provided by General Zia Huddin
waved their RPGs exuberantly. Their Toyota Hi-Lux pick-up
truck, a status symbol among Paktia's warlords, swerved from
side to side across a plain dotted with the gigantic mud-walled
fortresses of Pashtun clans. Several check-points on we reached
the edge of Shah-i-Kot to be told it was not safe to venture further. 'Five hundred British commandos are in there. There is a
bombardment going on,' said Mir Agha Khan, one of Zia
Huddin's local commanders. 'There is no guarantee of what
will happen.'

It was the beginning of the deployment of 1,700 British
Marines from 45 Commando; proof of the Blair government's
commitment to the war on terror. The call for help had gone out
from US Central Command in the frantic early days of March,
when Operation Anaconda threatened to go awry and the generals were getting windy about the headlines resulting from the
deaths of eight US servicemen. 'It was suggested that we might
be able to make a contribution with our Marine mountain warfare cadre,' a British officer diplomatically put it. The Marines
at Bagram camp were more outspoken: in their opinion
American infantrymen were not up to gruelling, guerrilla-style
operations at high altitudes. 'The Yanks are great with all the
bells and whistles and logistics but in terms of boots on the
ground they don't have the experience that we do,' said one
young Marine, his face windburned from a reconnaissance trip
in the mountains.

The British patrol had a more hard-nosed approach to the
problem of al-Qaeda than the American soldiers I had spoken
to. This war was not a personal vendetta sparked by the
destruction of landmarks in New York and Washington – the
Marines saw it as an opportunity to put their skills to the test

against a cunning and worthy adversary. With their mobile field guns and thirty weeks of intensive training 45 Commando were raring to get stuck in to the fight. 'They're just like us, they're a well-trained force; soldiers rather than terrorists,' said Second Lieutenant Grant Abbott of Whiskey Company.

'We want to confront the terrorists in the mountains and stop them dispersing into local communities,' said Lieutenant Colonel Paul Harradine, the British army spokesman. There was an understanding among officers and men that the British public would be more tolerant of casualties than the Americans; newspapers were already being briefed and carrying stories conveying the message that twenty deaths and sixty casualties could be the price the military would have to pay. 'If al-Qaeda can kill us they hope to provoke a backlash in the West so that we'll back off and give them breathing space to continue their terror campaign,' Matthew Waite, a Whiskey Company second lieutenant in his early twenties told me. 'I'd be foolish to say I was not afraid they might kill me, but I truly believe we have to beat them.'

Anaconda was the first and looked as if it would be the last set-piece, large-scale battle against al-Qaeda in Afghanistan. It had not 'smoked them out' as Bush had hoped, and it was not the 'unqualified success' that General Franks had claimed on a visit to Bagram base at the end of March. British military intelligence estimated that at least 2,000 of Bin Laden's fighters remained in the Paktia area and perhaps as many as 8,000 were not far away, across the border in Pakistan. The coalition forces had no option but to launch Anaconda when they learned the enemy was massing in the Paktia area but by stamping on the Taliban and al-Qaeda pool that had gathered in Shah-i-Kot, they had scattered droplets of resistance in a wider arc.

The coalition baton was being handed from the Americans to the British as Camp Gibraltar, the Marines' section at Bagram, expanded daily to accommodate the 1,700 troops. A Union Jack now fluttered against the backdrop of the mountains. 'I don't

see this as being a short-term thing,' Matthew Waite acknowledged, 'but everyone is prepared to be here for as long as we're
required.' His Russian military predecessors at Bagram would
have smiled cynically at those words.

The first few weeks of the Marines' deployment proved
frustrating. There was every sign that instead of meekly acqui-
escing to the British Army's desire to 'confront them in the
mountains', al-Qaeda had quietly melted away across the
porous border with Pakistan. Once more the enemy had
changed its tactics to mirror those they had used so successfully
against the Soviets over a decade earlier. Time was on their
side and they could afford to wait. The Marines could claim no
'kills', and not even a sighting of the enemy: just a succession of
captured ammunition dumps and caches of weapons. British
newspapers began to jeer about the 'Phoney War'. The commander of the British forces, Brigadier Roger Lane, openly
hinted that the Marines might not remain in Afghanistan for as
long as first planned, but Donald Rumsfeld pointedly said,
'There are still al-Qaeda and Taliban in the country and in
neighbouring countries . . . We have no intention of announcing
an end date or anything of that type.'

The British mission became mired in recriminations, accusations and confusion as Operation Ptarmigan gave way to
Operation Snipe and then Condor, all of them failing to root out
any 'AQT' – al-Qaeda/Taliban forces, in army parlance. The
only thing the Marines were catching was a mystery illness,
'winter vomiting disease', which swept through the medical
staff and forced the quarantining of Camp Gibraltar. Roger
Lane insisted that his troops had dealt a 'significant blow' to al-
Qaeda and that not finding the enemy was, 'from a strategic
point of view, an encouraging sign'. But this was not what ministers back in London wanted to hear. Tony Blair had stood
shoulder to shoulder with George Bush from the start, and
British intelligence had been ordered by Downing Street to
break their normal rule of silence and put together a public
dossier of evidence against al-Qaeda in the wake of the

September attacks. Chancellor Gordon Brown and the Treasury had been at the forefront of successful attempts to stop the flow of funds into Bin Laden's coffers. The Defence Secretary, Geoff Hoon, had stood up in the Commons and spoken about the Marines' high state of readiness for action in unforgiving terrain. When they arrived in Afghanistan, four companies of soldiers had marched off their transporters at Bagram base to the rousing sound of bagpipes: Britain was determined to play a significant and a glorious role in the war on terror.

A poisonous atmosphere soon developed on the hot, dusty and alcohol-free airbase as bored journalists grew tired of the gloss that was being put on the Marines' mission and the attempts to control access to the troops, lest they say something out of turn. An intrepid reporter was caught sneaking though a minefield at night to get a quote from soldiers, and other hacks were threatened with expulsion from the base for writing unhelpful stories. The journalists got their own back: 'Marines Losing War With Thin Air'; 'Arms Blown Up by Marines Were Mine, Says Afghan Ally'; 'Secret War Keeps Truth Away from Home Front' – the headlines got worse and worse. American forces on the base watched with some amusement and a tinge of satisfaction. They were still smarting at the Marines' claim, widely circulated in the British press, that they were harder, more suited to guerrilla warfare than their coalition colleagues. The whispering campaign in London against the unfortunate Brigadier whose talents were more suited to soldiering than spin came to a head on 19 May, when an anonymous 'senior defence official' told the *Sunday Telegraph* that 'the Marines have a morale problem and the only way to get rid of it is to get rid of the man at the top. Brigadier Lane had lost the confidence of his men . . . his tactical decisions look increasingly like the actions of a man desperate for some success.' A few days later the Brigadier's replacement was announced, a year earlier than planned. It came as a complete surprise to Geoff Hoon, who had just given a ringing endorsement of Roger Lane. Downing Street airily announced that the Defence

Secretary 'did not need to know' that the commander of British troops in Afghanistan was coming home.

The Marines at Bagram were furious that their chief had been stabbed in the back – it seemed to them he was merely a scapegoat who had taken the hit for the hype and the failed PR strategy which emanated from the Prime Minister and the top brass in England. Admiral Michael Boyce, Chief of the Defence Staff, admitted they had allowed expectations of pitched battles with al-Qaeda to be 'ramped up' and acknowledged the military was partly to blame for 'unhelpful' and critical media reports which had left the Marines feeling flat and disappointed when they failed to make contact with the enemy. 'I guess I am as responsible as anybody else,' the Admiral ruefully admitted. Tony Blair was silent about the fate of Brigadier Lane.

As summer's suffocating heat tightened its iron grip on the Afghan mountains, more details emerged of Bin Laden's plan to thwart the war on terror and ensure al-Qaeda's survival. Captives revealed that after Tora Bora the leadership had split their forces into two sections. The first, al-Qaeda's most proficient fighters together with surviving Taliban units and commanders, moved south to Paktia to engage the enemy in Operation Anaconda. The survivors then melted away across the Pakistan border. The second stream of al-Qaeda was comprised of men of many nationalities, trained in the terror camps. They were sent back from whence they came with instructions to bolster local extremist groups and – in Bin Laden's own words – 'to hit American and Jewish interests wherever you can'. Throughout the spring and early summer of 2002 al-Qaeda secretly fanned out – by boat from Karachi to Indonesia and Bangladesh, by land to Saudi Arabia, the Yemen and countries in Africa. North Africa was designated as the base from which terror attacks in Europe would be launched. Yemen became the new centre for al-Qaeda operations in the Gulf area. Soon the terrorists' handiwork was much in evidence.

The bombing of the Islamabad church and the deaths of two Americans and three Pakistanis was followed, on 11 April, by the killing of seventeen people in Tunisia. Twelve German tourists died when a truck bomb exploded outside a synagogue in the popular holiday resort of Djerba. The group claiming responsibility called itself the Islamic Army for the Liberation of the Holy Sites, the same name used by al-Qaeda in 1998 to lay claim to the bombing of the US embassies in Kenya and Dar-es-Salaam. The last act of the Tunisian suicide bomber before he drove the truck to the synagogue had been to phone a German national with known connections to radical Islamic groups. This time the German police were tapping the telephone and heard the bomber say, 'Don't forget to pray for me.' A search of the German man's apartment turned up the phone number of Ramsi bin al-Shibh, the member of the Hamburg cell who fled to Afghanistan. An Arab newspaper in London was told that al-Qaeda carried out the Djerba bombing and that the organisation was preparing for a 'more painful' strike against the Americans in the near future.

'It's not if, but when,' a Whitehall source told me when I asked how concerned the British security services were about more attacks on Europeans. On cue, the very next day, 8 May, a car bomb tore apart a bus full of French naval advisers in the Pakistani port of Karachi. Twelve Frenchmen and four local people died, including the driver of the car. In a turbulent city, long inured to ethnic violence, a suicide bombing was a new phenomenon. The sophistication of the bomb, with the explosive distributed along the chassis of the car, and the exact timing of the bomb blast – just as the foreigners were boarding the bus outside their five-star hotel – signalled the involvement of al-Qaeda. 'Far from ebbing, terrorism is stalking Pakistan with impunity,' announced the *Dawn* newspaper, a frequent interviewer of Bin Laden in the past. 'The government should realise that terrorists are now to be found in every corner of the country,' the paper warned.

Eight months earlier, amid the smoking ruins of Ground

Zero, George Bush and Tony Blair had stated the aim of their war on terror: for Blair, it was 'to eradicate Bin Laden's network of terror'; for Bush, it was 'to bring to justice those behind the September 11 attacks'. In a few months the coalition had succeeded in blowing apart what it had taken Bin Laden five years to build: the military camps which became the base, the training ground, for al-Qaeda. But eradicating the network and bringing to justice the leaders was still a distant prospect. A conservative estimate put the numbers trained in the camps at 10,000. A generous guess might have put the numbers of al-Qaeda and Taliban killed and captured in Afghanistan at 3,000, plus another 1,000 captured in other countries later. The others were still at large and now widely dispersed. As the first anniversary of the September attacks approached, the frequency and range of terror incidents increased. An American warplane was targeted by an al-Qaeda missile in Saudi Arabia and British warships were scouted by al-Qaeda boats in the Straits of Gibraltar, although both these plots ultimately failed. US soldiers in Kuwait and an aid worker from the American embassy in Jordan were gunned down, then a French tanker was bombed in the Yemen. There were more deaths and a sense of deepening unease spread throughout the West. Although in hiding, Osama bin Laden was fulfilling his ambition; al-Qaeda was no longer simply a terror organisation – it was becoming a worldwide movement.

24

Al-Qaeda Strikes Back

'We warned Australia before not to join in [the war in] Afghanistan and [about] its despicable effort to separate East Timor. It ignored the warning until it woke up to the sounds of explosions in Bali.'

—Osama bin Laden, audiotape broadcast on al-Jazeera television, 12 November 2002

A year, almost to the day, after President Bush launched his war on terror in Afghanistan, the party was in full swing at the Sari Club, a nightspot on the island of Bali in Indonesia. The twelfth of October was a Saturday and the strip of bars and restaurants that fringe Kuta Beach was packed that night with Western holidaymakers and expatriates, surfers, gap-year students and touring football and rugby teams from Hong Kong, Singapore and Perth.

Kuta Beach – and the Sari Club in particular – had always been a favourite haunt of young Australians. Attracted by Bali's natural beauty and its spiritual atmosphere, their hedonistic and flamboyant lifestyle had somehow been accommodated by the peaceful and tolerant Balinese. The locals' Hindu culture is unique among the many thousands of islands which make up the world's most populous Muslim nation, Indonesia.

There were also many Britons and Europeans at Kuta Beach that night. The Singapore Cricket Club had sent a touring rugby side to Bali, and Andy Douglas, a large, amiable Englishman with a broad grin, who played prop forward, was enjoying a drink in Paddy's, opposite the Sari. Ian Stafford and Ian Findlay, childhood friends from County Durham enjoying a lads' holiday away from their families, arrived just after ten in the street outside Paddy's and the Sari.

Just as Douglas was ordering another drink and Stafford and Findlay were trying to decide which bar to go to, an explosion ripped through Paddy's. 'I just felt a big flash of white light and I was thrown on to the ground – it seemed as if in slow motion,' recalled Andy Douglas. 'It was totally dark and I was on the ground, thinking, "That was a bomb."' Outside, Ian Stafford was rooted to the spot as he saw the bomb explode: 'A gigantic light filled the bar, you could see burning bodies and people flung all over and screaming – it was incredible. For five or ten seconds we thought, "What's happening here? It's not real." And then there was this really, really enormous bang.'

As a wave of people surged out of Paddy's and the Sari Club a second bomb, explosives packed inside a Mitsubishi mini-van, was detonated in the street outside, catching them as they fled. The blast and then a massive fireball swept through the club and along the street near where Ian Stafford and Ian Findlay were standing. 'It was directly in front of us, and then I felt everything hit us,' Stafford recalled. 'There was debris shooting into my legs, in my arms, all over. I went down and then I struggled up and there were holes all over me and I was covered in blood.' Stafford ran in panic, fearing another blast was imminent.

A young Australian tourist with a video camera filmed the inferno which quickly demolished the bamboo-thatched club. Dozens of people were trapped when the roof collapsed; mangled bodies and limbs were embedded with metal from bikes and cars that had been shredded by the blast. 'I had a massive lump of shrapnel in my throat – an eighth of an inch from my windpipe, and death,' Stafford told *Panorama* after undergoing an operation to remove the bomb debris. 'There was shrapnel in my chest and another piece took part of my arm away.'

At the local hospital in Bali, equipped with only a couple of dozen beds, the staff were overwhelmed by the mass of casualties arriving by every possible means of transport. 'That place was a scene of unbelievable carnage,' Douglas shuddered in recollection. 'Eighty to a hundred people, dead bodies on the floor and burnt people screaming out in agony while others died on the floor. There was blood everywhere.'

As dawn arrived, dazed and broken people wandered the streets searching through the wreckage and the makeshift morgues for friends and family. Ian Stafford could not find his friend in any of the hospitals but finally recognised Findlay's sandals poking out from under a heap of dead bodies in the back of a van. 'I believe he took the brunt of the blast standing in front, shielding me,' said Stafford, overcome with remorse. 'It was the hardest thing I have ever done, phoning Ian's wife – I just broke down and couldn't help them in their grief.' But his remorse quickly turned to anger. 'What have we done to them, that they just target innocent people, tourists?' he demanded.

An Australian man in the hospital, unrecognisable due to his burns, had a more succinct explanation: 'They know Bali is a place where many Westerners come. They just want to send the message – "We'll get you anywhere you are".' There was no doubt in any of the victims' minds who 'they' were. As forensic investigators began sifting through the wreckage for clues, the expectation was that they would find that al-Qaeda was once again responsible for this latest terror attack – and a third blast that night, a smaller one outside the US consulate in Denpasar, the capital of Bali, reinforced the belief that Osama bin Laden was behind the bombings.

Alexander Downer, the Australian Foreign Minister, was the first foreign politician to lay a wreath at the charred remains of the Sari Club. He was haunted by what he saw. 'As I looked at it I thought, how could anyone have survived?' he told me. 'I asked myself if there was anything else we could have done. Was a piece of intelligence just discarded and not properly examined?' In the national soul-searching that followed Bali in

Australia even the tough and taciturn Prime Minister, John Howard, was publicly moved to tears as the death toll of Australians was reported to have topped a hundred, over half the overall total. It emerged that his government had received warnings from the CIA, just weeks before the blast, that holiday resorts in Indonesia were one of the targets al-Qaeda might go for around the first anniversary of September 11. But there was no specific mention of Bali and the threat against an Australian embassy, not a 'soft' target like a nightclub, was judged more real.

Osama bin Laden himself had given a broad hint, eleven months earlier, that Australia could be next in line for a terror attack. It was a hint, though, to which no one paid enough attention. In the early days of the war in Afghanistan, Bin Laden's appearance on a video on 3 November made headlines around the world. But attention was still focused on whether he would acknowledge responsibility for September 11 and a couple of ominous lines buried in the speech went largely unremarked. 'The crusader Australian forces were on Indonesian shores and in fact they landed to separate East Timor, which is part of the Islamic world,' Bin Laden said. He was referring to the role played by Australia in spearheading a UN peacekeeping force which intervened in the civil war in East Timor in 1999, later overseeing the island's vote for independence from Indonesia. 'We should view [these] events not as separate links but as links in a long series of conspiracies, a war of annihilation,' Bin Laden warned.

The leader of al-Qaeda was sending a message to his supporters in Indonesia and south-east Asia, sanctioning them to hit a new 'crusader' target. It was a word he had used many times to describe his primary enemy, the United States; now it was being applied to her allies, in particular those countries, like Australia, which had contributed forces to the coalition fighting al-Qaeda in Afghanistan. Australia was already perceived by some to be the regional superpower and Bin Laden's words would have struck a chord with local Islamic extremists who already resented Australian dominance of an area of the world with a large Muslim population.

Bin Laden was on the run when he made the November video; his safe houses and training camps bombed nightly by the Americans. He had planned a strategy to ensure al-Qaeda survived the war in Afghanistan and even then his fighters were fanning out from their base there to carry on the struggle back in their home countries. Their orders were to re-join local extremist organisations which had sent them to train in Afghanistan with al-Qaeda. They were to recruit local members and direct new operations against American interests and also against a broader range of Western targets. Bin Laden's aim was to further polarise the world between Christian 'crusader' states and Muslims, and to further ethnic and religious schisms. It was an agenda which chimed with that of local militants in south-east Asia.

Bin Laden was opening a second front in his war against the West and the coming months would show that south-east Asia had become al-Qaeda's most active and dangerous centre for sub-contracted terror. The Australian government noted Bin Laden's words with alarm but in the months immediately after the attacks in New York and Washington, his game plan was not yet understood. 'We've learned more in the last six months, but we did not know just how closely al-Qaeda was linked to local groups in our region,' admitted Alexander Downer.

Singapore, December 2001

In a darkened room, intelligence agents watched a jerky video. The camera which captured the footage on screen was in a car sweeping along a broad boulevard lined with elegant colonial buildings, Singapore's embassy row.

The occupants of the vehicle, who called themselves 'Sammy' and 'Randy', were on a sightseeing tour with a difference. The white porticos of the American embassy were flanked on one side by the British High Commission and on the other by the Australian High Commission. The Stars and Stripes hanging from one flagpole were sandwiched between a Union Jack and the Australian flag. The old colonial masters now protected the interests of tens of thousands of expatriates in Singapore, one of south-east Asia's most modern and successful city-states. The video camera moved suddenly from the flags to focus on the ugly new concrete blocks at ground level, barriers designed to deter truck and car bombs.

This was footage the world was never meant to see – a terrorists' reconnaissance video made in 1999, exploring targets the group intended to hit, filming people they meant to kill. The scene switches to shoppers leaving a subway station; a line of motorcycles and a minibus are parked outside waiting to ferry US servicemen to the nearby naval base. A man's calm voice, speaking English with a Malay accent, gives a running commentary: 'This is the entrance to the building, with many vehicles parked there. They will not be suspicious to have a motorcycle or a bicycle there as well,' he says. 'This is the type of box they use on the motorcycles. These are the same type of boxes we intend to use.'

The video would ultimately result in the unmasking of the film-makers' group, members of a secret militant Islamic organisation called Jemaah Islamiyah, or JI. A copy was sent to Afghanistan where it was found by US military intelligence in late November 2001, in the wreckage of an al-Qaeda safe house near Kabul. Like many extremist groups which sheltered under the broad umbrella of al-Qaeda, they were seeking approval and financing from Bin Laden for a daring joint venture. It was to be a series of terror attacks in Singapore, involving seven trucks filled with explosives. These massive bombs, detonated almost simultaneously, would have killed hundreds, if not thousands, in a spectacular terror strike to rival that of September 11. The targets were the American and Israeli embassies and the British and Australian High Commissions.

The local US naval base and the bus carrying military personnel were also on the terrorists' list.

'The copy of this video was found in the rubble of the house of Mohamed Atef, one of Bin Laden's key lieutenants,' Wong Kan Seng, Singapore's Home Minister, told me. 'There is no doubt that there is a direct link between al-Qaeda and this attack planned here.' Citizens do not often step out of line in Singapore, a country known for its zealous policing and efficient security services. It did not take long for the authorities, once they had been shown the video, to track down those responsible. Within a month eighteen arrests were made and the original of the tape was found in one of the houses raided in Singapore.

The Singaporeans were perplexed – the suspects did not fit the usual pattern of Islamic radicals, in appearance or occupation. This is a country which prides itself on its Western lifestyle and modern outlook, and most of the arrested men were typical aspiring middle-class professionals who showed no outward sign of radicalism. One of them was a shipping officer who could have secured access to the US naval base. 'We were shocked and surprised because these men were not marginalised or down-trodden, but people with good jobs and university degrees. They had families and owned their own homes,' said Wong Kan Seng, shaking his head in disbelief at this very un-Singaporean manifestation of dissent in the heart of his prosperous state.

The men told their interrogators they were members of a cell formed in Singapore and Malaysia by the extremist group Jemaah Islamiyah. They were trying to purchase seventeen tons of explosives to create the truck bombs. It was a conspiracy that stretched across the Far East and some thirty more arrests were later made, not only in Malaysia but also in the Philippines.

The thousands of islands, large and small, which comprise Indonesia, the Philippines, Malaysia and Thailand are known as 'the arc of instability'. In the 1980s these countries, focused on building modern, post-colonial societies on a secular, multi-ethnic basis, failed to pay enough heed to the rising tide of Islamic fundamentalism among their large Muslim populations. *Mujahideen* from these countries were among the volunteers who fought the Soviets in Afghanistan. Bin Laden recognised the potential of this area back in 1988, sending his own brother-in-law to the region where the violent secessionist movements in the Muslim south of the Philippines provided the first fertile ground in which al-Qaeda planted the seeds of terror. Soon Malaysians and Indonesians too were among the recruits training in the Afghan camps.

It was in fact an Indonesian, Riduan Isamuddin, known as Hambali, who reached the highest ranks of al-Qaeda. The tubby religious student, bearded and bespectacled, was one of the few non-Arabs in Bin Laden's inner circle. As a teenager he had become involved with a network of local groups known broadly as the Islamic Association, but he fled to Malaysia in 1985 during a government crackdown. His hardline views were formed, like so many in Bin Laden's circle, when he fought the Soviets in Afghanistan. Hambali became a member of al-Qaeda's *majlis shura* or inner council and in the mid-1990s began actively to plan terror attacks in his own corner of the world. He took part in the failed Operation Bojinka, Ramsi Yousef's plan to blow up US airliners over the Pacific. And he worked closely with Khalid Sheikh Mohamed, Yousef's uncle, who dreamt up not only the first, unsuccessful, attempt to bring down the World Trade Center towers in 1993 but is also suspected of coming up with the idea for the September 11 plot.

Hambali despatched several dozen Malaysian recruits to Afghanistan for training and developed the country as an important staging-post for al-Qaeda. In January 2000 he hosted an important meeting at an apartment in Kuala Lumpur, the Malaysian capital. Two of the September 11 hijackers, Khalid al-Midhar and Nawaf al-Hazmi, made the trip there from California, where they were attempting to learn to fly. Two al-

Qaeda operatives in the process of planning another attack, the bombing of the USS *Cole* in the Yemen, were also present. The CIA knew this was a significant meeting of terrorists and tipped off their Malaysian counterparts, who covertly filmed the gathering. But the identities and purpose of the men were hazy and the video did not make it to the analysts in time to prevent the two Saudis re-entering America, with disastrous consequences. Hambali's group also provided a safe house for a visitor from London, and the letter from 'Infocus Tech' which later enabled Zacharias Moussaoui, the 'twentieth hijacker', to enrol at a US flying school.

The growing importance of south-east Asia and its home-grown militant groups to al-Qaeda was signalled in June 2000 when Dr Ayman al-Zawahiri, Bin Laden's deputy, and Mohamed Atef, his military chief, turned up in Indonesia. They visited Acer and the Maluku islands, places which had been wracked by sectarian violence, and were impressed by the lack of security and the large and supportive Muslim population. By now Hambali had returned to his native Indonesia, where a new and democratic government had been elected.

The truck bombs in Singapore were intended to be al-Qaeda's response to the war on terror they knew would follow the September 11 attacks, but the plan was foiled. The interrogations that followed the arrests revealed not only the threat posed by Jemaah Islamiyah but gave a valuable insight into how al-Qaeda was running its extended network through this affiliated group. Mohamed Atef had, in the time-honoured way, sent funds to Hambali through a Saudi charity. Hambali had used it to purchase four tons of ammonium nitrate in Malaysia. The biggest fish, though, had escaped the net – and so had his cache of explosives. As 2002 dawned it was apparent that he had other plots in the pipeline and many governments in the region were actively searching for him.

Hambali found a secret bolt-hole in another Muslim area, this time in southern Thailand. A member of JI who met him there in January later revealed to investigators that Hambali 'was so angry he swore revenge' for the arrests of the cell in Singapore. His determined that his next operation would not be thwarted and he gave the order to switch tactics from attacking fortified embassies and closely-guarded military personnel to hitting 'softer' targets – like tourists in holiday resorts.

Indonesia, autumn 2002

The location of al-Qaeda's next joint venture with local Islamic extremists would be very different from Singapore, with its vigilant security services and its pride in fostering good relations between different ethnic groups. Hambali's eyes turned to his own vast and chaotic country of 220 million people – the world's fastest-growing Muslim state. Indonesia was only just emerging uncertainly from the long shadow of the dictatorial Suharto regime. The government of President Megawati Sukarnoputri was still hesitant and shaky, her country vulnerable, as Afghanistan and the Sudan had been, to al-Qaeda's clutches. Yet tourists were still flocking to Bali's beaches, oblivious of the danger.

As the stunned Balinese held cleansing ceremonies to free the Sari Club of the souls of the dead which haunted their once magical island, attention focused on an elderly Indonesian with a snowy beard and a beaming but strangely vacant smile. Abu Bakr Bashir is the principal of an Islamic boarding school at Solo on the main Indonesian island of Jakarta. When the BBC visited him three days after the nightclub attack his students were clustered around a notice board crammed with newspaper cuttings; they were agog with the international notoriety their tutor had attracted. Dubbed 'the Bin Laden of the Far East', Abu Bakr was vigorously denying that he was the spiritual head of Jemaah Islamiyah, a charge made by many governments in the region. He was denying too that he had anything to do with the Bali bombing. 'I don't know anything about Jemaah Islamiyah,' snapped Abu Bakr. 'I don't know anything about al-Qaeda. I believe the bombing was the work of a foreign intelligence agency. I suspect that it was American,' he stated defiantly.

The Singaporeans, holding more than thirty members of JI, were not impressed by this rhetoric. 'Those we detained said that Abu Bakr is the "Emir", the chief, of the group,' Wong Kan Seng told me. 'Some of them even took the *bayat*, the oath of allegiance, to Abu Bakr Bashir.' His words echoed the evidence given to the US courts in the East African embassy bombings trial by the Sudanese defector who spilled the beans on the workings of al-Qaeda and how the *bayat* was sworn to the Emir, Osama bin Laden.

Under the Suharto regime Abu Bakr Bashir had been exiled to Malaysia in 1985 and spent fourteen years there, years investigators believe he spent setting up and expanding Jemaah Islamiyah with the aim of creating a pan-Islamic union stretching across Indonesia, Singapore, Malaysia and the Muslim southern islands of the Philippines. Abu Bakr has admitted that Hambali was one of his students during this time in Malaysia before he returned to run his school in Indonesia in 1999. Western and local intelligence agencies believe that al-Qaeda co-opted Jemaah Islamiyah into 'The Base' in the mid-1990s, providing money and training through Hambali, the link man. Abu Bakr is, according to investigators, the spiritual head of JI just as Bin Laden has provided al-Qaeda's inspiration. A colourful poster on the wall behind the Indonesian cleric, teaching his all-male class of children, some as young as ten, featured drops of blood and flames licking around hate-filled diatribes against America and Jewish people.

I watched a video of a secret JI training camp established near the Indonesian coastal town of Poso – a poor man's version of the Afghan camps featured in al-Qaeda videos. The recruits wield wooden guns, the setting is green jungle rather than barren desert, and faces are Malay and Indonesian, not Arab or Pakistani. Many governments want to know why this camp was not closed down by the Indonesians despite increasing warnings about the dangers, warnings underlined by a rash of bomb attacks in Indonesia and the Philippines in 2000 and after September 11. The Indonesian government consistently refused to confront and deal with the extremist menace in their midst until the Bali bombing. President Megawati's coalition government was only kept in power with the support of Islamic parties. The vast majority of Indonesia's population are moderate – the two mainstream Muslim organisations have 70 million members – but outlawing Jemaah Islamiyah and arresting Abu Bakr was still a political hot potato which the indecisive president was unwilling to handle, even in the wake of September 11.

The Australian Foreign Minister Alexander Downer confirmed that his government had consistently pressed both publicly and privately for Indonesia to deal with JI and its alleged spiritual leader. Singapore was also pushing for action, along with America, especially as the anniversary of September 11 approached and a rising crescendo of intelligence began to indicate that large-scale attacks were being planned in southeast Asia. The source of much of that intelligence was an al-Qaeda 'sleeper' who had been living unobtrusively for years in Indonesia until the war on terror gave him a rude awakening.

The sun was setting behind a simple minaret as the call to prayer sounded through the palms and banana trees ringing the small village of Cijeruk, on the island of Java. The Indonesian woman's eyes were glittering in the slits of her Arab-style head dress and her black *chador* swept the floor. 'I met him at nine in the morning and we were married early the same evening,' Mira Agustina told *Panorama*. It was five days after the Bali bombings and she had just returned after yet another marathon questioning session with the local police. Mira Agustina was the plain daughter of the local imam, in danger of being left on the shelf, when a stranger suddenly appeared in the village one day and told her father he wished to marry her. The marriage certificate showed a photograph of the dumpy, black-garbed figure and a stern-faced older man. Omar al-Faruk claimed to be Indonesian but in reality he was a Kuwaiti and al-Qaeda's agent in south-east Asia. A veteran of the Afghan camps, al-Faruk had been sent to Indonesia by Abu Zubaydah, al-Qaeda's head of recruitment. His job was to co-ordinate the activities of various extreme Islamic groups, not only in Indonesia but across the region.

Two daughters were born in quick succession and Omar proved a model father. 'He showed great respect to me and cared greatly for our family,' Mira Agustina said defensively. Just as Arab members of al-Qaeda had done in East Africa, in preparation for the embassy bombings in 1998, al-Faruk married a local girl to enable him to blend in to a small Islamic community. He taught the Qur'an and hung around the village most of the time, but it was also noticed that he spent a lot of time on his mobile phone. Later investigators would find Omar's number programmed into Abu Zubaydah's phone when he was captured in Pakistan. And it featured in the phone record of other al-Qaeda members from Chechnya to Camp X-Ray in Cuba.

Suddenly, in June 2002, Omar vanished. 'It was a Wednesday and he called at noon to say he was going to the mosque,' recalled Mira Agustina. 'I never heard from him again.' She denied all knowledge of her husband's real occupation as a terrorist co-ordinator. Within hours of what was to be his last phone call, to his wife or anyone else, Omar al-Faruk was being bundled off a military plane in the searing heat of Bagram air base in Afghanistan. He had been seized in Java by American agents and whisked out of Indonesia to that deserted-looking hangar with the broken windows and the black-out panels which I would furtively study during the weeks I spent in Bagram. For three months al-Faruk said nothing, but finally, on 9 September 2002, the psychological interrogation tactics, sleep deprivation and isolation began to tell, and he cracked. What he told his American captors set alarm bells ringing across south-east Asia.

Al-Faruk confessed to two attempts to kill the Indonesian President, Megawati Sukarnoputri, and revealed a direct financial link between al-Qaeda and Abu Bakr Bashir. He claimed that Bin Laden, using the name Sheikh Abu Abdullah Emirati, had transferred $74,000 to Abu Bakr. The cash was to be used to fund a campaign to kill Westerners, Israelis and Indonesians. US embassies in the region would again be a target and 'large-scale' attacks were planned around the first anniversary of September 11. US Navy ships on exercise in May 2001 in Indonesia had been another intended target. However, not enough men could be recruited to carry out the mission.

Omar al-Faruk never mentioned Bali, but he confirmed that Hambali, the JI operations chief, was an important figure in al-Qaeda's local network. Al-Faruk painted a picture of Jemaah Islamiyah and other extremist groups acting as surrogates of al-Qaeda in the region, encouraged to carry out attacks which served their own agenda as well as Bin Laden's wider purpose. Attacks against Christians were all part of the same campaign and al-Faruk had been behind a wave of violence which left eighteen dead and more than a hundred injured in Indonesian churches around Christmas 2000.

Al-Faruk's admissions sparked a frenzy of diplomatic activity as various governments tried to impress upon Megawati and her ministers the need to act against JI and Abu Bakr Bashir – and fast. The American ambassador to Jakarta confronted the Indonesians with al-Faruk's confession, and the Australian Foreign Minister pleaded with his Indonesian counterpart. But still they did nothing. They had sanctioned the seizure and deportation of al-Faruk, a foreigner suspected of terror links, but their own police had yet to question him in Bagram and they were still stalling.

The anniversary of the World Trade Center attacks was looming by the time al-Faruk made his confession and the US closed several embassies in the region the next day. The Australians closed their mission in East Timor, mindful of the warning Bin Laden had already given the 'Australian crusaders'. Their intelligence agency had intercepted conversations between JI operatives planning to attack Australians in the region but the government would later insist there was nothing specific indicating 'soft' targets. And so no warnings were given to Australian citizens about the risk of visiting tourist resorts in Indonesia.

The British, Canadian and New Zealand governments also put their embassies on high alert over the anniversary period. It passed off uneventfully, however, with only an isolated grenade attack on a US embassy residence. An uneasy calm descended as Western governments re-opened their diplomatic missions. The Indonesian authorities breathed a sign of relief, thinking they were off the hook.

Exactly one month later the Bali bomb wrecked not only the Sari Club but destroyed the lives of hundreds of families, shattering international confidence in Indonesia and obliterating Bali's lucrative tourist industry. A shaken President Megawati was seen tearfully picking her way through what remained of the Sari Club – and her country's tattered reputation.

'We received general warnings from the US but no specific information about whether there would be incidents – or bombs exploding in one place or another,' insisted Dr Hasan Wirajuda, Indonesia's Foreign Minister. I pressed Dr Wirajuda on his government's inaction over JI and the threat they had posed for many years. 'Certainly we need to do more, and more than in the past,' he conceded. Belatedly Jemaah Islamiyah was outlawed and efforts got under way to trace its assets. The Singapore government, who had been pressing for arrests since they uncovered the terrorist video and the truck-bomb plot in their country nine months earlier, was furious. 'It's unfortunate that it required a tragedy like Bali – which should not have happened – to be the wake-up call for some people,' Wong Kan Seng, the Home Minister, told me tartly.

Abu Bakr Bashir was basking in media attention when the Bali bomb exploded. *Time* magazine had leaked details of al-Faruk's CIA confession in late September and the accusations

he had made against the Indonesian cleric. Under the spot-
lights of television crews Bashir swept into court to sue *Time*,
the CIA and the government of Singapore when the axe suddenly fell. The Indonesians finally announced they would
detain him and the next pictures to emerge of the cleric showed
him motionless in his bed, surrounded by respectful acolytes.
He was 'too ill' to submit to questioning and there was a stand-
off outside his house between the police and his supporters,
who threatened violence if he was carried off to prison.

In the wake of the bombing a respected Indonesian general,
Made Mangu Pastika, was appointed to lead the investigation
with forensic and intelligence expertise provided by Australian
and British police officers and by many Western security agencies. Within days of the bombing it was established that both
bombs, the smaller initial one and the second, massive device
inside the mini-van, had been strategically placed to kill and
maim as many as possible. 'They created a killing ground,'
Pastika told *Panorama*. 'It was a very sophisticated and well-
planned attack and very professionally executed, with the
bombs set up tactically to create maximum casualties.' Pastika
revealed that the force of the blast had incinerated the mini-van
entirely, except for the roof which had blown on to the top of a
three-storey building a hundred yards away.

Under enormous political pressure from around the region,
the Indonesians announced, a month later, that they had
arrested one of the main perpetrators of the bombing. In an
extraordinary public interrogation, conducted behind a glass
door, in view of the press, the suspect, known only as
'Amrozoi', laughed and joked with his accusers. He then
pointed to the press, many of them Westerners, saying, 'These
are the sort of people I wanted to kill!' This scene caused outrage, especially in Australia, which had confirmed the loss of
seventy-eight of its citizens in the bombing and feared the real
toll was into three figures. Amrozoi confessed to being one of at
least eight members of Jemaah Islamiyah involved in the plot
and said he had procured the mini-van and the explosives to

make the bomb. The planning had been carried out in Solo, on the island of Java, during clandestine meetings at street food stalls and via text messages sent between him and two other plotters. One of them, Imam Samudra, was the ring-leader. He supplied Amrozoi with funds to buy a vehicle and certain chemicals, ingredients Amrozoi recognised were needed for a bomb.

Imam Samudra was another graduate of the Bin Laden terror training school in Afghanistan. A university graduate who spoke English, Arabic and Indonesian and who was interested in computers, he always wore a hat and carried a laptop, according to Amrozoi. In contrast Amrozoi described himself as a 'delinquent youth' who had worked on building sites in Malaysia until he returned home in 1992 and became a committed follower of radical Islam. He had been in Malaysia at the same time as Abu Bakr Bashir and Hambali and later attended religious speeches given by the cleric back in Indonesia.

Six days before the bombing Amrozoi made his way to Bali to meet up with others in the group and to buy a motorcycle, for use as a getaway vehicle. He saw two Nokia 5110 mobile phones wired up to trigger two of the smaller bombs, which would later explode outside Paddy's Bar and the US consulate in Denpasar. He then returned to his village where, on 13 October, he heard radio reports of the Bali bombing. 'He was delighted that his bomb had successfully exploded,' said national police chief General Da' Bachtiar, who conducted the public interrogation of Amrozoi. The Indonesian authorities also revealed that Samudra had hung around the Sari Club for several days after the bombing, watching as the investigation got under way. Another macabre touch had been the meeting held in Solo after the Bali killings during which Samudra distributed $1,000 among some of the men who had been involved in the terror attack.

On 21 November 2002, as a bus pulled up to a ferry in a Java port, police stormed on board and captured Imam Samudra. The young Indonesian, dressed in baggy jeans and a blue T-shirt with 'Converse Original' emblazoned across the chest, was paraded triumphantly before the television cameras by the Indonesian police. They hastily bundled him back inside the police station when he started shouting *'Allahu akbar!'* – Arabic for 'God is great!' Samudra's forehead bore a mark caused by repeatedly pressing his face against the floor while praying. He looked defiant and shouted, 'This is a sacred struggle, not a heinous one!'

Samudra revealed that the first explosion in Bali, in Paddy's Bar, had been detonated by a suicide bomber, a Muslim 'martyr' called 'Iqbal' who had walked into the bar carrying the device in a backpack. The theory until then had been that both the explosions at Kuta Beach had been detonated by remote control, using the mobile phones. Now the Indonesians faced the new and unpleasant reality that not only in the Middle East but in south-east Asia too there were people prepared to die for their beliefs. Even the death penalty in Indonesia would be a sanction unlikely to deter would-be local terrorists who could display such religious fervour. In a chilling echo of al-Qaeda's tactics Samudra said the Bali bar and nightclub were chosen as targets because 'a lot of foreigners' frequented them.

Samudra offered a tantalising clue as to the way Jemaah Islamiyah and al-Qaeda were interlinked and how the organisations shared both terrorist expertise and philosophy. According to the police, Samudra told them he had reached 'his leader and the people who have the same vision' by phone after the Bali bombing. He confirmed that he had spent several years in Afghanistan and that he had also lived in Malaysia, where he had taught at a school run by Abu Bakr Bashir. Samudra claimed to have financed the bombing himself using $40,000 raised by a raid on a local jewellery store.

The Indonesians and Western intelligence agencies had no doubt that Hambali, with his dual JI and al-Qaeda function, was the real mastermind behind the bombing. He was still on the run somewhere in the vast archipelago of Indonesia. So too was the elder brother of Amrozoi, Ustaz Muklas, a religious leader and another key JI operative involved in planning the bombing. The investigators also put out an alert for three other men, foreigners, including a Yemeni travelling on a forged American passport and a Malaysian explosives expert. A year on from the start of the war on terror in Afghanistan the network was proving wider, more committed, and more independent of al-Qaeda's day-to-day control than had previously been suspected. Samudra's confession implicated at least fifteen local individuals in the cell involved in the Bali bombing. Western intelligence estimates ran to at least 200 local activists in Indonesia and neighbouring countries.

'We hope that through Samudra we can get Hambali,' said the head of Indonesian intelligence, optimistically. The hunt was urgent, the Indonesians hinted, because 'there are indications Samudra has a new plan' in the pipeline. The four tons of ammonium nitrate believed to have been hidden by Hambali after the exposure of the Singapore plot were still missing and fears of a new and devastating attack haunted south-east Asia. But the hardened al-Qaeda men, the long-serving top operatives, continued to elude the grasp of law enforcement around the world. Just as Khalid Sheikh Mohamed, the architect of the September 11 attacks, had slipped the net in Karachi when Ramsi bin al-Shibh was arrested in September 2001, so Hambali vanished even though Imam Samudra had been seized.

Exactly a month after the devastating explosions in Bali, Osama bin Laden broke his silence on another tape, broadcast again by al-Jazeera television. For nine months the American administration had refused to admit that various tapes and statements filtering out through the press and on Islamic websites were genuinely from Bin Laden. This time the CIA declared it really was him and European intelligence agencies agreed. It was the first confirmed communication from al-Qaeda's leader since the radio broadcast picked up at Tora Bora proved he was still alive.

The CIA theorised that the slow and hesitant voice indicated a weak and sick man, suffering still from wounds sustained in

Afghanistan or from his long-term kidney ailment. Bin Laden's message, however, was direct and clear and meant for those who allied themselves with the United States. 'What do your governments want by allying themselves with the criminal gang in the White House against Muslims?' he demanded. 'I mention in particular Britain, France, Italy, Canada, Germany and Australia.'

If there had been any doubt that al-Qaeda was involved in the Bali bomb attack and that Australia had been a particular target, Bin Laden spelled it out: 'We warned Australia before not to join in [the war in] Afghanistan and [about] its despicable effort to separate East Timor,' Bin Laden said. 'It ignored the warning until it woke up to the sounds of explosions in Bali ... The Islamic nation, thanks to God, has started to attack you at the hands of its beloved sons who pledged to God to continue *jihad* as long as they are alive.' Bin Laden thus indicated that his aim of creating a global Islamic caliphate was now in sight.

In Australia itself there were indications of a cell of JI extremists who seemed amateurish but clearly had potential for deadly attacks. One member was a British-born soldier and former alcoholic, Jack Roche. He had converted to Islam, married an Indonesian and settled in Perth. Roche told a journalist from the *Australian* he had been 'seconded' to Hambali and undertook a journey to Afghanistan to deliver a note to Osama bin Laden. While there he had trained in the use of explosives 'in case he got bored'. Roche revealed that Hambali was specifically trying to recruit Caucasian agents and that his own job had been to form an 'operational cell' in Sydney with the aim of planning attacks against 'Israeli or US interests'.

Roche's case echoed that of Richard Reid, the British failed 'shoe bomber', another man with a troubled past who had converted to Islam and Bin Laden's doctrine. Reid did not fit the usual profile of an al-Qaeda bomber and was therefore especially valuable to the terror organisation. Now there were signs that this drive to recruit white Westerners had spread beyond Europe to Australia. From Phuket to Perth, Jakarta to Kuala

Lumpur, the warnings sounded daily following the Bali bombing. Embassies, an international school, resorts and hotels were
all tipped as targets.

In Singapore's Cricket Club the members slowly returned to
the bar which had been deserted for weeks after the Bali attack.
On the wood-panelled walls hung a new photograph, of seventeen smiling men in black and yellow rugby kit, the touring
rugby side which had been in Paddy's Bar on the night of 12
October. Eight of them – Britons Tim Arnold, Neil Bowler, Chris
Bradford, Chris Kays, Dave Kent, Peter Record and Chris
Redman, and Charlie van Rennen, an Australian – did not
come home.

For Andy Douglas, their team-mate who was injured that
night, the future for expatriates in south-east Asia no longer
seemed full of exciting promise. The trip to the paradise island
of Bali had turned into a nightmare from which he knew he
would never recover. 'The real tragedy will hit home when
we're down at the club training and you look round and see
those lads just aren't there any more,' Douglas said quietly.
'This attack has really brought it home to everybody that any of
us can be attacked – in any place.'

25

Where is Bin Laden?

'If they kill him they will create a thousand Bin Ladens, you will see!'

—Hassan al-Turabi, Bin Laden's Sudanese mentor,
1998

Osama bin Laden's distant and hesitant voice on a scratchy audiotape, claiming responsibility for the Bali bombing, electrified the debate about the war on terror and sparked anxiety in many Western countries. The tape provided near-certain confirmation that he was still alive and it contained an explicit threat to hit ordinary people in six Western countries as well as America and Israel.

The problem of Bin Laden had gnawed away at the coalition's sense of purpose right from the start, when President Bush's war aim had been 'to bring to justice those responsible for the attacks on September 11'. The administration had sought to play down the significance of the failure to deal with Bin Laden and his deputy, Ayman al-Zawahiri, at Tora Bora. In April a public row broke out between the American intelligence agencies and the Defense Secretary over whether the al-Qaeda leader had indeed ever been at Tora Bora; the Pentagon was sensitive to the rumours that they had let him get away. 'Nor do I know today of any evidence he was at Tora

Bora at the time, or that he left Tora Bora at the time or even where he is today,' protested Donald Rumsfeld. 'The armed forces are not in the needle-in-a-haystack business, we deal with armies, navies, air forces,' he went on. 'Finding single individuals is not easy.' He seemed to be suggesting that the CIA might examine its own failure to provide hard evidence of Bin Laden's whereabouts. President Bush kept trying to downplay the importance of Bin Laden: 'I just don't spend that much time on him, to be honest,' he insisted. 'Focusing on one person indicates to me that people don't understand the scope of this mission. Terror is bigger than one man.' But there were rumblings in the American Congress; Senator Bob Graham, pursuing his questioning of intelligence failures which had led to the attacks, told the press Bin Laden was definitely still alive. Tom Daschle, the influential Leader of the Senate, made it crystal-clear what he and most Americans believed the aim of the war on terror had to be: 'The bottom line is, we've got to find him.'

Where is Bin Laden? The all-consuming question haunted the coalition during the first ten months of 2002. There was no shortage of rumours and sightings: he had fled to Chechnya; he had been seen on a horse; he was hooked up to a portable kidney dialysis machine; he was even, somewhat improbably, struggling against Marfan's disease, an illness suffered by tall people. He was still in south-eastern Afghanistan, said the experts, sighted at a wedding, or perhaps just over the border at Mirimshah in Pakistan – or was it Maidan? Or Parachinar? Alternatively he had either been badly wounded at Tora Bora and nursed by his faithful physician, Dr Ayman al-Zawahiri, or he had survived unscathed – you could take your pick. The truth was that no one really knew.

Al-Qaeda's propaganda arm was still active and videos found their way via Pakistan to al-Jazeera Television's heavily-guarded compound in Doha, the capital of Qatar. In one tape released in December 2001, after the abortive siege of Tora Bora, Bin Laden looked pale, his left arm motionless, as if he had been hurt. But there was no certainty as to when the video had been made. Almost on cue, in April 2002, another tape appeared after the next bloody confrontation with the Americans, Operation Anaconda. It was clearly a morale-booster for Bin Laden's supporters, designed to prove to his audience in the Islamic world that al-Qaeda were not yet beaten. It contained the 'martyr' footage of Ahmed al-Haznawi, one of the hijackers, recorded six months before the September 11 attacks. Al-Zawahiri also appeared on the tape, acting as spokesman for al-Qaeda: he praised the 'nineteen brothers who left us and offered their lives for the cause of Allah'. Bin Laden was seen sitting beside the doctor, his face haggard, mumbling distractedly and stroking his beard. In the background there were rocky hills, a stream and patches of green grass, indicating the video had been shot many months earlier, before the winter started, although it was hard to tell if the setting was a real one or just a painted backdrop. Donald Rumsfeld believed the tape to be a patchwork of earlier clips. 'I have not seen anything about his activities, any videotapes of him that are reasonably certain to have been [made] this year,' said Rumsfeld. 'Maybe they exist – he may exist. But I just don't know it.'

An al-Qaeda commander hiding in Pakistan told an Arab newspaper in mid-May that Bin Laden had been hit in the shoulder by shrapnel at Tora Bora but had undergone an operation 'somewhere' and was recovering. Their leader was 'back to work', the commander emphasised, an attempt per-haps to reassure followers who had seen their gaunt and muttering *emir* in the April video that he was now back in full command. The same week a Pakistani intelligence officer handed a new tape to a Birmingham-based Islamic news agency. It contained a clip of a much more animated Bin Laden in a camouflage jacket exhorting his troops. Behind him a tree sprouted fresh green leaves, a sign that this video had been shot recently. The al-Qaeda propaganda machine seemed to be functioning more efficiently than the British and American PR effort. That day the coalition forces were embroiled in another row, accused of bombing innocent Afghans, firing guns in celebration at a wedding.

Bin Laden's family had no doubt he was still alive. The renegade son who had been rejected by much of the Bin Laden clan had always remained close to his mother, who continued to live in Saudi Arabia after her second marriage. At the beginning of March she received a handwritten letter from Osama, proof to her that her beloved son had not been killed. 'I am in good health,' he wrote, 'and I am in a very, very safe place. They will never get me, unless God wills it.' The letter ends with the phrase, 'You will hear good news very soon.'

Saudi sources revealed to me that videotapes of seventeen of the September 11 hijackers are also in existence – in addition to the one that appeared after Operation Anaconda featuring Ahmed al-Haznawi against the backdrop of the burning World Trade Center. They would be released one by one, 'at the right moment', I was promised, when the al-Qaeda propaganda machine deemed that it could reap maximum advantage and show its defiance by featuring its 'martyrs'.

By the end of 2002 the consensus among Western intelligence agencies was that Bin Laden had been wounded but was definitely still alive; the jungle drums which would have communicated news of his death were silent. It was not for want of trying. On 4 February a CIA Predator drone had loosed off Hellfire missiles at a group of fifteen or twenty people meeting on a hillside near Zhawar Kili, in a remote part of Paktia province. One of the men was very tall and the Chairman of the Joint Chiefs of Staff, General Richard Myers, said the pictures showed clearly the 'deference paid' to senior members of the group. The men were moving among outcroppings of rocks and trees and appeared to be aware the Predator was in the vicinity. There was excitement in the intelligence community for some days; the CIA had already got hold of another video of an uncertain date showing Bin Laden camping in the open with just a few followers, obviously on the run. But pieces of human flesh, retrieved from the scene and sent to the Pentagon for

DNA testing, confirmed that al-Qaeda's leader had not been among the group at Zhawar Kili. Airline schedules and credit-card vouchers were found in the wreckage of the site, which made local claims that a hapless group of Afghan scrap-merchants had been mistakenly killed unlikely.

I had met a group of DNA detectives on a military flight in Afghanistan. The four burly men in jeans and baseball caps, members of the US Army's Criminal Investigation Division, were accompanied by a professorial-looking colleague who was scribbling scientific formulae in a notebook. Their job was to comb the battlefields and other remote sites where bombs and missiles had killed al-Qaeda fighters and commanders, to collect tissue from bodies and send it to the Pentagon for analysis. The objective was to confirm the identities of the dead and their ranks within al-Qaeda and strike them off the wanted list. Similarly, blood samples were taken from the 300 detainees at Guantanamo Bay and other US detention centres to build up a database of suspected terrorists for the future. This time the data-base was part of a joint computer centre set up in Washington and shared between the FBI, the CIA, Justice, Immigration and other government departments; it was accessible to agents who had the relevant clearance. Some lessons, it seemed, had been learned from mistakes made prior to September 11. A source close to Bin Laden's family told me his brothers and sisters had not been formally approached by the Americans to provide DNA to use as a match for any tissue collected in the field. 'It would not, however, be difficult to get blood samples from oblig-ing hospitals, in Saudi and America, which had catered to the family's medical needs in the past,' said the source.

At the beginning of 2003 only nine of the twenty-seven top al-Qaeda operatives on US Central Command's wanted list had been killed, and four captured. The highest-ranking kill had been Mohamed Atef, the third in command, and his replacement, Abu Zubaydah, was under lock and key. But there was no sign of the two top men, Osama bin Laden himself and Ayman al-Zawahiri. Along with Jalaludin Haqqani, the commander of al-Qaeda forces during Operation Anaconda, the Egyptian doctor continued to play cat-and-mouse across the border between Afghanistan and Pakistan with US Special Forces. For a week they staked out a house where the fugitives were believed to be, but the two men had already gone.

There was no clue either as to the whereabouts of Mullah Omar, the fugitive Taliban leader who had also gone to ground, but one of his intelligence officials, known only as Obeidullah, emerged briefly from his hiding place in May – significantly, in Peshawar, in Pakistan – to give a warning. 'We are not unhappy, afraid or finished. We are just waiting, gathering our strength,' said Obeidullah. He revealed that Mullah Omar had been in the mountains around Shah-i-Kot in March during Operation Anaconda and claimed, 'There aren't just one hundred or two hundred of us . . . there are thousands. We know how to fight a guerrilla war.'

Karachi, Pakistan, September 2002

The West's campaign against al-Qaeda received a welcome boost on the first anniversary of the September 11 attacks. Pakistani forces, guns blazing, stormed an apartment block in the teeming and lawless city of Karachi while FBI agents, sitting outside in a black sedan car, kept a watchful eye on the proceedings. The occupants of the flat fought tenaciously, one even scrawling curses against America on a wall in his own blood before expiring. Screaming abuse at his captors, a slight, bearded thirty-year-old man with a bloody bandage over his eyes was eventually wrestled into the back of a van. It was Ramsi bin al-Shibh, Mohamed Atta's friend from Hamburg and one of the organisers of the plane hijackings a year earlier. The would-be pilot who had fled to Afghanistan had become a victim of his own thirst for an al-Qaeda propaganda coup as the anniversary of the Twin Towers attacks approached. A week before, al-Jazeera television had scooped the world's media again, broadcasting an exclusive interview with Bin al-Shibh in hiding. The reporter, Yosri Fouda, had been smuggled in to the Karachi apartment in June to find Bin al-Shibh sitting on the floor surrounded by three laptop computers, five satellite phones and hundreds of compact discs. He seemed to be co-ordinating the scattered network using the Internet, constantly 'fiddling with his laptops' according to Fouda, while he boasted of the part he played as a co-ordinator of the September 11 plot.

Ramsi bin al-Shibh described his role as one of 'connecting the cells to each other, forming a link between these cells and the general command in Afghanistan and determining the priorities . . . [and] following up the work of these cells until the conclusion of the work'. He confirmed that he and Mohamed Atta had been al-Qaeda 'sleepers' in Germany until activated for the mission in late 1999 on a visit to Afghanistan with Marwan al-Shehhi and Ziad Jarrah. He was full of praise for Atta, who was given the final say on the targets for attack and the timing. 'He was unbelievable – unbelievable!' Bin al-Shibh said reverently. 'God bless his soul and put Paradise under his feet for he is, God willing, among the martyrs.' Bin al-Shibh revealed he received the notification of the date of the attacks in a cryptic phone call from Atta in the USA on 29 August – only after the nineteen plane tickets had been purchased. The message had been passed to Bin Laden himself only five days before that September 11 would be the day – 'Holy Tuesday', as Bin al-Shibh called it.

The fanaticism of Bin al-Shibh became apparent as he described to Fouda how he was 'desperately sad' not to have obtained a US visa so he himself could take part in the suicide mission. Instead he had had to organise Zacharias Moussaoui's training which also failed when the French–Moroccan was arrested in Minnesota, fulfilling Bin al-Shibh's fears that he was a big-mouth, unsuitable for the task. Ramsi confirmed that the fourth plane, Flight 93, which crashed near Pittsburgh, had indeed been destined for Capitol Hill, as I had been told within hours of the attacks on September 11. Like millions of people around the world Ramsi bin al-Shibh had watched the tragedy unfold on television – but his reaction had been to cheer on his friends from Hamburg to follow Atta blindly to their deaths.

Bin al-Shibh was not alone in the apartment in Karachi. There was a second man, thirty-seven years old, portly with thinning brown hair. He had greeted Fouda warmly with the words, 'Welcome, I hope those intelligence dogs did not follow you here!' He introduced himself as the mysterious Khalid Sheikh Mohamed, now the number three in the organisation, the head of the military committee and the man Western intelligence had only slowly come to realise was the real architect of the September 11 attacks. The uncle of Ramsi Yousef, the first man to bomb the World Trade Center in 1993, Mohamed had melded together that iconic target with the passenger-plane bombings at the heart of Operation Bojinka. Adding a co-conspirator's idea of using a plane as a missile against US government buildings, Mohamed had come up with the blueprint for the September 11 attacks.

Western intelligence agencies had only just discovered that Khalid Sheikh Mohamed had visited 54 Marienstrasse, the nerve centre of the Hamburg cell. Now he confirmed the al-Qaeda thinking which lay behind the four near-simultaneous terror attacks which killed three thousand people. 'They were designed to cause as many deaths as possible and to be a big slap for America on American soil,' Mohamed said, adding, 'We were never short of potential martyrs – indeed, we have a department called the Department of Martyrs.' That uncomfortable piece of information was followed by an even more worrying threat. 'We first thought of striking a couple of nuclear targets but decided against it for fear it would go out of control,' Mohamed said. 'It was eventually decided to leave out nuclear targets – for now.' With this, another bit of the jigsaw fell into place for me – Mohamed Atta's presence near a nuclear plant in Alabama in early 2001. He must indeed have been scouting out other possible targets.

Khalid Sheikh Mohamed concluded his meeting with al-Jazeera with another warning – that the 'martyrs' would remain active 'as long as we are in *jihad* against the infidels and the Zionists'. The US had offered a reward of $25 million for the capture of Mohamed and yet he had the nerve to arrange this public taunting of his enemy courtesy of al-Jazeera. The propaganda exercise proved the undoing of al-Qaeda's new Karachi cell, however. The trails put out by al-Jazeera to advertise their programme contained audio clips of Bin al-Shibh's voice. Fouda had originally been allowed to video the two men but his tapes had been kept by them for weeks and when they were returned the images had been erased. The audio remained, however, and that sound, plus the information in the broadcast that the interviews had been conducted in Karachi, was enough to set the giant computers of the NSA, America's National Security Agency, whirring. They were put to work to scour the airwaves for signals coming from Pakistan sent by satellite phones in order to match the voice on the tape against millions of phone calls in an attempt to track down the source. The Pakistanis had also received information from two Burmese captives that two flats had been rented by al-Qaeda in a middle-class district of Karachi.

At 8:00 A.M. on 11 September the Pakistani commandos pounced in a raid conducted by the ISI, the Pakistani intelligence service. Eight men were taken captive after a bloody two-hour battle – but one man escaped. Khalid Sheikh Mohamed proved as elusive as ever, despite the massive bounty on his head. A Western intelligence official I spoke to was convinced that the same rogue elements within the ISI who had long been protectors of al-Qaeda and the Taliban had once again proved their loyalty by tipping him off. Mohamed had slipped away from the apartment only an hour before the raid, leaving behind a four-year-old child, his adopted daughter, with his partner-in-crime Ramsi bin al-Shibh.

At first Ramsi refused to speak to his interrogators but within weeks he was beginning to loosen up, as Abu Zubaydah had done before him. Their desire to boast to the enemy about the skills and effectiveness of al-Qaeda was a powerful tool which their questioners had learned to harness. Efforts by Western intelligence to thwart new plots depended on getting fresh information from knowledgeable captives like Bin al-Shibh. The information that even a top-level al-Qaeda detainee like Zubaydah could give soon grew stale. The organisation's cellular structure was becoming even more fragmented and hard to counter as al-Qaeda spread its operatives abroad and activated its many affiliates.

From cross-referencing Bin al-Shibh's interrogation with that of another prisoner, John Walker Lindh, the 'American Taliban' captured in Afghanistan, a theory began to emerge that there was originally intended to be a fifth plane targeted at the White House on September 11. It had been scuppered by Ramsi bin al-Shibh's failure to get a US visa. This first phase of terror would be followed by more operations worldwide. Lindh revealed that he had been told by a senior al-Qaeda operative that 'fifteen more operations were pending'. Alarm spread throughout the intelligence community, especially in Britain, when Ramsi bin al-Shibh claimed that Heathrow airport was one target. Mindful that he might be deliberately spreading disinformation, a worried official told me, 'We don't know exactly what they had in mind, but we think the plan was to hijack a plane just after take-off and then crash it into one of the terminals.'

Fears in Whitehall were sharpened even further after Bin al-Shibh's arrest when a new piece of information emerged: the fugitive Khalid Sheikh Mohamed had now been put in charge of plans to strike the enemy occupying the number-two slot on the organisation's hate list – Britain. No one knew if attacks would target UK interests and citizens abroad or in the heart of one of the nation's cities. Knowing Mohamed's predilection for iconic buildings and mindful of Bin Laden's threats to hit economic targets, the intelligence analysts focused on Canary Wharf, the tallest office block dominating the London skyline.

The British government had a problem trying to balance the

need to keep the public vigilant by issuing accurate warnings while stemming the tide of panic caused by each new piece of leaked, and sometimes invented, intelligence. The authorities came under attack, lambasted by a Parliamentary Select Committee, for not having raised the red flag in their travel guidance to holidaymakers visiting Bali. The island is Indonesia's best-known tourist resort and spies had been telling British intelligence a month before the bombing that attacks on nightclubs in Indonesia were being discussed by terrorists in the region.

In November, three weeks after the Bali bombing, the public's fears were dramatically heightened when an administrative blunder resulted in a draft of a speech by the Home Secretary being mistakenly issued to some journalists. 'Maybe they will try to develop a so-called dirty bomb or some kind of poison gas,' the document stated. 'Maybe they will try to use boats or trains rather than planes. The bottom line is that we simply cannot be sure.' Officials tried in vain to persuade the press to substitute the more anodyne version which replaced it. Then, ten days later, three North Africans appeared in a London court; they had been arrested in possession of a stack of false documents which MI5 believed indicated they were involved in the early stages of plotting a strike related to al-Qaeda. The newspapers carried headlines claiming 'MI5 foils poison-gas attack on the Tube'.There was no hard evidence for this but as 2002 drew to a close any scenario was considered possible, so febrile was the atmosphere.

British fears were realised just days into the new year when police raided a small flat above a chemist's shop in Wood Green, a North London suburb with a large immigrant Muslim population. Six men of North African origin were arrested and rudimentary lab equipment seized. It was found to contain traces of ricin, the deadly by-product of the castor oil bean, a poison without an antidote. Ricin has long been a bioweapon which al-Qaeda has tried to obtain for its arsenal. The terror manual found in Manchester in 1999 contained details of how to use this poison for assassinations. The al-Qaeda operative from Canada, Ahmed Ressam, who was arrested on the US border with explosives in December 1999, told his captors about the training he had received in the Afghan camps. Ricin was one of the toxins recruits had practised smearing on door-knobs to strike down unsuspecting victims.

The Wood Green case confirmed the continuing importance to al-Qaeda of the Maghreb connection. Five of the men arrested were Algerians and one Moroccan, confirmation that al-Qaeda was now running European operations out of North Africa, as Bin Laden had decreed in the spring of 2002. Two of the youngest Algerians were reportedly only teenagers, asylum-seekers who had recently arrived in England. The intelligence services were puzzled as to how the ricin was intended to be used and against whom. Unsuitable for use in food sources or water supplies, and difficult to convert to aerosol form for an airborne attack, the poison may have been intended to kill a single high-profile target. The Bulgarian dissident, Georgi Markov, had been killed in London in 1978 with a ricin-tipped umbrella – a victim of the Cold War. Security sources also suggested that perhaps the Algerians had intended to smear ricin on the doors of public buildings causing limited casualties but maximum panic.

The Horn of Africa, autumn 2002

In the autumn of 2002, as al-Qaeda made it clear it had opened another front against its enemies, in the Far East, America too was expanding its covert efforts in the war against terror – beyond Afghanistan and Central Asia. A thousand Special Forces and CIA units set up a new military base, this time in the Horn of Africa, in Djibouti, separated by only a narrow sea strait, the Bab al-Mandeb, from the Yemen and the hinterland of the Arabian peninsula beyond. Their target was the groups of al-Qaeda fighters who, since their ousting from Afghanistan, were establishing new bases in the Yemen and Saudi Arabia, Bin Laden's traditional heartlands.

In June, the normally secretive Saudi kingdom allowed the
news to leak that suspected members of an al-Qaeda cell had
been arrested. It was the first time that the authorities had publicly acknowledged the growing problem of Islamic extremism
internally; they admitted they had seized eleven Saudis under
the command of a Sudanese and an Iraqi who had smuggled
arms into the kingdom from the Yemen. Using two surface-to-
air missiles they had tried, unsuccessfully, to bring down US
warplanes using the Prince Sultan airbase, sixty miles from
Riyadh. Later, the Saudi interior minister would admit that his
security forces were holding around one hundred al-Qaeda
men in the country's jails. Relations between Washington and
the House of Saud, already badly strained by the revelation
that fifteen of the September 11 hijackers were Saudis, had
reached breaking point a year on.

The Saudis came in for a hammering in the summer of 2002
in the Congressional hearings into the intelligence failures
which led to the attacks in New York and Washington.
Criminal investigations in the US had revealed a series of links
between Saudi-based charities and al-Qaeda. American counter-
terrorism officials complained loudly that the Saudis were
unwilling or unable to choke off the flow of funds from the
kingdom into Bin Laden's coffers. A secret report was prepared
identifying nine key wealthy individuals behind al-Qaeda –
seven of them were Saudis. The Saudi government was
accused of being slow to freeze suspect bank accounts and
there were hints that the Bush administration would give them
a three-month deadline to stop the money or else military aid
to the country would be slashed and visas denied its citizens.

The final straw came when the smooth-talking Saudi
ambassador to Washington, Prince Bandar, once more found
himself in an unwelcome spotlight a year on from the aftermath of September 11 – this time facing an FBI investigation.
His wife, Princess Haifa al-Faisal, had been distributing financial
largesse to a Saudi woman who claimed to need funds for
medical treatment. About $2,000 appeared to have ended up

in the hands of a friend of the woman's husband, who in turn distributed the cash to two of the fifteen Saudis responsible for the carnage on September 11. 'I find that accusations that I contributed funds to terrorists outrageous and completely irresponsible,' the Princess said in a rare public statement.

While the Princess and her husband denied making contributions to the terrorists, the donation illustrated how the funding of al-Qaeda continued to be a major headache for Western governments. The vast sums which still flowed from Saudi millionaires into charitable coffers were not properly monitored and many donors in the Middle East seemed reluctant to question exactly where their money ended up. A highly confidential survey of members of the extensive Saudi security apparatus, in the autumn of 2002, revealed that 80 per cent of them sympathised with the aims of al-Qaeda, further illustrating the problem posed by the kingdom in the fight against terrorism.

A UN report, released in the summer of 2002 by a panel responsible for monitoring the enforcement of an arms, travel and financial embargo on al-Qaeda, revealed that while more than $112 million of assets owned by suspected friends and members of al-Qaeda were frozen in the weeks following September 11, only $10 million was denied them in the eight months that followed. Despite initial successes in 'locating and freezing' al-Qaeda assets, the network 'continues to have access to considerable financial and other economic resources', the UN report stated, adding that it had proved 'exceedingly difficult' to identify these funds. The terror group's financial backers in North Africa, the Middle East and Asia still managed at least $30 million in investments – perhaps as much as $300 million – and could draw on Bin Laden's own personal inheritance. Bank accounts, in particular in London, Vienna and al-Qaeda's tried and tested financial centre, Dubai, continued to facilitate the flow of money. Private donations of about $16 million annually were still pouring in 'largely unabated', according to the authors of the report, who concluded, 'Al-Qaeda is by all accounts "fit and well" and poised to strike again at its leisure.'

That sentiment was echoed by the Director of the CIA, George Tenet, struggling before the Congressional hearings to defend his Agency's failure to put the two Saudi hijackers, Khalid al-Midhar and Nawaf al-Hazmi, on a watch-list – until it was too late. 'Al-Qaeda is reconstituted – and coming after us,' Mr Tenet stated. As threats once more reached a crescendo around the first anniversary of the September 11 attacks, the US response was to go on the offensive against al-Qaeda in new countries which, post-Afghanistan, Bin Laden's lieu-tenants threatened to destabilise and hijack. Top of the list was the Yemen, where a weak government was struggling to satisfy America's demands for punitive action against al-Qaeda with-out enraging local tribal leaders, Bin Laden supporters of long standing. When eighteen Yemeni troops were killed in a gun battle while trying to arrest Qaed Salim Sinan al-Harethi, a top al-Qaeda operative, the President of the Yemen, Ali Abdullah Saleh, gave America permission to fly the Predator over its territory.

From the US base across the water in Djibouti the drones were launched, equipped with Hellfire missiles, to begin their sweep of Yemeni territory. America's presence in the Horn of Africa enabled them to keep the pressure on Saleh, reminding him that if Yemen would not act then they could strike from just across the water. On 6 October al-Qaeda sent an ominous warning to Saleh's government when al-Harethi and a group of militants attacked a French oil tanker, the *Limburg*, off the Yemen. The bombing, almost a carbon copy of the attack on the *Cole* two years earlier, killed one French crew member. But the repercussions were significant for the Yemen, threatening its very survival as insurance rates soared by 700 per cent for tankers berthing in its ports. Yemen depends on oil exports for three-quarters of its annual income, and is heavily reliant on the container and shipping trade – a fact well known to al-Qaeda. 'If they persist with this alliance, then they must be ready to pay a heavy price with their blood and with their interests,' the terror group stated. The *Limburg* attack was a wake-up call for President Saleh, who had long sought to reason with the terrorists, blocking the *Cole* investigation in 2000. Yemeni intelligence agents had been tracking al-Harethi for months, passing information on to their American counterparts, and within a week their moment came.

On 3 November, a bolt from the blue hit a jeep travelling in the vast wastes of the Yemeni desert. It was a Hellfire missile fired from a Predator by a CIA officer, thousands of miles away in Langley, Virginia, watching live video footage beamed from the drone. All that was left of the vehicle and its six occupants was a charred wreck. Al-Harethi had planned his last attack for al-Qaeda when his suicide bombers hit the *Limburg* a few days before. Among the dead was Kamal Derwish, the leader of a suspected al-Qaeda cell in Buffalo, America.

The rules of engagement had changed. This was an Israeli-style raid – reminiscent of the helicopter gunship attacks or the remote-controlled, exploding mobile phones which took out Hamas bomb-makers in Gaza or the West Bank. America was now playing hardball and there was no attempt to hide it. It was 'a very successful tactical operation', said Paul Wolfowitz, the Deputy Defense Secretary and a noted hawk. 'We've got to deny the sanctuaries everywhere we are able to – and we have got to put pressure on every government that is giving these people support to get out of that business.' President Saleh commented, 'We call on everyone from among our country-men who have been entangled in membership of the al-Qaeda organisation to repent . . . and renounce all means of violence.'

Djibouti was a valuable staging-post across the water, enabling America to hit directly at al-Qaeda on the Arabian peninsula while keeping its army off the holy soil which Bin Laden threatened would burn under the boots of US and British soldiers if he had his way. But three weeks after America launched its pre-emptive strike in the Yemen al-Qaeda proved its grip on the Horn of Africa itself had not yet weakened.

Mombasa, November 2002

The Anter family, Ora and Rahamin and their three children –
fourteen-year-old Dvir, twelve-year-old brother Noy and
their eight-year-old sister Edva – had dreamed of escaping
the violence and random killing in their homeland, Israel. And
so they booked a holiday at a hotel called the Paradise in
Mombasa. Owned by an Israeli businessman, the hotel specialised in package holidays to the East African coast and most
of its clientele was Jewish. Early on the morning of 28 November,
the two Anter boys were standing in the lobby of the hotel
having just checked in with their parents after the flight from Tel
Aviv to Mombasa. The children were enjoying the welcoming
African dance routine performed by Rizikizio Chengo and his
troupe of Kenyan dancers. As the rest of the tourist party moved
off towards the dining room the two boys ran back to request an
encore from the dancers. Just at that moment a green Pajero Jeep
burst through the wooden barrier in front of the hotel and
careered towards the lobby. One of the passengers jumped out
and ran into the building detonating explosives strapped to his
body as the car exploded in a ball of flames.

Ten Kenyan dancers, the two Israeli boys and their 61-
year-old tour guide were blown to pieces by the blast. The
tropical hotel was gutted by fire within an hour as more than
eighty people were ferried to hospital with gaping wounds
caused by flying glass and metal. Casualties at the Paradise
would have been far worse if the explosion had happened
minutes earlier before the Israeli guests had left the lobby to
unpack and have their breakfast.

An even worse scenario should have unfolded in Mombasa
that morning. As the Pajero approached the hotel an Arkia
Airways Boeing 757 was beginning its take-off at Mombasa,
ferrying 260 Israeli tourists back to Tel Aviv. Ninety seconds
into the flight, at 3,000 feet, Captain Rafi Marik felt a 'bump'
which he thought was a bird strike. One of the passengers,
Machluf Amsalem, knew better. He had seen a trail of smoke

sear past the wingtip of the Boeing and knew that it was a heat-seeking surface-to-air missile. A second missile shot by on the other side. The group of five men who had fired them from two kilometres away jumped into a white four-wheel drive and roared off.

It was an audacious attack, intended to rival al-Qaeda's spectacular of September 11: two near-simultaneous strikes, the first al-Qaeda's trademark vehicle bombing, the other a daring attack using missiles against a passenger plane. If the terrorists had not missed, and if the hotel attack had happened a fraction earlier, three or four hundred people, mainly Israelis, would have died.

Once again, poverty-stricken Kenyans, people trying to eke a living from foreign tourism, had suffered most from al-Qaeda's murderous spree. Their countrymen would suffer still further as tourists fled East Africa, undermining the economy. Israeli reaction was decisive; Prime Minster Ariel Sharon promised his Cabinet that 'our long arm will catch the attackers and those who dispatch them'. The new head of Mossad, the Israeli intelligence service, Meir Dagan, was tasked with that responsibility. As military planes arrived, within hours of the attacks, to carry all the Israeli survivors and injured home, Israel Army Radio announced that al-Qaeda's fingerprints were all over this atrocity. The prime suspect was Abdullah Ahmed Abdullah, an al-Qaeda bomb-maker wanted since the attack on the US Embassy in Nairobi in 1998. There was a strong suspicion he had acted, in the usual al-Qaeda way, in concert with a local extremist group – the Somali al-Itihaad al-Islamiya, a long-time ally of Bin Laden's.

The serial numbers on the Russian SAM 7 missile launchers, recovered later, showed they had been manufactured near Moscow in 1974. They were in the same series as the missile fired at the Prince Sultan airbase in Saudi earlier that year. Intelligence experts believed this indicated that al-Qaeda still had significant command and control over its far-flung empire – shipping arms around the Middle East and across to Somalia and East Africa. The use of missiles was a dangerous escalation of the war being waged against the West and the target, Israel, was a propaganda coup for al-Qaeda designed to strengthen their support in the Arab world. An Islamic website was soon claiming the attack as al-Qaeda's and threatening more strikes against Israel.

For more than a year Israel had claimed its internal battle against Palestinian suicide bombers had put the country in the front line of the war against terror. Now Israeli citizens too had become victims of al-Qaeda, but that posed problems for the Bush administration. In its attempts to build the widest coalition to destroy Bin Laden's organisation, the Americans had persuaded Arab regimes, including Jordan, Saudi Arabia, the Yemen and Egypt, to interrogate al-Qaeda suspects and hand over intelligence information. That arrangement was now jeopardised with Israel's entry into the war zone and the impact it had on domestic opinion in the Arab world. And no one was under any illusions that Israel would not hesitate to strike first and hit hard if it perceived any chink in the armour of al-Qaeda. Palestinian terrorists had learned a bitter lesson when they challenged Israel on East African soil – the daring raid on a hijacked El Al plane at Entebbe in 1974 left none of the terrorists alive. And in the wake of the massacre of Israeli athletes at Munich in 1972, Mossad had patiently tracked down those responsible over many years. 'Operation Wrath of God', as their mission was called, had resulted in the assassination of many Palestinians believed to have been involved in the Munich massacre. But no one believed that dealing with the hundreds of al-Qaeda 'sleepers' and thousands of would-be terror recruits or penetrating the hiding places of Bin Laden and his top lieutenants would be that easy.

The question of Osama bin Laden's whereabouts is still unanswered, but in a way also irrelevant. As Dr Hassan al-Turabi, Bin Laden's Sudanese friend, had told me four years earlier: 'If they kill him they will create a thousand Bin Ladens, you will see!'

Epilogue

Shah-i-Kot, Afghanistan, April 2002

Two small girls in pink and green quilted skirts flicked their reed switches and called out reassuringly as they herded their flock of goats along the narrow path high above the valley of Shah-i-Kot. Behind them men trudged silently after the camels, new-born lambs peeking out from straw cages lashed to the beasts' humps. The Kuchi tribes were on the move, driving their animals from winter pastures in Pakistan across the mountains into Afghanistan and hundreds of miles north to the livestock markets at Mazar-i-Sharif. A tall, slender figure on a horse brought up the rear, shrouded in a black *burkha* with a mesh allowing only a flash of her eyes to be seen. Who was she? I wondered. There was speculation that Bin Laden continued to escape detection riding remote mountain paths, dressed as a woman. Below me I could see all the way to Khost, the town on the border with Pakistan.

As 2002 unfolded it became increasingly clear that al-Qaeda

had not only established itself in many corners of the world but still retained the skeleton of a base in the North-West Frontier province of Pakistan and in neighbouring Baluchistan. District elections had resulted in the victory of a coalition of Islamic parties which opposed the hunt for al-Qaeda's leaders and demanded the withdrawal of US troops. Quietly, on a small scale, al-Qaeda was able to set up new training camps around the town of Mirim Shah, and to recruit impressionable young men from this deeply conservative area where tribal leaders had long supported Bin Laden and the Taliban. From the autonomous tribal region of Waziristan men and arms were being infiltrated back across the border into Afghanistan to harass US forces which were still prevented by political constraints from pursuing cross-border operations. Iran too was secretly assisting at least one extremist Islamic group in the region, whose numbers had been bolstered by refugee fighters from al-Qaeda. 'The whole problem has just moved south-west and south-east a bit,' sighed a Western intelligence officer, describing to me the frustrations of stamping out the remnants of 'The Base' in central Asia.

The war against terror was running out of steam, as the Chairman of the US Joint Chiefs of Staff, General Richard Myers, admitted in November. The US military campaign in Afghanistan had 'lost a little momentum, to be frank'. The Bush administration had its eyes elsewhere, gearing up for a war against Iraq in 2003. The President and some of his top advisers were convinced that there was a real risk that Saddam Hussein would provide al-Qaeda with chemical or biological weapons, and even nuclear material, to cause even greater devastation in American cities than on September 11. While Bin Laden had always made clear his desire to obtain such weapons, the CIA was sceptical that any hard evidence existed so far to link the extremist Islamic al-Qaeda with the secular Iraqi regime. That, however, did not stop the hawks in the US government, led by Defense Secretary Donald Rumsfeld, from claiming there *were* proven ties between Bin Laden and Baghdad. In fact the one group of Islamic extremists operating in northern Iraq, Ansar al-Islam, which was known to number al-Qaeda fugitives among its ranks, was being sponsored by Iran, not Iraq. Ansar had conducted small-scale experiments with biological poisons and crude chemical weapons, but the area of mountains and caves in which it operates is on the border between Iraq and Iran, beyond Saddam's reach and controlled by Tehran. Democrats criticised their government for allowing Iraq to distract them before the main enemy, al-Qaeda, had been neutralised and its leader captured. 'By what measure can we say this has been successful?' demanded Tom Daschle, the Democrats' leader in the Senate, referring to a list of unmet objectives in America's war with militant Islam.

President Bush was still ticking off his scorecard in the autumn of 2002. The notable successes were the arrest of Ramsi bin al-Shibh in Pakistan and the capture of the head of al-Qaeda's Gulf operations, Abd al-Rahim al-Nashiri, in November. A longtime associate of Osama bin Laden and a mastermind of attacks at sea, al-Nashiri had been involved in the USS *Cole* attack in 2000, the bombing of the French tanker in the Yemen and the thwarted attacks on British warships in the Mediterranean in 2002. More than 3,000 suspected al-Qaeda operatives had been rounded up in 98 different countries, but nearly all of them were low-level members of the organisation, with little inside knowledge – no great loss. Osama bin Laden, his deputy Ayman al-Zawahiri and the head of the military committee, Khalid Sheikh Mohamed, remained defiantly at large along with at least five mid-level al-Qaeda managers identified by the CIA and other Western intelligence agencies. This command structure still retained a significant degree of control over unknown numbers of operatives in cells in many countries.

The US joint Congressional hearings into the security lapses that made September 11 possible issued its final report in December 2002, sharply criticising intelligence agencies for their failure to prevent the attacks on New York and the Pentagon. The agencies had 'missed opportunities to disrupt the September 11 plot by denying entry to or detaining would-be

hijackers; to at least try to unravel the plot through surveillance and other investigative work within the United States;
and finally to generate a heightened state of alert and thus
harden the homeland against attack'. The Directors of the CIA
and the FBI came under fire for failing to ensure the country
was as prepared as it should have been. The panel urged the
creation of a cabinet-level director of national intelligence to
oversee the entire intelligence community and put an end to
decades-old turf battles. Senator Bob Graham, the co-chairman,
made it clear that Congress could not afford to maintain the
status quo. 'I come back to one number – 3,025 – the number of
persons who were killed on September 11,' said Graham, 'and
I do not believe that members of Congress are going to want to
take the position, let us stand by, let us allow the gaps and
weaknesses in our current system to continue, to cross our fingers and hope that we are not in the next few months again
picking up the pieces and, sadly, the bodies of yet another successful attack inside the United States.'

As the cumbersome systems of America and other Western
countries tried to counter al-Qaeda with new laws and new
bureaucracies, The Base, showing its customary nimbleness,
was still one step ahead. Al-Qaeda was not only becoming a
movement with worldwide appeal but a 'virtual' terror organisation in its methods. It still depended on old-fashioned,
secure ways of communication – couriers and word of mouth –
in the Afghan and Pakistan tribal areas where US satellites
could quickly put Special Forces on the trail of the source of a
mobile phone call. But al-Qaeda was also increasingly waging
a cyber-battle in its global operations. The Internet and mobile
communications enabled a small core of leaders spread
throughout many different countries to co-ordinate the terror
network. It no longer needed a physical base. The 'tree of training, the seedling al-Qaeda planted in its camps in Afghanistan
has grown in the hearts of Muslim youth and has yielded fruit
in all parts of the world', boasted one of the organisation's
strategists.

The significance of al-Qaeda's use of the Internet was revealed when US officials finally found over 2,000 encrypted messages and data files in a password-protected section of an Islamic website, which had been downloaded on to the computer Abu Zubaydah used to communicate with Mohamed Atta and the hijackers. The messages began in May 2001, peaked in August and ended on 9 September, two days before the attacks in New York and Washington. A year later, the discovery of Ramsi bin al-Shibh in Karachi, surrounded by laptops and mobile phones, showed again how the network utilised Internet links. A Kenyan witness who noticed the Mombasa bombers sitting in their Jeep minutes before the attack on Israeli tourists saw ten mobile phones lined up on the dashboard. The Bali bombers two months earlier had used mobile phones to co-ordinate and trigger their attack on the Sari Club.

Al-Qaeda was not only using websites to conceal instructions to its followers, but also defiantly pumping out propaganda via the Web, most notably on *www.alneda.com*, hosted by servers in Malaysia, Texas and Michigan. 'The US campaign in Afghanistan has catapulted al-Qaeda on to a dangerous and effective level,' warned the website in October. 'Its chaste presence in Afghanistan has disappeared. Instead of stationing itself in one known place, it has become a secret program and a project for martyrdom worldwide. Eradication of al-Qaeda has become impossible. Let the [US] Administration reap the results of its foolish acts!' No sooner did the authorities identify an al-Qaeda website and block it than a new one popped up, or supporters were advised to congregate in chat rooms, which are almost impossible to monitor comprehensively.

From Moscow, where Chechen extremists holding a full theatre hostage wore headbands emblazoned with Arabic slogans echoing Bin Laden's teachings, to Jibla in the Yemen, where an Islamic fanatic gunned down three Americans in a missionary hospital; from Charles de Gaulle airport in Paris, where an Algerian baggage-handler was found with explosives in his car, to Daska in Pakistan, where a grenade thrown into a church killed three young girls at a Christmas Day service: al-Qaeda-inspired attacks multiplied as 2002 drew to a close. Prisoners continued to alarm their interrogators with half-heard fragments, hints of a new and devastating attack still in the pipeline, bigger than Bali or Mombasa – more ambitious even than September 11. 'We renew our pledge to Allah, our promise to the [Muslim] nation and our threat to Americans and Jews that they shall remain restless,' Bin Laden warned on alneda.com in October 2002. 'They shall not feel at ease and shall not dream of security until they take their hands off our nation and stop their aggression against us and their support for our enemies.'

I had reached the end of my journey in search of al-Qaeda, for the moment. Behind me in the mountainside above Shah-i-Kot there was a narrow opening in the sheer rock face, the entrance almost blocked with fallen shale loosened by an American bomb. I climbed over the pile of stones and slithered down into one of al-Qaeda's caves. It was cool and dry, ten feet high in the middle, a tunnel stretching back almost a hundred metres with tyre tracks still visible on the sandy floor. The roofs and walls were pitted with thousands of indentations, the laborious marks of chisels wielded over twenty years ago, when the caves were built to shelter the fledgling al-Qaeda from the Soviets. Hidden deep within the mountain the cave had been undamaged by the American bomb, its explosion glancing off the sheer edge of the hillside. The cave waited for someone to reclaim it – perhaps Commander Arbos, the al-Qaeda man whose domain it had been and who had fled to Pakistan, wounded but not killed or captured yet.

The shadows were lengthening outside the cave. The Afghan guards who had brought me here took out small mirrors to catch the sun's last rays and direct the slanting shafts of light along the dark walls that led into the heart of the mountain. Those shifting beams seemed like al-Qaeda itself, flaring intensely as they struck one spot on the rocky wall, then disappearing only to strike elsewhere, always moving on. The sunlight eventually faded into dusk but al-Qaeda has not faded away under the onslaught of the war on terror. It has proved itself capable not only of surviving, but of re-grouping and re-shaping itself to stage further attacks, as events in Bali, Mombasa and elsewhere have shown. It is not a question of whether the world will ever see another al-Qaeda terror outrage rivalling the ingenuity or the scale of the September 11 attacks, but when and where – and how many innocent lives it will claim.

Acknowledgements

I should like to thank many colleagues at the BBC, who have worked with me over the years on *Panorama* to investigate al-Qaeda: Aidan Laverty, Thea Guest, Kerstin Fischer, Kevin Sutcliffe, Fiona Campbell, Nicole Kleeman, Amanda Vaughan-Barratt, Kath Posner, Kate Redman, Rosa Rudnicka and above all John Thynne, who gave me so much help in collating research, both for my recent films and for this book. My thanks also to Mike Robinson for allowing me the time to put everything down on paper.

There are many other individuals around the world who have helped me try to unravel the secrets of the terror network over the past four years – diplomats, fellow journalists, members of the military, civil servants, politicians and a host of ordinary – but in reality extraordinary – people who have been witnesses to the events I have described. They are too numerous to mention, and some prefer to remain anonymous, but am grateful to you all.

Bill Hamilton, my agent, has been, as ever, an enthusiasti

supporter and astute in his observations about what this book should be about. Thanks also to Andrew Gordon.

My biggest debt is to my family, my husband John and my children Tom and Rose, who have hardly seen me since September 11. Not only have they been self-sufficient and uncomplaining, they have also understood that this book was something I had to write.